YET MORE VOICES FROM PRISON WALLS

by
WILLIAM CAWMAN

Author of
Voices from Prison Walls
More Voices from Prison Walls

SCHMUL PUBLISHING COMPANY
NICHOLASVILLE, KENTUCKY

COPYRIGHT © 2018 BY SCHMUL PUBLISHING CO.
All rights reserved. No part of this publication may be reproduced or used in any form or by any means—graphic, electronic, or mechanical, including photocopying, recording, taping, or information storage or retrieval systems—without prior written permission of the publishers.

Churches and other noncommercial interests may reproduce portions of this book without prior written permission of the publisher, provided such quotations are not offered for sale—or other compensation in any form—whether alone or as part of another publication, and provided that the text does not exceed 500 words or five percent of the entire book, whichever is less, and does not include material quoted from another publisher. When reproducing text from this book, the following credit line must be included: "From *Yet More Voices from Prison Walls* by William Cawman, © 2018 by Schmul Publishing Co., Nicholasville, Kentucky. Used by permission."

Cover image copyright: <a href='https://www.123rf.com/profile_albund'>albund / 123RF Stock Photo</a>. Used by permission.

Published by Schmul Publishing Co.
PO Box 776
Nicholasville, KY USA

Printed in the United States of America

ISBN 10: 0-88019-613-0
ISBN 13: 978-0-88019-613-0

Visit us on the Internet at www.wesleyanbooks.com, or order direct from the publisher by calling 800-772-6657, or by writing to the above address.

Contents

Foreword 4

1. "His Compassions Fail Not" 6
2. "Grace Did Much More Abound" 24
3. In Prison and Out of Prison 42
4. Watching Christ being Formed in Them 62
5. "And Such Were Some of You…But!" 81
6. "And Yet There is Room" 100
7. Wheat and Tares 118
8. Impossibilities…Except for God 136
9. One More for Jesus 155
10. Prison and Beyond 173
11. Department of Corrections, They Call This 191
12. My Savior has my Treasure 209
    Interlude 222
13. Dramatized Choices 227
14. Broken Pieces 247
15. Grace Greater Than My Sin 264
16. Is it Just Jail-House Religion? 281

Foreword

AT THE TIME of this publishing, God has given over eighteen precious years of labor among the men in prison. Often in travelling around the country in evangelistic work I hear precious members of the family of God say to me, "God has given you a wonderful ministry in that prison." Yes, He has, for which I bow in gratitude and unworthiness. But they miss a very vital link in what they say thus. God has given a ministry among men in prison to which many, many have responded in faithful prayers. This, be it clearly understood, is the heart throb of all fruit from this ministry. God answers prayer!

This, the third volume of these monthly letters, is filled with answers to those prayers. My heart's desire is that no one attribute an undue amount of gratitude or acknowledgement to the one who wrote them, for without those prayers there would have been no miracles to write about. When Paul in one of his epistles wrote about entering into other men's labors, I am reminded that such is exactly what I have been privileged to do. You have prayed; I have witnessed the answers to those prayers, and that to such an extent that sometimes I actually feel selfish that I cannot more effectually share the joy with you. Rest assured, eternity will bestow no misplaced laurels. The Scripture says, "The Lord knoweth them that are His." Furthermore, He knows who has been faithful in the secret closet without any lust to be rewarded openly. The best we can do now is to say Thank you, but heaven will not be that bankrupt!

This volume of the monthly letters covers a four year period: 2009-2012. During those four years not every effort was as rewarding as may have been hoped. Some have slipped through our fingers and for that we plead the Blood of forgiveness for any element of it in which we could have done better. For any eternal good done, we give all the honors to Him who is Faithful and True, and to the faithful ones of His children who have obediently responded to the pull of prayer and the ministry of the Word.

Let me share a glorious thought with you. In that Great Day growing ever closer, there will not be a single name in that roll call that you and I will not know."For now we see through a glass, darkly; but then face to face: now I know in part; but then shall I know even as also I am known" (1 Corinthians 13:12). I confess that some of the men you have prayed for even I have forgotten their names, but on that Great Day I will not need to be there to introduce to you the answer to your prayers. You will know them!

I trust you will recognize in the pages that follow what a value God places upon a single soul. Truly, "The Lord is not slack concerning his promise, as some men count slackness; but is longsuffering to us-ward, not willing that any should perish, but that all should come to repentance."

—WILLIAM CAWMAN

1
"His Compassions Fail Not"

January 1, 2009

ANOTHER YEAR HAS PASSED forever into history, and as I think back on it I sense such a mixture of emotions. I thank God for a year of His presence and grace. I do want to live closer to Him and be more useful to Him next year. I would desire your prayers to that end. Will we have this whole year ahead to love and labor for Jesus?

The dying man in the hospital is dead. He died shortly after writing the last letter to you. Thank you for all your prayers for him, but let me put it this way: Paul said in 2 Co 2:16, "To the one we are the savour of death unto death; and to the other the savour of life unto life. And who is sufficient for these things?" The poor man left hardly a ray of hope that he made it to heaven, but he will meet your prayers for him on the Day of Judgment, and that is not comfortable for any of us. It is, however, a part of our ministry that we cannot avoid. To give false hope is worse than to face a person with the truth, even if they choose not to take the truth. There came a definite point where, due largely to false witnesses, he made a choice to avoid the cost of confessing his sins, and from that time on he was different.

Do you remember that Felix trembled when Paul first spoke to him of coming judgment, but he desired Paul to go away until later? We read that he talked with Paul many times after that, but there is no record that he ever trembled again. There you have the picture. One of the good inmates who visited him just before his death said that all he was focused on was the arrangement of the food items on his tray. The last time I visited with him, just a day or two before he died, I looked one last time into his sunken eyes and thought of the awful fact that they would soon be lost in hell. He did not want to hear or believe the truth, but he does now—after it is too late.

I have something to tell you with a sense of urgency—a prayer request that has come back after a long time. Those of you who have been reading these letters from the beginning (more than nine years ago) would remember the many times we asked prayer for a very promising man, C——, who God delivered instantaneously from heroin and he was seeking to be sanctified. The devil succeeded in getting his eyes off of the goal and onto his release from prison. Although I tried to faithfully warn him, he went out and from that time has been in and out of prison, deeply depressed, and he even tried to slit his wrist more than once. Some of the sparse letters I would receive almost wrenched the tears from my soul. *But God*—oh, bless His name—He has a hold on him again and here is a letter:

> Dear Brother Cawman,
>   It was a blessing to hear from you. I hope all goes well there where you are. Now, to the good stuff. God be praised for opening my eyes to the error of my ways. Do you remember that anticipation you had with me concerning the second work of grace? I can't forget how you always mentioned in your letters to me of how you were waiting for the good news of my sanctification. Unfortunately, I kept sin in my heart believing that I was going to get through. Satan had blinded me by appearing

as an angel of light. Also, I wouldn't listen to you, in terms of the right choices for my sanctification. I thought that I had all the answers. I know now how unwilling I was to release all sin and the worldly concerns that did nothing but lead me back to jail eight times since my release in June of 2004. Oh, how I remember my first attempt at seeking that Blessing! I misled myself and all of you who prayed for me because I regarded sin in my heart. You see, I thought that I could still be the con man and hustler that I was raised to be. I deceived myself believing that I was prepared to live in a world that I only knew how to live as a drug addict and thief in. To make matters worse, I was quick to blame my mother and the things that happen to me as a boy for my relapses and returns to prison. They were all excuses that God wouldn't accept. Included in all those excuses was a false sense of concern for my children and reuniting with them. You warned me. You said that I could do nothing good for them until my heart was right with God. I refused to cooperate and do my small part in the work God has prepared for me. It was a simple part that only required for me to look to Jesus and follow His example no matter what. I confess my awful sin of disobedience to God and you this day. Yes my brother, the Lord has brought me back to the place it all started. That place in my heart where I am left with the soul-saving decision to follow the Lord unto Christian Perfection. This time there's no confusion to set in. Every bit of heart-held sin is going to be placed at the altar, and left there despite the consequences.

Recently I received three small books. "Holiness for Ordinary People" by Keith Drury; "Sparks from Seven Hammers" a compilation of reflections on holiness. The writers include: B. Carradine, GA McLaughlin, Catherine Booth, William Smith, A.M. Hills, W.B. Godbey and C.W. Ruth. Needless to say, that I didn't even finish that book before I fell before the Lord in shame, guilt and confession. The last book is Samuel Logan Brengle's "Guest of the Soul".

What reality set in, in terms of every part of my willful disobedience after I first believed. God, in His unfailing mercy, has played each aspect of that refusing state of being over in my head and heart until I pled for His mercy again and promised to do it right this time. Not only did He grant me this opportunity, but He revealed to me the very purposes of why He sanctifies us. It's not for me! I wasn't supposed to believe that I would reach new heights and accomplish great things for myself! It's for passing it on to all nations, to make believers out of everyone else. Everything is for us to point others to Christ while remaining at His feet looking up to Him for our needs. He also granted that I have no concern for the world and everything in it. When the Lord called His Apostles, He didn't include their families, businesses or luggage. He told them to forsake all and follow Him. That's where I failed. I couldn't let go of this world. I couldn't think straight unless I could get a driver's license, see my daughter or start a business.

I have humbled myself in His Way now. Please bear with me as I get back to my first Love. I pray God to give you that anticipation again. Look for my letters to answer that call again. I believe in getting through now and know that it is for me. The only thing that I know now is Him. I have about a year to go and don't mind staying here until I get the Blessing. However, God willing, I will make my way to Vineland for strengthening this believer for the Lord's work. Amen.

With much love and respect, C——

He failed once, I did several times. Let's pray again, and let's pray in faith! I believe there will be some good news coming.

A few more men have died recently in the hospital. One of them prayed with tears before he slipped into unconsciousness, and after he died the inmate who sat and prayed with him felt such a warm glow of witness that he had made it. What a merciful God we serve.

During the month of December I am usually home and I try to make the rounds of every man in my classes for a personal visit. It has been so rewarding—and otherwise. Some visits are disappointing and I wonder if we have gotten anywhere, but then some are just the opposite. One dear man who has been faithful in attending sat down and began to open his heart about what the Lord was doing for him and I just sat there amazed as I listened. I would never have dreamed that truth was sinking in to the changing of his life like it was. He is a tug boat captain up and down the eastern seaboard, and during the time in prison God has been awakening and talking to him and he seems to be just saying "yes" to it all. There was a ring of reality to all that he was saying and I thank God that a man is being rescued from the path of sin, hopefully forever.

Another man came in who hasn't been in this prison very long, but came from one of the other prisons. He began to tell me of his awful life (23 years old) and the pain and suffering he has grown up with. He pulled a gun on a policeman and the police shot him through the hip and it came out at his stomach. While he has been in prison another inmate poked his right eye out with a broom handle and so now he wears a glass eye which is very obvious even from a distance. He has always had a severe learning disability and has never been able to read. But for all that, he began to testify about how he has let Jesus come into his heart and how much he loves Him. He asked God to please help him to read his Bible, and with a big smile he said, "I can read it! But I still can't read anything else." Did you need any other proof that our precious Bible is divinely inspired? If so, that ought to do it! Whether this is totally reliable or not, when some of these men sit and begin to tell of what God is doing for them, it just rings a bell way down deep in my own heart.

And then there is another man that comes from Peru and has sat in on the class for some time now with a very unresponsive, perhaps somewhat cynical look on his face. He was a civil engineer in Peru and then spent some years in France doing the same thing. When I scheduled him for a visit, he started right in and spent the whole half hour talking himself. He started with the delivery that we must keep all of the com-

1: "His Compassions Fail Not" 11

mandments, so that meant that we should be worshipping on Saturday instead of Sunday. When he had run out of steam and all that he knew on that line, he began to descry the awful malady of eating meat. That point covered, he moved on to the observation that God was too merciful to let anyone burn in hell for all eternity, so there was no such a place. Then his half hour was up and he left without indicating that he had any need of listening to anything.

Another young man comes from Honduras. He is very bright and enthusiastically responsive in classes and Bible studies, and I was eager to get to know him more. For a while he shared with me how much he really loves God now that he has come to Him, but then he began to go back also into his past. Before long he was in tears of pain as he told me how he had left a beautiful young wife and baby girl all alone in Honduras and come to this country. The reason for it was that a gang had shot and killed his sister who was very close to him. It so devastated him that he almost lost his mind and just ran off and left the country. Then he got into drugs and ended up in prison. He finds it hard to forgive his past, but yet he obviously really loves the Lord now. He also needs prayer as well as his wife.

Christmas time is an emotional time for many of the men and they react in many different ways. The other day two men in one of the few four man cells boiled water in a hot pot and then dumped it all over another cellmate. He had to be airlifted to a burn center and was in serious condition.

In one of my classes there is a young man who just recently got saved. You might want to ask how I know that, so I will tell you. One morning recently he spoke up and asked if he could testify, so of course I granted him leave. He said that before he got saved he always had the idea that there were some sins that were such a part of his life that if he ever got rid of them it would take a long time. He said that other people he had talked to agreed that it was just that way. But he said when he let Jesus come into his heart, those very sins were the first ones to disappear out of his life. He found that he had complete deliverance from them. That's how I know—and I expect you do too, now. He is amazing as I watch him latch on to deeper truths concerning holiness of heart and freedom from all sin; his face just lights up and his head nods ascent like he really believes it. I believe he does believe it.

In His love,
William Cawman

February 1, 2009

LET ME START WITH a recent development here in the prison that seems very promising. Several weeks ago a man from Haiti came to visit with me. He has been very faithful in the Bible studies and classes and it has been so rewarding to watch him grow in grace and in his experience with God. As he visited with me he told me that after God began to get his heart right, he felt the desire to bring all of his life into obedience to God's will. He had never completed his high school education and he felt he should do it to please God. It was hard at first, but with encouragement from other of the Christian men he finally made the grade and received his GED. He said that he felt a big smile from God that he had done this, and it inspired him with a hunger to study more, so he wondered if I knew of any Bible college that would have a study course in Bible and Theology that he could take. He said that whether he stayed here or returned to Haiti (he may be deported there) he did not want to lead others astray. I told him I would look into it for him.

I contacted the presidents of two Bible colleges and both of them were very eager to help and offered outlines of what they had to offer by correspondence. One of them indicated that for men in prison the cost of materials could be covered by their ministerial group. Then I remembered that a couple of pastors had asked me to let them know if there were any needs in the prison that they could help out with. In short order a plan fell into place that would allow churches to contribute or sponsor one or more of these men wanting to do this and it would not cost the inmates to study.

The man from Haiti was not the only man wanting this, for it seemed that all of the sudden several men asked me about the same thing, and I know they were not in contact with each other. The man from Haiti came back to see me after about a month and he had a rather distressed look on his face. He started in: "Chaplain, I have a decision to make and I don't know which way to go. I told you that I wanted to take some college Bible studies, and I do, but I know that if I am going to make enough money to pay for the courses I will have to drop out of Christian Living Class and Bible studies and work hard to earn the money (Top wage in prison is about $2.60 per day). I really don't want to drop out of what I am taking because it is helping me so much, but I do want to take the college classes too. I have been praying about it but I don't seem to get an answer, so I was just praying, 'Lord, please give the chaplain an answer for me.' I don't want to make the wrong decision."

I said, "Well, Brother, let me tell you something. I have contacted two presidents of Bible colleges and both are willing to provide college courses in Bible and Theology at no cost to you." He looked at me for a few seconds and then put his hand over his eyes and began to sob. "I never knew God would answer me like this.Do you mean that I can do both? I have my book here for Christian Living Class in case you thought it would be best for me to drop it, but now I can do both. Oh God, You are so good! Chaplain, I've never had God answer me like this before." The next Bible study he was on his feet giving testimony to God's goodness to him. Since then several more have very excitedly asked to enroll and there are now two from each of the three facilities that are starting, and it would remind you of little boys on their first day of school. My heart praises God and all those involved for making this possible, for it is not only precious to the ones taking it, but to my own heart as well, for I sense God honoring it.

There is another development that I am eager to tell you about, but it also has a sad side to it. It starts several years back, but I will try to give it as briefly as possible. Many of the men who come out of this prison are returning to their "homes," whatever that means to them, and many of those places are in the Camden/Philadelphia area. During the first few months of 2007 a young man came and did an internship with me in the prison, feeling the Lord calling him to do inner city work in those two cities. He was only 21 years old and the officers looked at him with misgivings, asking my supervisor if he was trying to feed lambs to the wolves. But in very short order he won the confidence of the officers and more importantly, the love of the men. It really spoke to them that a young man would be so on fire for God. After he finished his internship, he continued to the present time to fill in for me in the weekly classes while waiting on God to open the doors in the inner city. It has been a number of years ago that I wrote to you of this need— men needing a helping hand after going back to these areas. It has been a painful lack to have no one in those areas to point them to, so this ray of light has been exciting to us.

The time has come that God seems to be opening the door for him to actually move onto his mission field, and while that is a long standing need being met, yet he will not be able to do as much as before in filling in at the prison. We will miss that very much, but we all know that God has primarily called him to the inner city work and to minister to them after they get out. Many of you also receive the newsletters he has been sending out, telling of the opening doors in this area, and so now it is time to connect the two ministries in a newsletter the way God has connected them in His wonderful workings. The following paragraph is a beautiful example of how God is connecting the two ministries and answering prayer for this great need.

In 2003 a young man was put in prison at the age of 18 and soon thereafter became a Muslim, even though he was never one before. Last June, five years afterward, he was playing basketball and when he jumped into the air someone knocked him over and he landed on his head and fractured his skull. He was in a coma for some time, and as he began to come to himself he began to think seriously about who it was that had brought him back. The faithful Holy Spirit was knocking at his heart's door, and thank God he listened and began to seek the Lord. God came and saved him and changed his life until he could not keep it to himself, but felt like telling everyone how much God meant to him. The accident, however, left him subject to sudden blackouts without any warning and he would fall and endanger his head again. They simply put him in a wheelchair and left him in the prison hospital. He wanted to talk to me so I went over to visit.

After he had told me with a smile on his face what God had done for him, he said that he was very shortly to get out of prison to go home and he wanted to follow the will of God when he got there. He expressed the need for a new set of friends instead of those he had before. I asked him where home was and he said it was in Camden. I asked him if he would like for someone to come to his house and visit him and he immediately latched onto it and said he would like to have a Bible study in his house and he would invite his friends too. Please pray for this new contact and open door, and please pause a moment to thank the Lord that He is answering prayer in providing this follow-up ministry. Then help us pray that it will be mightily used of God to help many men continue in the grace they have found.

The month of January has been a longer absence than I usually take. I left on Jan. 5 for a youth conference in Guatemala and from there to Bolivia for a conference and a visit to mission points. When I return, Lord willing, on Jan. 28 I will take pictures and reports of the work on these mission fields to share with them. I have pictures of groups of churches waving their hands in greeting specifically to the men in prison, and I can't wait to show them to them. When prayer requests or greetings are shared with these men, they are so moved by them. You must remember that many of them never had any family values, have never known about caring one for another, etc., and for it to dawn on them that someone (let's say from way down in Bolivia, if they even know where that is) cares enough to wave to them—well, it is just very melting to them. I have had them come to me even several years after hearing of a need on the mission field and ask, "How is ——, I pray for them every day." It reminds me of Jesus' words, "Wherefore I say unto thee, [his] sins, which are many, are forgiven; for [he] loved much: but to whom little is forgiven, the same loveth little."

Could I give a note of personal thanks to God right here regarding meetings we hold outside of the prison? For some time after I followed the call of God into prison ministry, I thought that at some point the prison ministry would become a full time employment, but God had something else in mind, and my time is about equally divided between prison ministry and evangelism. I look back over several years and feel so melted with gratitude to God that He knew (as He always does) what was best. To spend every day, all day, year after year in prison, no matter how God meets hearts there, could become a very wearing experience of which I will not elaborate. On the other hand, so can back-to-back meetings in evangelism become a temptation to discouragement. But the combination is not only healthful to my own spiritual outlook, but it brings much prayer support to the men in prison. And it brings much prayer to revival efforts because of the faithful prayers of these precious men. I often wonder if any pastor or evangelist has as many praying for him as I do.

Now since I have said that, let me give you a few excerpts from the lips and hearts of these precious lambs God has committed to our care. You will please grasp the love of their hearts while you go ahead and laugh at their expressions. One man was praying in a Sunday night service and as he covered the territory it came about that he wanted to ask the Lord's blessing on the chaplain's message that was to follow. "Oh Laud, now bless ah chaplain as he is about to break da word to us. Oh Laud, please make him a sounding brass and a tinkling symbol!" I endeavored to keep a straight face as I implored the Lord to allow the Holy Spirit to interpret his desire to my Father. Another man in praying for his chaplain said, "Oh God, bless ah deah chaplain, bless his shortcomings and his longcomings." To that I said a hearty "amen," as I knew God would understand without any interpreter.

Just as it happens in any group, expressions get started and then spread through the whole group. One of them must have read the passage where it is said that Christ "thought it not robbery to be equal with God." Apparently that expression caught fire as a high sounding phrase and in very short order I was hearing it in prayer all through the prison, and it was being applied to every petition about anything. "Oh Lord, we want to thank you that our chaplain 'thought it not robbery' to come in today to speak to us." Other petitions as well were replete with heartfelt thanks for the "thought it not robbery" factor.

Another man in beginning his prayer prayed a phrase that I have loved ever since. "Oh Lord, I want to thank You for being God all by Yourself." Aren't you glad He is? Sometimes these simple heartfelt prayers get at the heart of things more than all the tongues of the learned. But then, Jesus said it would be that way, and He thanked His Father for it, too.

Thank you each one, so very much, for your faithfulness in prayer for us.

In Christian love,
William Cawman

March 1, 2009

"The LORD is my shepherd; I shall not want. He maketh me to lie down in green pastures: he leadeth me beside the still waters.

He restoreth my soul: he leadeth me in the paths of righteousness for his name's sake."

Blessed be the Shepherd who is so willing to restore our souls, and thank each one of you who prayed for the man I told you about who fell from such a beautiful walk with the Lord a few months ago. In a recent letter I told you of such a heart-breaking disappointment, that a man who had been without a doubt walking in the beauty of holiness for over a year, suddenly fell into the trap of the devil. BUT GOD! He has restored his soul, and now let me tell you more about His wonderful mercies.

This man is serving a life sentence for killing a girl when he was only seventeen years of age. He is now in his early forties, probably of Italian heritage, and has been by his own admission raised in prison mindsets. When he was sent to this prison he began attending church and immediately told me that he was completely convinced that the way of holiness I was teaching was the right way. He sought and professed to have found it and went on for some time. But perhaps a year and a half ago one night in a Bible study he got up and confessed out with a broken heart that he was not living in the blessing, and that there were things in his life that shouldn't be rising up, but they were. He went down before God and that very night prayed through clearly and God cleansed his heart.

From that night on I watched with delight as he grew in his walk with the Lord and as God led him into deeper cleansings of that prison mindset he had been brought up in. He confessed these areas of fault often and begged the men to pray for him; yet at the same time they all saw nothing except the beauty of holiness in his heart and life. Just a few months ago I may have related to you how he came in to visit me and told me that a year ago when God sanctified his heart, he had asked God to give him wisdom to know how to walk with Him and live a life of holiness. He then said that just the other day it dawned on him that God was answering that prayer, and that the sum and total of the wisdom God was giving him was that he didn't know anything. He knew he must remain utterly and completely dependent on God. It was so precious to hear him say it with such humility and meekness.

Then not long after that he suddenly just seemed to drop out of everything. He gave all of his holiness books to one of the other men and wouldn't talk about it and quit coming to all classes and services. The men tried to help him but he just told them to change the channel; that he didn't want to talk about it. At least twice I put him on the appointment sheet to come and visit me, and once when I met him coming from work I told him that he was on the schedule and told him not to cop out. He smiled and nodded his head, but he never came.

Then just as suddenly, he turned around and started coming back to class and said he wanted to visit. It was about a week or so before we got an appointment set up and he came in and sat down and I looked again into the face that I had rejoiced to see so often before. He began to tell me that two weeks ago he had come back to the Lord and God had forgiven his fall and given him the clear witness that he was forgiven, and then he said that very morning God had witnessed clearly to him that his heart was again cleansed from sin. Then he began to tell me in detail what had happened. First of all, the facility he is living in has been pretty desolate for a while. We are having the weekly Christian Living Class each Thursday morning, but apart from that we had not been assigned to that facility for Bible studies or Sunday services for some time and they had been afflicted with the absolutely worst of Biblical teaching by those who were coming in.

One "Bible teacher" told them, and then left it behind in pamphlet form for them to study, "We all know that after we are born again, we still continue to sin. The reason for this is that when we are born again, only our soul is born again; our body still continues to sin." Week after week, month after month, this doctrine of devils was about all they had to partake of outside of our Christian Living Class. He said he began to allow a bitterness to spring up in his heart toward all of this sinning atmosphere around him. Then the devil jumped on him and began to discourage him in saying that it would always be that way, and that since he was in prison for the rest of his life, why struggle to stem the tide of what was so strong about him? He didn't catch it and finally just threw up his hands in despair.

He said that now God is going back over that and pointing out to him that there is a human defect that needs to be corrected and dealt with in him, and it is this. He said he can now see that all of his life he has had a tendency to self-destruction when he gets started in the wrong direction. He said that in response to the devil's accusations and taunts he almost felt justified in walking away from God as a type of self-punishment for what he had done to put himself in prison for the rest of his life. He told me that God is dealing directly with that and telling him that he needs to put that mindset and tendency out of his heart forever. While he is determined to do this, he is rejoicing in the mercy of God that has restored his soul and saved his feet from falling, and it feels so good to him to be back home in God's house. Surely "His mercy endureth forever!" Don't you welcome him back too? My heart surely does, and the other men in class heartily did too.

These men have their own type of battles that many of us know nothing about, but let's not limit the grace of our God. Some of us who can attend a good holiness church each Sunday and prayer meeting night, and who know the precious atmosphere of a family altar, and have revival meetings and camp meetings to attend where others of like precious faith can gather around us, might want to try for a moment or two to imagine all of this being taken away. Then add to that loss the thought of living day after day in the middle of a hellhole of not only worldliness, but out-broken sin of the basest sort.

Imagine having to listen, instead of to family prayer, to cursing and profanity and dirty stories and gross uncovered sin, all around you every moment of the day. Imagine having no one on your tier who is like-minded with you. Imagine having an officer over you who has no respect for your God and openly mocks and makes it difficult for you. Do you realize that there are a number of men who are not only overcoming all of this, but who are living closer to God and walking in holiness of heart and life in measures that perhaps would put to shame many professors of the same grace?

On a personal note that humbles and keeps me running for my life—how can I as their chaplain and shepherd live in some flimsy powerless state of a form of godliness that denies the power they are finding? I thank God for these men, and I am not reluctant to confess that they have been perhaps more than anything else, the salvation of my soul from the Laodicean luke-warmness of this church age. I will thank them and God for all eternity that I have seen the grace of God and holiness work where it would seem the most challenging that it could. It does! "I want that kind of blessing," the song writer said, and my heart answers, "I do too!"

One morning recently I was asking the men again to pray much for our daughter who is trying to establish a holiness mission in Mozambique, Africa. One of the men (one that I am learning to have more and more confidence in) prayed in his Ebonics style, "Oh God will You please help them over there in Africa and just let the Gospel do what it do?" Aren't you glad it does something? That same brother then went on to pray, "Oh Lord, we want to be just like Jesus. If we begin to become otherwise; if we begin to get a little harsh in our spirits or words, or anything like that, will You please send a brother along to talk to us about it?" I began to examine my own heart as to my willingness for that same desire, and I found my heart loving that prayer. "Oh God, 'if in anything [I] be otherwise minded,'" please send a brother along to talk to me." Brother indeed would he be.

I sometimes wonder—and I know I'm sort of rambling now, but my heart is really in it— whether these men, my brothers in prison, have not given me more than I have ever been able to give them. I know one thing, they are truly my brothers, and I love them for the grace of God that has been obviously shed abroad in their hearts. My supervisor tells me, "Your men really miss you when you are not here." Well, I miss them too, and I doubt any pastor's congregation prays for him as diligently and as fervently as these men do for theirs. They also fervently pray for any need brought to their attention.

It has been such a blessing to have volunteers from our church as well as visiting evangelists, pastors and missionaries come in to speak to them. Long after they are gone, they will mention something they have said that has helped them, or ask about a need they presented to them. Perhaps it is not all that bad to be shut away from the demanding agendas most of us have hanging over us.

After a number of years I have noticed something rather interesting, and which just reminds me more and more that this battle is God's, not mine. We have one whole unit of the prison set apart for a drug program that the state sponsors and seems to feel essential. Notwithstanding, I have never heard one positive good come out of it. The program itself is conducted by ex-drug users, probably about two-thirds of whom could best be labeled by removing the "ex." Many men whose crimes are involved with drug using or dealing are sent to the program and as a reward are granted quicker release upon completing it. I have noticed for a long time that some of the Christian men seem to be able to sit through the several months of the program and keep the victory and let it do whatever it does to them; others are only there for a short time when they come to me in distress and say that they cannot keep clear with God and go on with it. I just advise them that God is first. If they cannot keep clear with God and stay in the program, so what of an earlier release? A number of them have just asked to be dismissed on the grounds that they cannot keep a clear conscience and sit all day long under programming that forbids them to make reference to God as the effective Power that has changed their lives. And to think that penitentiaries were named such because they were first started as a forum for men to become penitent before God until He changed them.

I marvel at the compassion God has given to some of the men who work with dying men in the hospital. The common concept that is perhaps normal to have of a man in prison is that he is a hard, unfeeling, calloused individual. Some of these men have such a love and compassion for their dying fellow prisoners that it amazes me. One today was telling me of one of his patients who has such a wasted and broken-apart body that one can actually thrust his hand into the open bedsore on his back side. He is covered with them and has a bad case of Alzheimer's until he is just as broken emotionally, yet this man will go in and take good care of him and then pray over him and just say, "Dear Jesus, You know this man's heart; You know what he would like to tell you but he can't anymore. Would You please hear his prayer and get him ready for heaven?" They will have their reward.

In Him,
William Cawman

2
"Grace Did Much More Abound"

April 1, 2009

Greetings once again in the love of Jesus and all that He is. I find more and more the depth of preciousness in the opening words of Hudson Taylor's favorite hymn: "Jesus, I am resting in the joy of Who Thou art..." After all is said and done of what we think we have done for Him, it is enough to know that we are entirely buried in Him and that He is all in all. I hope and trust each of you are enjoying Him as much as my heart is.

It has been a while since I updated you on the spiritual journey of the man who used to be a Mormon. I will not relate his story here as it is at length in letters of the past, but it is a blessing to sense his continuing growth in the knowledge of God and holiness after all the years of teaching by the demonic cult of Mormonism. Let me give you an excerpt of a recent letter he sent to me.

> ...God is cleansing and refining my mind and soul from the false doctrine that was force-fed to me since I was a toddler— changing my entire approach, understanding, and experience toward what/who God is and how to seek Him.

He's also moving in me to fuel the desire for Him. I experience that as a cleansing force because it overshadows and overtakes all other desires. (Which may sound like a "tame" process, but it's not, it's a wild and savage burning out, letting go, and in the case of certain people, a grieving process that can be extremely painful.) …

…the best way I've had to describe it is Oswald Chamber's statement, "What is my vision of God's purpose for me? Whatever it may be, His purpose is for me to depend on Him and on His power *now!*" That is the polar opposite of Mormonism, where the goal is to no longer need God, but to become a god myself. Perhaps that's why the first aspect of sanctification for me has had to include the intellectual and emotional cleansing methods of meditation for an extended period, and several years of re-introduction to the Scriptures, a new understanding of Christ, a legitimate repentance process and simply experiencing God and the Holy Spirit.

I'm being shown a healthy suspicion of myself; that my personality and proclivities have a different feel than God's guidance— not that my natural tendencies are all bad, just often misplaced and miss-timed, and are perfumed with too much ego….

An example of my natural personality is that after reading your letter I was thrilled that a 4-year course is available! I nearly jumped off my bunk. If you'd been here in person I'd have hugged you and praised the Lord in gratitude and asked if I could start the program right there on the spot. What a blessing to have a Bible-centered educational experience available. It's exactly what I've been praying for. I have a little note on my shelf that has the question the Lord asked Lazarus' sister, "Do you believe I am able to do this?" When I look at it I say, "Yea, Lord, I believe!" Then I slow my natural man down, and respect His timing.

I'm very grateful to you, and praise God and bless His name that a door has been opened for me to be guided through God's Word by good men. Yea, Lord, I believe! Thank you.

Let me tell you about another miracle of God's grace. I think I already mentioned this man in a previous letter and how one day he stood up to testify in class and told us about his getting saved a few months before. He had been a wicked sinner in heart and life and some of those sins had such a grip on him that he was sure it would take a long time to get loose from them if indeed he ever would. But he said when God saved him those very sins were the first ones to leave him. God immediately took away the cigarette habit and the cursing and the filthy appetites and he went forth rejoicing in new life.

After a few months of learning to walk with God, the system wanted him to enter a drug rehab program, telling him that it would hasten his release from prison. He told them that he would try it, but that if it began in any way to interfere with his relationship with God, he would drop out of it. They looked at him and said, "What do you mean by that?" He told them very clearly that he is not the man he used to be and that he doesn't ever want to be that man again. He said he was enjoying his new relationship with Jesus and that he never wanted anything to cause him to go back to what he was. He said they looked away into the air, but he had a feeling they knew what he was meaning. Then he went on to tell me with emphasis, "Chaplain, I cannot even stand to think about what I used to be. I was so terrible that I hate it now. I never want those old sins again."

Now he has even more to rejoice about, so listen to his further story. I asked him about his family, and immediately his face lit up. He had lived with a woman for thirteen years and they had two children together, but they had never gotten married, even though they planned to someday. He had spent some time in prison and after he got out, she told him that if he ever went in again she was done with him and would leave him for good. He didn't really think she would, and besides sin had such a hold on him that he went on with his lifestyle and was again arrested and sent to prison. She wrote to him and told him she was moving to another state and would never be in his life again as well as the two children.

For around two years he never heard a thing from her, but after God saved him one day a letter slid under his door. He opened it to read that his "wife" had also gotten saved and she was forgiving him and wanted to give him another chance. She immediately put the children back into his life and is contacting him regularly. Of course, he plans to get married immediately when he gets out and not continue to live in sin. He also wants to find a good church where she is living and live for God. Have you ever heard the little chorus with a great big message: "He can move the highest mountain"? You know who that "He" is, don't you? Why don't we ask for more and believe Him?

Let me tell you of another part of the prison where God is working that I don't often speak about. We not only have a broad spectrum of criminals in prison but a real variety of officers as well. Among the several hundred officers that cover the three shifts you can imagine that we see many drastically different personalities as well as many other differences. Among the lot, however, there are a few who really seem to be enjoying whatever it is they have found in their relationship to God. There is one black officer whose position it is to escort the medicine carts as they are moved from one clinic to another within the facility. He always has a very pleasant smile and as well, never fails to stop to greet me with a handshake and the latest Scripture that he is feeding on. It is very obvious that not only is he not putting his candle under a bushel, but he is "thinking on these things." It always brightens my pathway to meet him. Just how complete his relationship with God is I do not know, but I often wonder why everyone that knows Jesus doesn't manifest it like he does.

Another very tall white officer is also very vibrantly ready to greet me anywhere and around anyone. His face lights up when he sees me coming down the corridor and he comes with a handshake and a hug and wants to know what the latest word is— and he is not referring to any other word than what I have been hearing from God. He is always wanting to know where I have been in meetings and how it went. There are regularly scheduled Bible studies that are held in the administration building of the prison for these officers and staff members who care to attend.

They usually take place at shift change so that officers from all three shifts can come if they want to. They are always small groups, but those who attend seem really zealous about it. This tall officer is always begging me to attend and share something with them. I am not there every week, and even when I am I often have so many men needing a visit that I cannot always get there; yet I do go when I can. They listen to what I have to say to them about God's marvelous works in my own heart and life and never seem to resist any truth. They beg me to come back again as soon as I can.

I could tell you of others among the officers also who really seem to be open and unashamed of their faith in God, but I wanted to tell you this much for two reasons. One reason is that you will pray for the officers. Oh, how I wish they were all Christians and loved Jesus and their fellow men. What a difference it would make in the rehabilitation of the men under their care. The other reason is that I see in these few men one more evidence that while the Antichrist is moving in with alarming pace, so also the Holy Spirit is hovering still over this old world, calling everyone that will listen to come to Him. There is definitely an awareness in the world that time is short, and God's Holy Spirit is being so faithful. It makes me long to be at tip-toe to hear His voice and be useable to Him in this dark hour.

There is another special need I would like to make request for. Several years ago a tall, very good looking black man came to this prison from another one and immediately began to show unusual interest and faithfulness in all the services and Bible studies and classes. It soon became evident that he was a real missionary at heart. He has a very winning bearing about him that draws men to him (not at all in a wrong way) and wherever in the prison he is residing, he brings a good group to services with him.

One day I came around the corner of the courtyard which was full of men out getting exercise, etc., and there he was standing in the middle of them all with his arm around another man praying with him. For all of that he told me over and over that he just could not see that what I was teaching them of a life free from sin and a cleansing of the nature of it was in the Bible. After a while he was released on parole and within about a year was back in prison again with a fresh charge and another twenty years to serve. He immediately began coming back to services again, and to be really honest was a blessing in many ways. But he still said he could not see that it was possible to live free from sin. I asked him if his way of believing had kept him from sin and he dropped his head for a minute and then said, "No, it didn't."

Over the past couple of years since coming back, he has come little by little to a much clearer head acceptance of that grand Biblical teaching, and often I believe he does live a justified life and really loves the Lord, but please pray that he will allow God to give him a personal Pentecost. What a power he could be for God and holiness if he were only cleansed from sin! He loves to study the Word, and often comes up with deep thoughts and findings from it that enriches the classes or Bible studies, but he needs a pure heart. He realizes that much more than he did a while ago, but believing it is not enough. (The devil believes in holiness too, with all there is of him; if he didn't he wouldn't put up such resistance against it.) But I long that he could really get sanctified wholly. Will you lend your petition to the prayer of Jesus, "Sanctify [him] through Thy truth, Thy Word is truth"?

Your Brother in Him,
W. Cawman

May 1, 2009

> And an highway shall be there, and a way, and it shall be called The way of holiness; the unclean shall not pass over it; but it shall be for those: the wayfaring men, *though fools*, shall not err therein. (Isa. 35:8)
>
> In that hour Jesus rejoiced in spirit, and said, I thank thee, O Father, Lord of heaven and earth, that thou hast hid these things from the wise and prudent, and hast revealed them unto *babes*: even so, Father; for so it seemed good in thy sight. (Luke 10:21)

OUR GOD IS THE BIGGEST entity in the entire universe, of whom Solomon declares, "But will God in very deed dwell with men on the earth? behold, heaven and the heaven of heavens cannot contain thee; how much less this house which I have built!" Yet He will literally move inside of a child's heart. Our God is such a complicated and intricately detailed Being that angels stand in awe and wonder, yet He makes Himself perfectly known to the simplest mind, that it need not err in the way to heaven.

For several weeks now a man has been sitting on the front seat of the Bible studies in the minimum camp of the prison. He has been listening intently although often with knit brow. He often has asked questions that would easily identify him as being totally— yes, totally— ignorant and untutored in the way of righteousness and holiness. In a Wednesday afternoon Bible study recently he came to the front at the close of the class and with hunger written on his face said, "Chaplain, would you please pray with me? I want to ask Jesus to come into my heart." Immediately I instructed him that as we prayed he should lay all his sins before Jesus and ask Him to forgive them and to come into his heart. We then prayed, but of course the time is very limited as they are to go directly to their bunks for the late afternoon count. I then told him as he was leaving to keep asking Jesus until he knew without a doubt that He had come in.

2: "Grace Did Much More Abound" 31

The following afternoon when I could have a little more time with him I went back and called him into the chapel. He said he had been asking Jesus to come in and that he did not want sin anymore. He said he did not want to enter into the conversations and pictures being passed around and that he did not want to watch television anymore. He said the men were making fun of him but it didn't matter, he wanted Jesus to come in. We had prayer again as I urged him to believe that Jesus would do it.

Of course, as you know, the devil was not silent and kept saying in my ear, "It won't happen; he doesn't understand; he isn't really awakened enough... blah, blah, blah..." I'm not sure what all else he said, but it doesn't matter, for ere long the man's eyes were wet with tears and he said he felt Jesus had forgiven him. I gave him a hug and told him that now we are brothers. So let me just shout right in the face of Satan— "So there! One more for Jesus!"

The next week when he came into the Bible study I was immediately attracted by the wonderful change in his face. There was no question but that he was a changed man and that there was a new light lit up in him. I went in later just to try to strengthen and encourage him and as he spoke to me I was just melted that Jesus so loves us that He will entrust us with the treasure of His grace and life, even though we might be the most untutored soul on earth.

I could easily sense that he is somewhat slow of learning, totally a stranger to the language of the Bible, and has not the smallest foundation of experience of how to walk with God; but Jesus is teaching him and helping him to love and serve him. He was pondering over his Bible and then pointed to a word and asked me how to say it— the word was "Naphtali." We solved that problem quite quickly, and he practiced saying it three times— on to the next step!

Several letters ago I think I told you of a man from Haiti who was so melted to tears when I told him that a Bible college president had offered to give him a four year course and it would not cost him anything. The other day this same man at the beginning of class said, "Chaplain, could I say something? I know I have not sinned, but my heart is so heavy. I feel such a burden on my heart for so many lost souls all around me. They are not rejecting me, they are rejecting Him. It seems my eyes have suddenly been opened up wide to what they are doing. This is not about me anymore; I feel such deep pain over sin. It brings tears; my heart is so heavy and broken over the many who are rejecting Him. I would like to ask all the brothers here in class to pray for me that I will be able to respond to this like God wants me to."

These statements were coming, not as from one who had learned somewhere that his heart should be broken over sin, but out of true brokenness itself. I felt like asking God to get my own heart closer to Him that I too might feel as deeply as I should the lost estate of the multitudes around us. Please do help this man pray that God will use him to bear the burden unto fruit for God's kingdom.

You might be interested in a follow up of a prayer request from some time ago. Some time back I had asked for prayer for the situation with the Islamic chaplain and his never-ending aggression and unethical shenanigans. He had, totally contrary to very strict ethics which we are all to follow, gone directly to Trenton to the commissioner and complained about our supervisor in order to try to get his position. If you understand anything at all about the mindsets of Islam, you can see how irksome it would be for him as the leader of the Muslims in prison to have a white Christian over him.

At times it looked really serious from the fact that from our White House down, the philosophy is to tiptoe on eggshells with Islam and trample Christianity ruthlessly under foot. Along with his desire to take over the position of supervisor, he constantly for years had agitated that the prison should hire more help for him as he said he was overworked (!!!!). Well, finally, a few months ago the system granted the request and hired a part time Imam to help him. The new Imam seems to be a very friendly and congenial fellow and the inmates like him better than the first one, so now there is a measure of jealousy springing up that is keeping the first chaplain busy keeping it under control. The first one is now seen always accompanying the second one everywhere he goes so as not to let him get ahead of him, which of course demonstrates quite clearly how much he needed him.

Do you remember the Biblical story of the enemies that surrounded Judah, where God told Jehoshaphat that he would not need to fight in this battle? Then the enemies of the Lord turned their attention to each other and self-destructed? Well, I guess it won't be amiss if you want to derive a little amusement from this answer to your prayers, for we did. The years of agitation from that quarter have quieted down amazingly, for he is so busy keeping abreast of the new chaplain he wanted for so long, so as not to let him get the edge on him, that he has at least for now forgotten all his other areas of discontent. Carnality would provide first class entertainment if it weren't so ugly.

Due to the fact that God's pathway for me personally has led to almost equally divided time between the prison ministry and evangelism, I feel so thankful for the volunteers from our church who faithfully take their time to go and fill in when I am gone. For several years my classes were just dismissed when I was not there, but now that hardly ever has to happen. When I first began sending out these letters I was instructed by the State to leave names out of them for the protection of both volunteers and inmates, and I have tried to follow all the instructions I was given in writing them, but that does not decrease the gratitude I feel for them.

A young man who took an internship with me a couple of years ago, and who includes a letter of his own now, has been so faithful in filling in the weekly classes, and our pastor backs him up at times. Then another couple faithfully fill in the Friday evening Bible studies and different ones take the Sunday night services when I am gone. I must tell on my pastor a bit.

Recently he must have preached a good red-hot message on a Sunday night to a group in the prison. I returned on Tuesday and heard from several of the good sanctified men about it. They were thrilled with it and said there was a lot of talk about it going around the courtyards. The report was that the men who were finished with sin loved it and some others were angry over it. Praise the Lord! I love reports like that!

A while back a volunteer minister preached to the same group that our pastor had that Sunday night. He told them, and then left pamphlets behind to reinforce it, that "we all know that after we are born again, we continue to sin. The reason for this is that when we are born again, it is only our soul that is born again; our body continues to sin." When the men told me about it I suggested that they try telling the judge that the next time they had to appear before him. "Oh, Judge, I didn't do that, it was just my body that did that." I told them that I would suppose the judge might answer, "Well, perhaps we will lock your body up for a while for doing it."

You can see that these men in a captivated setting get a real smorgasbord of instruction. Sadly enough there are those who love the doctrines of the devil. Some time ago I was visiting upstairs in the hospital and as I passed by a cell I noticed a large man sitting in a wheelchair. As soon as he saw me he got excited and asked me to come in. "Oh, Chaplain, I'm so glad to see you. I was just sitting here watching a preacher on television and he was saying that he can't quit sinning. Every time he sees a beautiful woman he just falls on his face. I got so blessed I was just shouting, 'Yep! That's me! That's me!'"

When you pray for these dear souls— and I know that many of you do and I thank you and so do they— pray that the Holy Spirit will be enabled to get through all the false shepherds and hireling voices and convict men of truth. Sometimes it seems we are fighting a losing battle against the dynamically aggressive sinning doctrines and the emotionally frenzied charisma of those who are "sensual, having not the Spirit;" but God is gleaning a few souls for the Bride of His Son, so we will battle on. The battle for souls is a battle, no matter where it is. We read of the revival efforts and the missionary efforts of the Philadelphia Church age and marvel as whole tribes and villages and towns would be swept into the kingdom and into the church. We are living for sure in the gleaning hour, but let's be faithful.

If God was only interested in big numbers, He would have ended the church age before this generation came along. But as long as He tarries the challenge is ours— "To serve the present age, our calling to fulfill," and— "Oh, may it all my powers engage, to do my Master's will." Aren't you thrilled to be counted worthy to be His witness to this generation? The harvest will soon be ended, and we will be so glad that we did not lay our armor down just because the world is not being won for Jesus. After all, did not our Great Shepherd say that the angels in heaven rejoice over one sinner that repents? Do you suppose that they are just watching and looking, all around the world and in every unlikely place even, and when they see another soul cry out to Jesus and let Him come into their heart, say— "One more for Jesus!" So there, devil!

Keep praying and there will be more victories to rejoice over!

Your Brother in battle,
William Cawman

June 1, 2009

GUESS WHAT? OUR SCHOLARS from behind prison walls have finally discovered where God came from! And it was confirmed by several voices from here and there in the prison classes. A "teacher" came in who seems to have a piece of knowledge that no one has ever had heretofore, for he told the men that the Bible says God came from Teman. Now if you don't believe that, you can find it yourself in Habakkuk 3:3. Isn't it wonderful that our dear men are learning such profound truths that will help them become more like Jesus? 2 Peter 2:1 says, "But there were false prophets also among the people, even as there shall be false teachers among you, who privily shall bring in damnable heresies, even denying the Lord that bought them, and bring upon themselves swift destruction."

And so, after having to waste valuable class time undoing this exciting discovery, we proceeded on with something more profitable. Sometimes one wonders just what motivates some people to want to try to teach the things of God when obviously they don't know Him themselves, but I'm sure the devil loves the whole business and gladly promotes it.

But now let me follow up on our dear brother from the minimum camp that we told you about in the last letter. On a Tuesday afternoon he came into class, and he usually now comes a few minutes early just in case we are there so that he can talk about his new life. We sat down for a few minutes before class and he said, "Chaplain, the devil is fighting me! I don't want all that old music and pictures and stuff and to act like I used to, but the devil is trying to bring it all out against me." I said, "Well, my brother, you didn't expect that Satan would let go of you that easily, did you? Do you remember reading in your Bible about the Children of Israel coming out of Egypt and how Pharaoh denied them permission to leave ten times, and then when they did leave how he followed after them? The devil isn't happy about you leaving his camp and he is going to put up a fight, but you just need to look to Jesus and plead the Blood against him."

The next day he came back to Bible study (first one to arrive again) and said, "Chaplain, it's working! God is giving me the victory." We started the Bible study and after we had sung a couple of songs and had prayer I noticed him sitting there with such a look of peace and rest on his face. He looked up and said, "I just love this new man God is making me. I don't ever want the old one again." Isn't it glorious to watch Christ being formed in a soul? It's even, I confess, somewhat entertaining, and far better and more wholesome than any other entertainment. Please pray for this man that he will allow God to get him through those initial hurdles that are such a vital part of being transformed from darkness to light and from the kingdom of Satan to the Kingdom of God. The gulf between those two has never been greater in any generation.

There is also another man I would like to give you an update on. Do you remember that a few months ago one of our best and most promising men who I had utmost confidence in suddenly dropped clear out of the picture and for a time wouldn't even talk to anyone about it? Well, thank God that I could write later and tell you that God helped him to see his error in listening to the discouragements of the devil and he sought his way back again to God and never stopped until he knew he was fully sanctified again.

The other day I asked him to open the class in prayer. He said, "I'd like to say something first. When I failed God a while back I brought reproach to Him and I'm not proud of that, but He has restored my soul and I am living in present victory. But I want to say to all the men, 'Keep your eyes on Jesus; this is not about me; it's all about Him. I can fail, but He can't.'" One could feel not only the true repentance in his words, but the set of his will also that he will never fail again. Our failures do nothing to magnify His grace, but His grace is certainly greater than all our failures.

Now I have another combination victory and prayer request to share with you. Several years ago a tall, very good looking and intelligent black man came into the prison from another one and immediately began to shine in the classes and Bible studies. He is a real student and loves the Word and often comes up with very thought provoking questions as well as observations. He is a talented missionary and whatever unit he is on, you can count on a good number of men coming to religious services from that unit.

For all of that he is very much like Paul's brethren of Israel who "have a zeal of God, but not according to knowledge." For over a year he came and listened intently to the teaching of complete deliverance, not only from the guilt of committed acts, but also from the very nature of sin as well. He couldn't see it. He listens to every preacher available on the television and does a lot of reading and kept saying that he just could not see that such a deliverance was possible.

The day came when he was released on parole. He still had the nature within that he did not believe it possible to be delivered from and in about a year he was back in prison for twenty more years on a fresh charge. Very broken, but very much determined to be right with God again, he repented and sought God and no doubt found forgiveness. He continued to say that he did not see it the way we were teaching it, so I asked him if the way he believed had worked. He hung his head and admitted that it had not. Still he could not seem to grasp it. Perhaps he was too much akin to the wise and prudent to have it revealed to him.

But one day in class this month the subject was "Holiness and Heaven," a chapter in Yocum's book, *The Holy Way*. As I spoke to them that morning about how pure heaven was and how unthinkable it would be that God would allow a single sin spot to enter there, I entered into an unusual degree of liberty and help from above. There was vibrant interest from nearly every man and many questions. I felt thoroughly thrilled while speaking on it and at the close of the class after all the others had passed out, he came to me with the most intense look on his face and said, "Chaplain, all the times I have sat under you and heard you speak of purity of heart, it never got through to me like it did this morning. I see it. It is right."

Please pray now that he will find it, for his condemnation will only be the greater for understanding it if he fails to get it. I often wonder what God could do with this man for the next twenty years in that prison if he were totally sold out to God. I'd be willing to find out, too.

I left the class that morning and started out of that compound into the main compound. Coming from the opposite direction was the man I told about in a letter a number of months ago who had prayed through to complete victory in holiness and was then made to root through a dumpster to try to find a toilet brush he had mistakenly thrown away, and how the officers standing guard over it heard him singing in there and couldn't believe it. He has not been attending class for the last while because of a conflict with another class, but plans to return soon. I said to him, "Brother, you missed a good class this morning." He said, "I can see that because your face is all aglow. I'll be coming back soon."

A few days later I was visiting with him and he told me that a short while back he had nearly slipped away and become careless, but that I had called him down and asked him how he was getting along, and he realized what was happening and caught himself, and now he is living in perfect victory. It is not only a constant battle to snatch souls from the kingdom of Satan, but it is a battle as well to keep them stirred up to not let the fire burn dim, especially when they are living in the worst cesspool of sin and shame imaginable.

It is struggle enough for saints who are members of a good church to stay awake and filled with oil in this sleepy church age; all the more so for these who have no church, no Christian family, no Sunday School. They need continual prayer that they will keep what God has done for them. And some of them are; all glory be to God!

The following day after that precious class time, we were teaching the same material in another facility and again God was really helping and the tide was exciting. We were studying further in that chapter of how holiness is an added strength against backsliding. As I was speaking to them of the lifelong quest and desire to become more and more like Jesus and how suddenly, when we step into heaven, "we shall be like Him," a glorious new (to me) thought occurred to me. I had always envisioned that when we step into heaven we would suddenly be changed into His complete likeness, but that is not at all what it actually says; it says, "we *shall be* like Him," not "we shall be made like Him." Then I thought of the Scripture that says that "in a moment, in the twinkling of an eye... we shall be changed." That moment is just before we see Him, and that means that when we shall finally look upon Him we will suddenly realize, "I am like Him!" Won't that be thrilling beyond any power to express? Won't it be worth it all then, as if it isn't worth it all even now?

I had to stop and tell them about the little girl whose daddy went away in military service before she could remember him. Her mother set a picture of him on the table and constantly told her little girl that it was her daddy. She loved the picture and hugged and kissed it. After several years daddy came home, very eager of course to pick up and love his little girl, but she didn't know him. Patiently he waited for her to get used to him. One day as they sat in the living room both parents noticed that she was looking at the picture and then at him; back again to the picture and then at him. Suddenly she burst into tears and ran and jumped into his arms saying, "You're my daddy!" Can you even faintly imagine what it will be when we "see Him as He is"? Can you imagine the unspeakable thrill of that moment when we first see His face and rush to meet Him, realizing that it is He into whose likeness we have been transformed? I don't want for anything in all the world to miss that, do you?

Do you remember the two sanctified men who were living in the same cell and then one of them was sent to another state to serve several more years there? I received a letter from him filled with fresh and glorious victory and when I shared it with his former cellmate and another brother who knew and loved him it brought a powerful sense of communion between all of us, even though we were separated by many miles. We got to talking about the communion of saints and how precious it is, even though they may be separated by vast miles and space that is filled with corrupted airwaves of all that hell can belch out.

Then we wondered what it will be like in the Millennium when there will be nothing that shall "hurt nor destroy in all my holy mountain: for the earth shall be full of the knowledge of the Lord, as the waters cover the sea." What a level of communion of saints will we experience then? The longer we talked the sweeter and more sacred the atmosphere became until it felt like we had been "sit[ting] together in heavenly places." The two precious brothers and myself just sat there in heavenly love and perfect harmony with nothing between us and nothing between us and Jesus. Holiness works!

I want to say again that I and these men thank you ever so much for your faithful prayers, and if you continue faithful in prayer there will be more to write about next month.

Yours for Jesus' sake,
William Cawman

3
IN PRISON AND OUT OF PRISON

July 1, 2009

THIS PAST MONTH HAS HELD a few new horizons as far as prison ministry is concerned. We spent part of the month in South Africa and Mozambique and on the way across the Atlantic we witnessed a future prison inmate in rapid development. A boy of perhaps two years of age was thankfully on the opposite side of the Boeing 777 from us, but was controlling the atmosphere notwithstanding. He had the complete mastery of both of his parents who spent their time walking the aisles with him while he threw himself around in tantrums of discontent and anger and slapped them in the face, endeavored to yank their hair out with both hands at once, and tried to bite them in the face. We kept thinking, "God have mercy on both parents and child, and what correctional measures will be effective when he arrives at the door of some penitentiary in a few short years?"

In Middleburg, SA we had the privilege of visiting a prison where we spoke to the women on one side and then to the men on the other side. How pathetic to see a cute little baby with his mother in prison. After we had spoken to the men they sang for us, and I wished that I had taken a recorder to capture it. It was absolutely beautiful. The warden of the prison was in the service the next Sunday morning and after I had preached on the glorious reality of the New Birth, he came with tears to the altar. Afterward he was begging for help, for he confessed that he had never been able to live a life of consistent Christian victory. Please pray for him.

I must also tell you that on Monday morning before we left SA for Mozambique I was asked to speak to the students of the local high school. Very few of them were black Africans. The majorities were Afrikaners and there were about 1200 enrolled. As I walked into the courtyard, hundreds of them were packed into standing room only and they were dressed in beautiful uniforms. As soon as I mounted the podium they hushed into perfect attention and listened as I begged them to care enough about the beautiful gift of life to give themselves to no one but Jesus Christ. I tried to warn them that many bidders were reaching for each of them, but none of them were worthy of their choice except Jesus. After I finished several of the young men came up and thanked me for the message. What a contrast to our own beloved nation, which for many years has sent missionaries to try to enlighten them.

But even though there is much more we could say about that, let me get back to prison where we left you last month, and let me follow up on a couple of stories. In the last letter I told you of the man who had listened for a long time and finally the real truth of heart purity dawned on him— almost the same as the truth of salvation by faith dawned on Martin Luther many years before.

Being a very dependable and looked-up-to man, he was the inmate representative for his tier. There is one on each tier who is authorized to bring any complaints or concerns from the inmate population to the administration. There was a legitimate concern that he had expressed to the administration and the officer in charge of that tier took it personally. Late in the afternoon, the officer called him out of the dayroom and began to "give it to him."

When he had said what he had to say, the inmate began walking away and the officer threw a punch at him. He turned and asked why he did that and the officer then began to attack him and told him to get down. A code was called and officers came in to back him up. They got him onto the floor and began to kick and hit him with handcuffs while one of them stood on his arm and another on his head. They did not break any bones, but they bruised him up badly. They then handcuffed him and sent him to another prison where he is being held under camera observation with the label of a "cop killer."

This all happened within full view of many of the inmates on the tier. Immediately grievances began to enter the administrator's office and special investigators were sent to the unit to interview the inmates who saw it. Over sixty men testified with one voice to what we have related above, and they all witnessed that the inmate acted the part of a Christian through it all. By the way, the officer who started it all is out on sick leave now claiming that the inmate hit him in the shoulder.

One of the precious sanctified men on the tier (in fact it is the man I have told you about who was made to search the dumpster and while doing so was singing with joy) has received several letters from the attacked inmate in the other prison. He says he forgives them all and refuses to allow any bitterness, and that God allowed it so he is going to find what God has for him in it. If this is part of what it takes to drive him to the cross of his personal crucifixion, he'll thank God for all eternity for it all. Will you pray that it will be so and that he will not only let this be the time of his complete sanctification, but that God will help his light to shine where he is?

And now, I absolutely must tell you more about the dear man out in the minimum camp that got saved last April and is growing in grace conspicuously. As I have already told you, this man is not an Einstein, but don't forget, God didn't choose many Einsteins anyway. In fact, listen to the prayer of Jesus: "Father I thank thee that thou hast hid these things from the wise and prudent, and hast revealed them unto babes: even so, Father; for so it seemed good in thy sight."

This dear man has never been the victim of preconceived ideas about how he is supposed to act or respond as a Christian, but it thrills my heart to see grace working just like God's Word says it will. After three weeks away in Africa I walked back into the minimum camp and there he stood at the top of the stairs with a glow all over his face and his hand waving greeting. He is getting more beautiful and lovable with every passing day. Never can I be convinced that the genuine grace of God does not work, and work just like God said it would.

As we started into the class discussion he said, "Chaplain, somebody told me that I can just talk to God just like I would talk to a person; that I don't have to make prayers— is that right?" "Oh indeed it is," I said, "You can just tell God anything at all and He will talk back to you too, and you can trust Him with all your secrets." "Oh, that makes me feel so good, I can do that!"

We went on further and as I looked back at him I was just overwhelmed at the change grace has made even in his countenance. After a while longer he said, "Chaplain, what does the word 'defile' mean? I was reading here in the Bible where Dinah the daughter of Jacob went out to see the daughters of the land and Shechem took her and defiled her— what does that mean?" I explained the meaning of the word and his face took on instant pain as he said, "Oh no, oh no!"

The man next to him said, "Remember, we used to be like that too Do you remember all the times we sinned like that?" I saw again a look of utter agony come over his face and then it changed to a violence of righteous anger, "I tell you, man, I don't ever want anything to do with that man again!" I instantly jumped to the occasion and said, "Men, right before you is a wonderful witness of real repentance. Repentance is not simply shedding a few tears and feeling sorry; it is a radical, violent turning from what we once were to walk an entirely new pathway."

And all this is not the product of an effort to try to match the teachings of some theology book; it is the spontaneous reactions of inward grace, imparted into the soul by faith in the precious Blood of Jesus.

For some weeks now, God has really been moving on hearts in the minimum camp and there has been a vibrancy of response that pulls on your heart. There has been another man that I have noticed often coming into class and getting on his knees and staying there for some time. It is obvious that he is really in earnest prayer to God. He has never said much until the other day when he put up his hand and said, "I need to give a little testimony. I have been praying and praying that God would put the pieces of my life back together as well as for other of the men too. This week I got a letter from my wife after a long silence. She told me the wonderful news that I am once again a father to a little seven pound eight ounce girl. And then she told me that she wants to change her ways and if I do too she is ready and willing to give me another chance."

We had a time of rejoicing and I said, "Man, do you realize how deeply in debt you are?" He said with a glowing smile, "Yes, I do."

In case you are ever tempted to think of these men as hardened criminals incapable of heavenly emotions, let me tell you that I often see more tears in prison than in many churches. Here is a man in his early forties who murdered a girl while in his teens and is serving what will probably be a life sentence. As he sits in class and listens to truth his eyes over and over brim with tears and his face evidences deep emotion. A more tender heart it would be hard to find anywhere. He is humble and teachable and pure in heart and life, and God loves him, for he is not the man he used to be but is a completely new creature in Christ Jesus. Isn't the grace of our God wonderful?

But in spite of all that God is doing for many, there are those who are struggling and cannot seem to break the chains of bondage. The enemy is cunningly aware of our weakest point and he doesn't waste any time or effort to aim his arrows at it. Several years ago I told you of a man who was walking so beautifully with God and had gotten out of prison and started coming to our church. For months he was such a blessing and was a brother in the family. But Satan waited his chance and through the open door of discouragement brought him down and back into sin. He went back to prison and he has struggled ever since.

For seasons he comes out on top and walks with God and hope rises that he will this time go all the way and never fall again, but in a short while he is clear down on the bottom again. Satan knows his besetting sin, and every time he gets tripped up he plunges into discouragement, self-abuse, and hopelessness and goes for another round of tragic defeat. All the men know that he never wants to depart from the way and he never loses his desire for God, but Satan has nearly beat him out of confidence in God. He has all but made shipwreck of his faith and he really needs prayer. He has a tender heart toward other men and never wants to see anyone else fail or go without God, but he has fallen so many times that now he lives down more than up, and Satan is laughing. Oh how I long to see him make one violent break forever with spiritual failure and start for heaven and never turn back again.

Just the other day he came to see me and was so discouraged and full of self-pity that even his face was a picture of torture. I did not make it easy on him, but warned him that if he does not set his will and take the hand of God and get out of this wilderness, he may go under one too many times and never come out on top again. He knew it and as I laid out before him the seriousness of the vacillating state he was living in he once again began to feel a spark of hope and desire. I'd love to see old Satan thoroughly defeated in his life and I know it can be so if he will let God do it for him.

In the more than eleven years that I have worked with some of these men I have seen two vast extremes. I have watched some come from far off places and begin to draw up close to God and then watched as Christ was formed in them and they became like Him. It is precious beyond words to watch this. But I have seen others who in the eleven years have backed away and aged until they hardly look like the same man that they did a few years ago.

One of them I have tried again and again to help, and at times it seemed he did want to get out, and he even seemed to get saved once, but he missed his chance to go home after all these years because during his exit exam he was discovered to have drugs in his system. Why, oh why? "When the living well is so nearby, Oh why will ye die?" Surely there is still much work to be done before Jesus comes back.

By the way, I had a glorious visit with the dumpster singer today and he told me with beaming face, "Chaplain, this thing works!" Hallelujah, it does too. Once again we all thank each of you for your prayers.

William Cawman

August 1, 2009

"I will worship toward thy holy temple, and praise thy name for thy lovingkindness and for thy truth: for thou hast magnified thy word above all thy name." So reads Psalm 138:2. Did you get it? "...thou hast magnified thy word above all thy name." Think of that! Indeed, if His Word is not true, His name is meaningless. This is the appraisal God Himself places upon His Word. Now let me tell you about a demonstration of that.

For a number of months which really has stretched into a few years, we have been studying the Book of Hebrews in one of the Friday night Bible studies. It has been rich beyond words as you can imagine. As we have neared the close of the epistle, I was searching to know what we should take up next and had even asked a few of the spiritual men in the class if they had any leadings or desires. Suddenly, I knew beyond doubt where we needed to go next. James follows Hebrews.

The first Bible study in which I was going to begin the study of James I sat down to open my heart to that most valuable epistle. For some reason, just as Jesus held the eyes of the two on their way to Emmaus for a season, it seemed the Book of James closed up right before my eyes. It seemed that a veil or a seal suddenly passed over it and— could I say it?— it seemed as if the words Daniel heard were applied: "...go thy way...for the words are closed up and sealed..."

I went to the Bible study wondering what I would give to the waiting men. When it came time for the study, not a moment before, I sensed a still small Voice saying, "Read the whole book." I announced to the men that we were going to do something different for a bit; that I was going to read the entire Book of James without making any comments as we went. They opened their Bibles and we began. It was never richer to my own heart as I read it very carefully and slowly, and whenever I would glance up, the men were buried in their Bibles taking it in. Every little bit I would hear an acknowledgement to the truth, but other than that, it was absolute concentration.

When I finished I asked if anyone had received anything new from the reading, and it looked as though nearly every hand went up. I then turned to the beginning of the book and the seal disappeared! We never got beyond verse 2. Oh, the value of the Word of God. God esteems it above all His precious name.

After the class a man came up from the back of the room and said, "Chaplain, God was really speaking to me tonight in a way I've never had Him do it before. I had so many questions answered..." and he seemed reluctant to leave the room. I walked away saying, "Give us less of man and more of Thy Word."

I think I told you that we also started a new book in our Christian Living classes. After finishing the precious book *The*

Holy Way by Dale Yocum, we had a wonderful thing happen. Someone alerted us to the fact that a publisher had printed a number of copies of the book *Our Own God*, by G. D. Watson, that had the page numbers out of order. The publisher sent us one hundred copies for simply the postage. The men began to study that book and the man I have written about who was so singing happy while being made to rummage through the dumpster for a toilet brush came to me and said with a gleam in his eyes, "Chaplain, this book is the best one I have ever read. I've read a lot of books, but never one like this one. Do you know, I've been witnessing to one of the officers and telling him about God and I told him about this book. Is there any chance I could have an extra copy to give to him?" I went and got one and handed it to him and said, "I wish you would give one to each of them." Will you pray for that officer?

Now I must tell you about the week of July 20 through 24. In a previous letter I mentioned that several inmates (seven at present, to be exact) have enrolled in a four year correspondence Bible and theology course with one of our holiness Bible colleges. Again, forgive the necessity of keeping state rules and leaving names out of the letter. One of the required courses consists of a study of proper Bible study methods. The president of the Bible college felt that it would be well if he could come this summer for a week and teach that class in person so that the men could get the most out of their other courses. Of course I welcomed this, but there was much background work to get it accomplished.

I presented the concept to the supervisor of chaplaincy and immediately he was in full favor of it happening and went to work on it. This was a little more (let me correct the word "little") than simply bringing in a visiting pastor which we have done many times; it constituted what the prison would term a "special event" which requires approval from not only the local administration but from the main offices in Trenton as well. Our prison is so large that it is divided into three identical facilities and there were students enrolled from all three.

So that required a special escorted provision to bring men from the other two facilities into one spot so that they could have class together.

At this point let me insert that the political atmosphere in Trenton, our state capital, has been in a sad state of moral deterioration for a while, since the man who was in charge of all state chaplaincy and was in favor of Christianity has retired. This moral deterioration is happening at an alarming pace. The first reactions were, "What is the purpose of this? What if we let you do this and then the Muslims want to do it? How can we allow something expressly 'Christian' in nature?" These sentiments and fears would have been unheard of five years ago. We prayed and sent back explanations of just what and why we wanted to do it, and thank God it was finally approved.

The day came and the men were anticipating it almost like it would be their wedding day. The classes started and what eager little birds they were to learn all they could. The classes were held from 8:30 to 10:30 and from 12:30 to 2:30 each day of that week. As the week went by, more and more positive comments and sentiments were expressed and the officer in charge of the education department which had given us a classroom to use became so friendly that he hugged the teacher and was ready to do anything he could to help us.

I was not personally present at many of the first class sessions as I had my own classes to teach in the chapel, but the last day I was with them and by Friday afternoon it honestly felt that we had been on the Mount with Jesus. The men expressed with deep emotion how much the class had meant to them and that they would never be the same again. We felt reluctant to leave, much the same as we often feel at the close of a camp or convention where God has moved in power. It was honestly one of the most single effective things that have ever happened for the cause of true holiness in this prison. At the close of it all the supervisor of chaplaincy threw the door wide open for it to happen again next summer, so please pray to that end.

Perhaps it would not be amiss to try to answer a question that will inevitably arise as to how these men can afford to be enrolled in Bible college when their top wage is perhaps between two and three dollars a day. Several churches, God bless them, have offered to send offerings to the college book store to defray the costs of their books, and the college is not charging tuition. This is an area that I stay out of as much as possible because it would never work for the chaplain to be involved in the inmates' finances, so whether the entire need is being met I have to leave with the college themselves; but one thing I know, God always supplies a way to get to hungry hearts and this is no exception.

It is one of the most encouraging things I have seen happen in these men's lives and I wish you could have been there on that last class. You would have seen your prayers being answered, and you would not have been dry-eyed, either. It is a marvelous thing how God works to get a soul prepared to be a part of the Bride of His Son. It would be the utmost demonstration of prideful folly for anyone to take an ounce of credit for bringing another soul to Jesus, for there is usually a chain of contacts and dealings that finally culminates in someone dropping in the final link and a soul is won to Jesus. My heart rejoices in every single person who has said a prayer, paid a visit, preached a message, sung a song, or even as Paul expressed it, "made mention of us in your prayers." God has used it all and has brought a little band of men into the truth and experience of heart holiness, and they are now a part of that glorious church that will make up His Bride.

Here is another update. Do you remember the man I have been telling you about in the minimum camp who came to us at the close of a Bible study in April and said, "Chaplain, would you please pray for me, I want Jesus to come into my heart?" He came in, too. Well, he has been walking in the light and learning to fight battles and keep victory, and this last week at the close of another Bible study in which I had been speaking very specifically about how pure our heart must be to enter heaven, he came up front again and said with the same deep simplicity as before, "Chaplain, would you please pray with me? I want a pure heart." I can't tell this like it really is, but will you pray for him too?

Recently a man sent a request to see a chaplain, with a letter stating that he wanted to be baptized because he wanted to enter the Kingdom of Heaven. My supervisor put it in my mail slot with a request that I see him and explain baptism to him and then we would talk about it some more. My supervisor also included a face sheet of the man so that I would know without looking him up myself just what background I was dealing with.

Let me say here that neither one of us favor baptizing men in prison. We feel it belongs to the community they came from to give that testimony after they have proved that they are walking a new pathway. I consequently have only baptized one man in the eleven years I have ministered in prison.

Oh, you say you would like to hear about that one? Well, he was a very bright and vibrant young man who really did seem to have experienced a change in his life, and he wanted ever so badly to be baptized. I explained to him as to many others why it was not really the place to do it in prison, but he must needs be baptized, so I told him if he would come to my office we would take care of it.

Now please forgive me for failure of total immersion, for it would require a "special event" to escort him to the drainage pond at the rear of the prison for such to happen. I went into the restroom next to my office and filled a Styrofoam cup with water and then after talking with him and hearing his testimony (very good) and again explaining the meaning of what we were doing, I began the prayer. At the prescribed moment in prayer I dumped the cup of water down over his head. He gasped and jumped and opened his eyes with, "Wow! I'll get you back sometime!"

I think I finished the prayer, but have never repeated the ordinance in prison.

Well, back to the man we started with. I took a few minutes first and explained the meaning and purpose of baptism and he readily agreed that it could wait, so we then proceeded to his desire to enter the Kingdom of Heaven. I asked him if he had ever had a time when he confessed his sins to Jesus and felt His forgiveness. He thought he had. I then asked him if Jesus had come into his heart and given him the power to live above sin. He readily confessed that he had no power at all to stop cursing and getting angry. I said to him, "What you need is to let Jesus come into your heart. Let's pray and ask Him to come in." I prayed and then I asked him if he wanted to pray and he said, "Yes, what shall I say?" I will visit him again this week; will you please pray for him too?

I mentioned that some time back the man who had held the door open and encouraged effective chaplaincy in NJ prisons retired. He was bucking more and more opposition from all around him. It did not help our cause at all for him to leave and this past week my supervisor was scheduled to attend a critical stress management seminar at the state offices in Trenton. He hoped to be able while there to speak to the commissioner regarding the move to take away our chapel officers. Instead the atmosphere was so charged with darkness and oppression he could not wait to get away. The emphasis was strongly on Buddhism and meditation arts. Pray for our country!

Until He comes!
William Cawman

September 1, 2009

ONE OF OUR POETS so beautifully wrote:

*Full many a gem the dark, unfathomed caves of
ocean bear;
Full many a flower is born to blush unseen, and
waste its sweetness on the desert air.*

And unbeknown to you and I there may be people we meet in the most unlikely places, and who would not at all appear to be such, who are gems just like this. Whenever my list of appointments gets caught up with the men who are waiting to sit and talk, I put a few names on the list of men who are in my classes, but who I've never had a visit with. You certainly never know what to expect. So many are less than serious enough to really come into contact with God and the way to heaven, but every once in a while you discover one who turns out to be such a blessing because of being so much farther up the road than you would have thought. I want to tell you about two of these in the same day, back to back.

The first one had been in class for several months and when I put his name on the list for a visit, he was very pleased. I asked him to tell me about his life and he eagerly began. He is now twenty-eight and had been a very popular young man and had lived his fill of girls and drink. At the age of about twenty-five his wild fun was stopped for drug dealing and he went to a county jail. By the time he was locked up he was having pain in his abdomen and the doctors performed some tests and discovered his liver in such deteriorated condition that his only hope was a transplant.

He begged the doctor to do something for him as there was little hope of receiving a kidney while in prison. The next time he went for a test there was a very kind nurse in her seventies that took his vital signs and then she told him she would like to pray with him. She asked the officer if she could and he told her not to touch him, but that she could pray. She did. The next time he went for a blood test, all was normal. He couldn't believe it and so asked them to test him again. They did and the test came back normal. His parents were amazed and requested that another test be given to him. It showed he was normal.

The young man began to seek God and the Lord saved him. As he told me this his face glowed with deep peace and he told me all he wants to do now is live for Jesus and that he is seeking God to give him a pure heart. Such witness accompanied his testimony that I felt my "heart was strangely warmed" with it and I am eagerly watching to see what more God is going to do in his life.

As soon as he left another young man, age twenty-six, came in and again I asked him about his life. He was just as eager to tell me his story. He has spent a total of fourteen of his twenty-six years in prisons. He grew up (or has he yet?) in an extremely dysfunctional home where his stepmother beat him for everything that happened, whether he was even home when it happened or not. One day when he was very small he wanted to go to church. He went all by himself and while he was there someone ate his father's cookies. When he got home his stepmother beat him for it because his older siblings said he had done it even though his stepmother knew he was not there.

He was first sent to jail when only eight years of age. He drowned his troubles with drugs and drink and lived a miserable life in and out of prison until just about six months ago. One day his cell mate who was in my classes told him he really needed to go to the classes. He decided to give it a try. I don't remember whether he said how long he had been coming, but one day, sitting there in class, he looked up into the corner of the room and he saw Jesus coming toward him. A great light shined into his heart and everything inside of him changed.

Now he is so happy that I was getting blessed listening to him. He said he has no un-forgiveness in his heart toward anyone, not even his stepmother, and he just wants to help others now to find the peace he has found. He went on to tell me that he knows that when he gets out in a few months from now he will need to find help to get free from all of his prison mentality, for he has actually been raised by prison culture, as inglorious as that is.

He told me that the last time he was out for a while he struggled to even adjust to seeing trees and smelling the grass. Yet in spite of it he really wants to just live this new life completely and never go back to the old life again. Will you please help these two young men in your prayers?

Wouldn't it be wonderful to meet them in heaven someday, where all the tears from their damaged lives will be wiped away and they will remember it no more? Heaven will be unspeakably rich for any of us, but imagine what it will be for a young man who never knew what it was to be a child, to love a school teacher, or a mother or father; to never have planted a garden or mowed a lawn or played with a dog or to have been tucked into bed at night with any sense of security at all. Such is the cruelty of that awful thing called "sin."

I would like to add a bright note to a story. It has been presented in parts and pieces of several letters of a man. Living in the beauty of holiness, he has now taken the place as tier rep for the man who was attacked and sent away by a revengeful officer. This man who took his place as tier rep is the same one who sang so beautifully in the dumpster. I won't repeat that story, so some who have not been getting the letters until recently will have a gap here.

Anyway, he came to see me one day and told me that the officer who had roughed up our good Christian brother and had him sent to another prison to get even with him was coming back to the tier the next day. He has been out on "sick leave" because he claimed the inmate wounded him, even though many witnesses testified that the Christian inmate never lifted a hand to strike back.

He wanted to know just how he should act to him, whether to avoid him or just what? I said to him, "Oh no, Brother, that would be exactly the opposite of what you should do. As soon as he arrives on the tier, just go right over to him with a big smile and welcome him back and ask him as the new tier rep if there is anything you can do to help make his job easier." I said, "What if you, by heaping coals of fire on his head, could win him to Jesus?" He said, "I like that, and that is just what I will do." You might remember him in prayer, and the officer, too.

Then, a day or so later someone dropped a note about his cell mate and so the officers came in and took his cell mate out. They asked our Brother to pack up his belongings for him. He began to pack them up and a female ombudsman, who was sent to investigate the situation, walked over to him.

She said, "K——, sometimes you might feel all alone in this place, but you are not alone." He looked into her face and knew exactly what she was trying to tell him. He said it was just the encouragement he needed and he felt God had her there just then. He took advantage of his empty cell that night and stayed up until two in the morning to worship the God he has come to love with all his heart. "Chaplain," he said with the sweetest and most contented smile, "He is a 'very present help in trouble.'"

And also let me continue the ongoing miracle of the simple man in the minimum camp. By the way, he told me the other day that he struggles to understand everything in the Bible because he only went to the fifth grade. I told him that God understands that and to just keep reading and get all that he can, and God will keep opening more.

One of the best signs of genuine divine life in him is that everything which he hears is available in the grace of God, he wants it! I told you in the last letter how one of our class discussions was about the pure in heart, and at the close of it he came up— with the same hungry look on his face as when he came up a few months ago and asked for prayer because he wanted to let Jesus come into his heart— and asked if I would pray with him because he wanted a pure heart.

Well, a couple of weeks later we were discussing the necessity of a real change of nature if we were to live the Christian life. Some of the men had asked for us to discuss that subject and many were really getting help as we did. Again at the close of the class he came to the front and said, "Chaplain, would you please pray with me? I want my nature changed." We prayed.

The next day in Bible study at the very beginning, he was sitting there with a smile that would have reminded one of Moses' shining face, and I am not exaggerating. He said, "Chaplain, when we prayed yesterday, something really happened; it's been better since." If I should preach ten works of grace, he would want them all!

Oh, how my heart loves to minister to men like that. And don't you think Jesus is enjoying pouring out His grace upon him? I can almost hear the conversation around the throne: "Holy Spirit, —— is hungry again, would you go and fill his cup?" "Jesus, I have been down to the prison and filled ——'s cup." "Holy Spirit, but he is hungry again, will you go again and fill his cup?" I deeply feel that heaven is enjoying this, and so am I. Aren't you?

I often find such readiness and support in prayer from these precious men, many of whose prayers might raise eyebrows in the more cultural settings of our churches. Aren't you glad God hears prayers that others might scoff at? This August was to be the eleventh year of an outreach effort on the boardwalk along the ocean in Wildwood, NJ. The week before it I asked the men in the minimum camp to pray for us and the next thing I knew they were saying, "Let's pray for you now."

They gathered up around the front of the chapel and joined hands and began to pray. Not long into their simple prayers I became gloriously conscious that God was hearing in heaven and was going to answer on earth. From that moment on I had an assurance that God was going to bless that week of ministry, and He surely did. To Him be all the glory and praise, but to them also thanks are due for their earnest prayers. I have made note of it before, but there is probably not a pastor anywhere on earth that has any greater blessing of backing in prayer than I find from these faithful men in prison.

A week or so ago I received two letters from two men who used to be in our prison here, but were moved to one of the northern prisons. They have both felt that they prayed through to sanctification while up there in that prison, and it surely sounded good, too. The one who was so close to getting sanctified before he left to go north felt for a while that he was stalled because of the dearth of spiritual help where he is, but he had heard of full salvation and he wanted it with all his heart. God answered his cry.

Just recently both of them have been earnestly seeking to draw nearer to God and they felt God showed them that there was still something in their hearts that did not belong there and would show itself under pressure. They began seeking God again in earnest. Listen to parts of their testimonies in their letters:

> Recently I came to the horrible realization that I was not sanctified. There was a root that occasionally bore rotten fruit. Many were the vain hopes and misunderstandings about sanctification. I boldly claimed it and refused any thought to the contrary. I thought the "rising up" was "normal." I thought willful sin was ignorant sin and thus not accounted...Thanks be to God the Father, Jesus the Son, and the Holy Spirit for illuminating me to the truth.

I wish I had space to tell more, but as he earnestly sought God for deliverance, suddenly it came and he found his soul all on fire for God with a new power over all inward sin.

The other brother writes:

> I do believe I will enter into His rest. He has brought me far enough for me to know that there is nothing behind me and everything in Christ. Jesus lies ahead of me. Amen. The Lord has blessed K—— to enter in. Hallelujah! Lord, let me be next!

Thank you each one for your faithful prayers, and as you keep praying God will do more.

William Cawman

4
WATCHING CHRIST BEING FORMED IN THEM

October 1, 2009

"For the grace of God that bringeth salvation hath appeared to all men, Teaching us that, denying ungodliness and worldly lusts, we should live soberly, righteously, and godly, in this present world; Looking for that blessed hope, and the glorious appearing of the great God and our Saviour Jesus Christ." (Titus 2:11-13)

So wrote Paul to the young preacher Titus, and we must admit over and over that there is no teacher that can be compared to the *grace of God*. If we can simply bring men and women into grace, so many otherwise impossible difficulties are solved so easily. Let me point out one that came to us in such a beautiful manner.

An inmate from Haiti, who has been walking so tenderly and closely with God for a good while now, told us this in class one morning recently: "Chaplain, I don't know why I do this, but I just do. I have saved a new set of clothes (prison garb just like all the others) and a new pair of boots, and I set them aside and only wear them to church. I really don't know why I do that except that I just feel like I want to do it."

Of course, I knew why immediately and sprang to the soapbox with the following observations. Until this last generation of lawless and empty "Christianity," saint and sinner alike had enough respect and reverence for the house of God to put their very best clothes on to go there. This is exactly what gave birth to the folksy expression, "Sunday-go-to-meetin' clothes." It was unheard of and un-thought of to go to the house of God in casual apparel, for we were going to meet with the King of Kings.

Do you see that *the grace of God* is teaching this man what many people are now despising even in holiness churches? But then, I'm supposed to be giving you praise and prayer requests from the prison, not preaching to you. Well, not all that was said on the soap box was printed here, but I guess enough that you can guess that this man is at war with the spirit of disrespect for God and His house and holiness that is sweeping our churches like a tidal wave while very few seem to see any problem with it.

This same dear man also said another morning that he had witnessed an inmate on his tier get jumped by the gang and saw him beat up. He said, "My heart has suffered ever since with a deep heaviness over what happened. Should I feel that way?" *Grace* is teaching him how to feel, how to act, how to live and how to love God with all his heart. And this man is a prisoner, not a Bible college student.

We have sustained a very disappointing blow from one of our best men—at least, so it seemed. One of the men who would have given the clearest of evidence and fruit of being fully sanctified, suddenly just dropped out of communication with everyone and just quit. It seems he simply succumbed to despair and discouragement and let the devil drive him to give up. He told one of the other men when they asked him what had happened that "the light went out on the inside." The man replied, "It went out on the outside, too."

Please help us pray for him. We cannot let him stay out

like this for he has known too much to ever successfully doubt the reality of it. Whether there was an inherent flaw in his foundation or whether he fell that quickly from genuine holiness into defeat, I cannot say, but surely God is not finished with him. It was a really serious blow to many who know him.

Another prayer request I would like to leave with you is for a 47-year-old black minister who is in prison. We have been visiting, and as I have probed into whether he has really experienced genuine salvation from sin, he says he is not sure himself. He is indeed a rare case in this respect: nearly every minister I have ever talked with who has been indoctrinated in Calvinistic theology, which allows a man to continue in the commission of sins, is very adamantly closed to hearing any other interpretation of Scripture, for he is in love with the darkness that allows him to sin while feeling he will go to heaven. This man is not. He is very open and ready to admit that he has failed and that if there is truth that he is not acquainted with he wants to hear it.

I wonder if he is not hearing for the first time, at the age of 47 and having ministered to others, what it means to be born again. I gave him some booklets and we have had a couple of good visits. Please pray that he will not be offended by the true Gospel, but will continue to open his heart to the truth.

I also want to tell you a little update on the man who took the place as tier rep for the one who was so mistreated by the officers and was sent away. I put him on the list for a visit the other day and when he came in he said, "Oh Chaplain, God always knows just when to send you along. I was crying and praying nearly all night last night because it seems I am so alone and there is so little God here. I think I am going to resign as tier rep because it seems so many evil men want me to be a partaker of their sins, and I cannot do that. God is so good, for it seems just when I need Him and can't go on any longer, He sends someone to give me just what I need."

As you can imagine, I cannot myself know all that these

men face so as to give an adequate or accurate picture to you of their battles. Most of us on the outside find it an ever-increasing battle to fight off the darkness around us and the evil spirits that would press against us; how much more these men face who have no Christian family close by to encourage and help them, but instead are living shoulder to shoulder with the most depraved and willfully sinful men imaginable.

For this, among other reasons, let me thank each of you once again who are faithfully remembering them in your prayers. You will have your reward, for it may be that your prayers are what is swinging the balance in their lives to enable them to find that promised renewing of the inner man in conflicts that otherwise would overwhelm them. Thank you, thank you, thank you!

One of our most steady sanctified men has just had a new area of ministry committed to him. This man is not chafing or repining over the remaining years of his thirty-year sentence for killing his wife and mother-in-law. He is so happy in the love of Jesus that he is just taken up with ministering to others right where he is. Many of you have probably heard of a program started within prisons called "Scared Straight." It consists of bringing wayward young people into a prison so that the inmates can talk with them and tell them just what prison life is like in an effort to scare them into better behavior. To what extent this has been effective, I cannot say, but our prison, some time back, proposed a similar program and is offering it to judges and detention programs as a hopefully helpful way to change the course of young lives before they have gone so far as to be committed to prison.

Our dear brother was one of the ones selected by the administration of the prison to talk with these young offenders. They have developed a format over the past few weeks and now have had their first opportunity to present it to seven young men who were ordered by a judge to take it. The young men are brought in through the same intake procedures that a prisoner is subjected to; they are made to dress in orange jumpsuits so that everyone recognizes that they are under correction. Then they are escorted by the few inmates who have been trained for this, as well as officers, to one of the tiers where men are housed.

On the way into the unit men in the courtyard are yelling at them with threats and unkind words which in itself ought to scare them into better thoughts than ever coming to a place like this. Then after they have seen for themselves what life is like in prison, they are taken to the hospital and allowed to see men who are dying of diseases caused by the same life of sin that they have started playing with.

Lastly they are taken to the visit hall and each of the inmates who have accompanied them is allowed to talk to them. Our brother said that for his first time in giving them his testimony, he wondered all the way through how soon they would shut him down, because he was testifying clearly of how nothing but the grace of God had changed his life from what it was to what it is now. But he was thanking God as he told me about it, that they allowed him to say just what he wanted to, and he is praying that God will be able to use him and his testimony to bring a turnabout in young lives. I know he would appreciate and beg for your prayers that he can be used of God to shine into darkened young lives.

This man has lived a consistent testimony of holiness of heart and life for a number of years now. Some of you may remember how he actually allowed his hungry heart to find full cleansing in the Blood of Jesus before he ever understood it theologically. When he heard the truth of holiness and began to read and study it, his whole being lit up with the realization that it was exactly what God had already done in his heart. He is now both possessor and believer; and beyond that he is a missionary and preacher of righteousness in word and life wherever he is.

While some men are struggling with the very idea of how long they must stay in prison, he is, while in prison, proving that *godliness with contentment is great gain*. This man needs your prayers, not that he is on shaky ground, but that God will continue to use him to shine as a light in this dark place, more and more.

Just the other day we had another victory that was very precious. A man who has been in prison for just a short time had joined my Christian Living classes and had been coming for a few weeks. He has a wife and children and a very good job as an elevator mechanic but he had become ensnared in sinful activity on the internet. He wanted to visit with me and told me about his sin, but he said he was completely finished with that type of activity and was doing all he could to get his life straightened out and do just the right things.

I told him that all of that was good, but I asked him if he had ever had a time in his life when he asked Jesus to forgive him and come into his heart until he knew that he was forgiven. He said that he did not know that he ever had. I told him that Jesus living within us is the only way to effectively stop sinning and that he really needed to ask Him to come in. He said, "I want that to happen. I want to let Him come in and change me."

We had prayer and then he prayed and then I urged him to keep seeking until he knew beyond any doubt that Jesus had saved him and was living in his heart. A few days later I put him on the visit list again so as to see how he was making out. When he entered the room he said, "Chaplain, thank you for calling me down again. I've been wanting to talk to you, because the next day after we talked, Jesus did come into my heart, and I know it. This is wonderful and I never want to lose it. I really love Him with all my heart; and do you know that the very next day I was called down by the parole officer and they gave me a date to go home. Now I want to know where there is a good church so that I can take my wife and go, because I want to live for God now."

This is one of the most painful questions I am ever asked unless I know of a good holiness church where the inmate is going. Many times I don't. The state of New Jersey used to have holiness churches scattered everywhere—now??? There are only three in the whole state that I am aware of, and being that most of our men are released into the northern part of the state, I do not know of a church that will be of any help to them, for if that church allows a grain of leaven to remain, it soon leavens the whole lump again. When I told him where our church was, he said, "That's not a problem, for I drive all over in my work anyway. We'll just make a day of it and come." Pray for him like Joseph advised his brethren, "See that ye fall not out by the way."

With gratitude and love,
William Cawman

┼┼┼

November 1, 2009

AND YOU DID PRAY, didn't you? Thank you so much in Jesus' name. Now let me tell you of how God again is answering those prayers. In the last letter I told you about one of our most promising and bright men who seemed to have a clear testimony of holiness suddenly falling out of the picture. I want to thank every one of you who prayed for him, and I had also told the men in his class that they should just gang up on him in prayer until he couldn't stay that way. A few days ago he came again to class and told me that he needed an hour to talk with me.

We sat down and he began to unload to me just what had happened. First let me say that every one of us has our peculiar battles and we may very seldom understand another person's battles as well as we think we do. As he unfolded what had happened I understood clearly just how the devil had tripped him up, even though I could not begin to understand it before.

He had grown up, that is until he went to prison at the age of seventeen, in a broken home and then in foster homes from which he had at times run away. From seventeen years of age until now he has been entirely molded by prison mentality, which is difficult to even relate to at all if you have never been there. God had done a lot for him and he believes firmly that he was walking in holiness of heart for some time, but then he began to have dealings with a lawyer with a view to bringing his case back to court. Whether he instigated it or it just came up automatically, I'm not sure, but he said that as he went back over his case, old feelings began to resurface and instead of praying through and getting the victory over them, he tried to cope with them in his own mind. When he originally went before the judge, he told the truth about the murder he had committed, but then he received charges for things he had not done as well, which lengthened his sentence. He actually has a life sentence with a minimum of 30 years.

He does not want to be in prison any more than you or I, and the desire to have the whole truth come out in order that his sentence could be reduced was strong. He grows so weary of the terrible atmosphere of sin all around him with no escape from it. But the more he went back over the details of his crime, the more he found himself plunged into despair and pain. The lawyer told him he did not see much hope of a change of sentence.

Then he began to look at the effects of his crime. The weight of what he had done came back afresh—he had taken a life. And besides, because of the nature of the other charges brought against him he is not eligible to help out in the hospice program in the hospital and he is not allowed to participate in the new program to help young offenders that I wrote about in the last letter. He felt so worthless and so hopeless, and instead of praying through he just began to mull it over and over in his mind. It only got worse. He said that when he was living with his eyes only on Jesus and was lost in His love, those things did not bother him, but he took his eyes off of Jesus and they all came crashing back down on him.

He then reacted like he had always done all of his life—he ran away from it. He simply cut himself off from all of the Christian brothers and quit coming to classes, etc. But oh, thank God, and God's praying family, he could not stay out in the cold. He had known too much of the joy of God to live like that. He realized what had happened to him and humbled himself and began to go around to the brothers and ask their forgiveness for cutting himself off from them.

He wants to ask the church to forgive him for his bad example and failure, but he wanted to talk with me first. He has asked God to forgive him and he feels He has, for he senses a relationship with God again, but he said that he knows his heart is not yet fully right. He said, "I know that I am not sanctified, and I want to be."

I urged him to press with all his heart back into the full favor of God. I warned him about allowing the devil to add to godly sorrow, the despair that cripples one from getting back to God. I mentioned to him the Scripture in Hebrews 12:12,13, "Wherefore lift up the hands which hang down, and the feeble knees; And make straight paths for your feet, lest that which is lame be turned out of the way; but let it rather be healed." And then of course that is followed by these words: "Follow peace with all men, and holiness, without which no man shall see the Lord." Whatever the weak place in his fortifications that allowed the enemy to get a foothold and cause his backsliding, it needs to be healed so that it never happens again. He fully agreed and said he wants to do whatever he has to in order to be fully right again. Thank God!

He wrote to the lawyer and told him to drop the whole case. He said that it was only leading him away from God and he is going to just leave all of that in God's hands. He wanted to know if that was the right thing to do. I told him it definitely was for if it had been the right thing it would not have brought a cloud between him and God. I reminded him of the promise in God's Word that "no good thing will

He withhold from him that walketh uprightly." I said, "If God wants you out of this prison instead of in it at any point in your life, He will pay no attention to the Department of Corrections; He will get you out. Just trust Him with it all." His eyes filled with tears as I could literally see him dumping the whole situation into God's keeping.

We had a good time of prayer and then he said, "I finished one year of college work with the Bible college (the wonderful courses I had told you about a few months ago), but I've probably disqualified myself from taking any more, haven't I?" This time I wanted to cry. I said to him, "Is that the way God treats us? I know the president of that Bible college and I know they will never cut you off for what you have done. That is not the way God's children treat each other. I know their arms will be wide open to welcome you back." He bowed his head into his hands and burst into tears. I do not believe he will stay long at all outside of the fullness of God's holiness. You have prayed him back into the kingdom, now will you pray him into the fountain of cleansing and the healing of his backslidings?

Another inmate who has lived a wonderfully sanctified life for a good while now is being released to go home. I had my last in-prison visit with him and he told me this: "Chaplain, I love you and want to thank you for all you have done in leading me in the right way. For a long time I leaned on you instead of on God. One day you had come back from a journey and as I was visiting with you your head began to nod and I could see you were very tired. God spoke to me and said, 'See, he is just a man.' I want to tell you that it only made me love you and respect you all the more. But from that time on I realized I was to lean on Jesus and not you. I would think to myself, Oh, I need to talk to the chaplain as soon as he gets back, and God said, 'Can't you talk to Me?'"

Isn't God good? Do pray for this man that he will be kept through the power of Jesus' Blood. Fortunately he is going to where there is a good holiness church that is welcoming him. I wish this could happen to all of them.

Starting with October, all of my classes inside the prison have been moved from 8:30-10:30 to 2:00-3:30. It seems to be working much better in regard to getting an officer so that we can have them back in the chapels again. It also seems that there is much less conflict with other appointments so that the enrollment in all three facilities has increased wonderfully. The first week, as we were opening one of the classes, my supervisor walked into the rear of the chapel. I asked him to come to the front and then I told the men that they should thank him for all the work he has gone to in order that classes like this could meet. I then asked him to open the class in prayer.

He said, "I will pray, but I want to say something first. Men, the book you are about to learn from under Chaplain Cawman is a very good book. He gave me one of them and for a while it laid on my desk, but then I began to read it as I did my treadmill at home. The more I read the more I liked it until finally on one chapter I had to get off of the treadmill and onto my knees." Then he led us in prayer. When you pray for us, don't forget him. He has done so much to open the way and keep it open for this work to go on.

I want to tell you something else as a follow up from several months ago. Many of you will remember the dying man in the hospital who was afraid to die, but afraid to confess his many murders. Do you remember that I told you that one of the professed Christian inmates went in and told him that I was wrong in telling him that he had to confess his sins if he wanted God to forgive him; that all he needed to do was confess to God?

Well, sometime shortly after that I put that inmate on the list for an interview and when he came into the office he said, "Did you want to see me?" I could tell he was apprehensive as to what was coming. I never mentioned his affront, but just began to visit with him and to let him know I cared about him. Shortly after that he asked to be enrolled in my classes and has become a firm supporter of everything I am teaching—at least, so it seems.

Many times a person has been so taught by the damnable sinning religious teachings of the doctrines of devils all around us that they are wrong, but perhaps not knowingly wrong. What they do with further light when they encounter it tells more about their real heart than their theology does.

Pray that he will go all the way into whatever he yet needs from God. Of course, sadly enough, it is too late for the dear man who chose to believe him and reject what I told him from God's Word and is now in hell. And if that sounds too blunt, I can't reverse it, for that is where he is. He deliberately chose to go to hell rather than face the shame of confessing his sins. Oh, that he would have listened to what he had to know was the truth, for he actually told me so, but he counted the cost and rejected mercy.

One more note of encouragement and at the same time a prayer request. Ten years ago or so, I wrote several times about an inmate designated C——. God instantly delivered him from the king of drugs, heroine, and left him with an appetite for the Word of God. He became a very avid student and has taken classes by distance learning from a Bible college and has graduated; but for all that he has never paid the price to get sanctified.

He was released for a time and fell dreadfully back into drugs and sin, and life became so heavy that he tried several times to take his life. He would not listen as we strongly pled with him to settle it and go through with God. He is now about to be released from prison and it seems that after all the prayers that have been prayed for him (my own mother prayed for him like he was her own son) they are finally taking hold. He has been very different for months and is ready to listen and obey. He just told me that there is no other course for him to choose—he must come and be able to get to our church. Please do pray for him that he will go all the way with God this time. God does answer prayer.

In Christian love,
William Cawman

☩

December 1, 2009

THERE ARE TWO THINGS I never cease to marvel at in working with men in prison. One is how perfectly the grace of Jesus works regardless of outward circumstances, and how it keeps men from every form of sin while living almost immersed in it twenty-four hours a day. But it does! It saves and sanctifies and keeps, even in the lives of those whose backgrounds are as far from Christian home and church influences as could be.

The other marvel is that many men can seem to sit in the same services, attend the same Bible studies and classes and seem just as ignorant and empty of grace as years ago. One wonders where all the truth goes in such lives. I don't know if they are stony ground or thorn infested ground or just how to classify them, but they could easily discourage the one trying to minister to them.

Now a third marvel is this: once in a while, one of these who for so long has looked so hopeless, breaks through all of the sudden into light from heaven and the whole scene changes. I just wish it would happen so much more often.

One such man I had a visit with again just the other day. He has not been in the prison long and does not have much longer before he returns home, but it is evident that his life has, up to this point, been lived in heathen darkness. His cell mate asked him to come to classes and right there he gave his heart to the Lord and now is so radically different.

He is so happy with God's presence in his heart that he says from now on all he wants is God to direct his life and he will obey Him. He will be going home to his waiting wife and a good job, but he says from here on things will never be the same and he doesn't want them to be. Do pray for him.

Another man is one of the first marvels I mentioned above. I have often said to my wife that if ever I have met a man who literally lives in Psalm 91, it is him. He verily shines all over with peace and contentment and joy unspeakable. He is the man that I told you about at the start of this year who said, when asked what he wanted more than anything else for this new year, "I want to be honest in answering that; I tell you that I am really enjoying my walk with Jesus and all I want is more of it!"

The other day we were visiting and he said, "Do you know, I read Psalm 91 every day. It is one of the portions I need every day." I guess that explains why he keeps living there, doesn't it?

In the Bible study group in Facility Three there is a little group of Hispanic brothers who really seem to enjoy the teaching and preaching immensely. They just beam as they listen to the truth preached, and so I decided to call each of them down and visit with them to see how they were coming. Let me tell you about two of them. One is from Mexico and lived most of his young life along the Gulf of Mexico. He was definitely living for sin and self and was going from one wrong path to another.

He came to this country, and I don't remember whether he said it was legally or not, but he got himself into trouble here and was put in prison. Even after that he continued to seek out the wrong path and then his brother died. That really shook him up and he began to seek God and he found Him, just like God promised we would. He is so happy now that it shows all over him. He says he knows that he is saved. He then told me with a beaming face that couldn't hide his joy that he is overwhelmed every time he thinks of the thought, "sons of God." He said he is not just forgiven, but that he is a new man; he is a "son of God."

The other man came from a home almost at the end of the airport runway in Guatemala City. He too has given his heart to Jesus and is changed from all that he used to be. He will undoubtedly be deported back to Guatemala when he finishes his prison sentence. He has a wife and two daughters and a son up here in this country, but he said he will leave it all up to God as to where he goes when he gets released. Please pray for him too, and we will certainly try to put him in contact with some of the good brethren in Guatemala when he is about to be released.

Here is something more from our good brother who had the spell of singing in the dumpster while being required to search for a missing toilet brush. (For those of you who are new to these letters, he was singing because it dawned on him, while being required to look for the brush amidst all the garbage in the dumpster at shortly after 5:00 am, that nothing ugly or un-Christ-like was coming up in his heart, and it made him start to sing.)

Well, the other day he told me with great concern that his young son has been given a cell phone. He says that makes him very uneasy because a cell phone is not just a telephone. It is a link to all the garbage that the devil has out there. He then began to express his concern over the internet and similar devices that make it so easy to fall a victim to temptation. He said that he knows he cannot be too careful because the sins that once possessed him will be looking for him again.

Then he said, "Chaplain, do you know, I want to avoid even all appearance of evil. The other day another inmate was waiting for the officer to push the electronic button to unlock his cell door and then he was intending to come right back out and go out to the yard. He saw me coming by and asked me if I would hold his book for a minute while he went in to get something. I said I would and took it and no sooner was he in his cell than I realized it was a magazine of pornography. And do you know what? Just then the officer came by and saw it. I felt terrible, but how could I explain myself. Chaplain, do you know what? We Christians just don't have any wiggle room, do we?" I agreed.

The other night in Bible study a man who has been so graciously helped of God and is growing conspicuously in grace stood up and wanted to say something. He started his testimony by saying, "Brothers, I was praying today and I just started to cry. I just can't understand why God loves me like this." Well, one thing is for sure, God's grace has certainly made him more loveable.

And then here is another testimony. God has been moving for some time out in the minimum camp. There are several hearts that are really reaching His direction and growing in their relationship to Him. On the day before Thanksgiving I told the men it would be a good time for them to each express their gratitude to God for what He has been doing for them.

I felt as though I had been in a very good and refreshing church service within a few minutes. But one brother in particular stood up and it was evident that his heart was full of thanksgiving. He began to thank God, but then just stopped and said, "Men, when I try to get it out my words just get all tangled and don't express it right, but down in my heart God is really working and I'm glad for it. It's real. And I tell you that I'm not trying to live with one foot in and one foot out; I'm all for Jesus!"

There was a tangible witness from heaven as he gave witness from earth, and I felt my heart joined to him in love. Another one stood up and said, "Men, I find more and more that this thing has to be real. God expects more than just to come to church and clap and sing and praise; He wants our lives to be right; completely right. It's getting too late in time to be playing around with this; I want to be right. And also, it's not like I have to be someone or be heard; I want to be less and less and let God be my all."

In one of the classes on the inside we had just been discussing the difference between loving God with merely a human love—which is not wrong as far as it goes, but how far short it falls of what is acceptable to God when He has made all provision to impart divine love into us to love Him with.

We spoke of the fact that not one of God's attributes is a standard or criteria that God lives up to; those attributes are God—He is infinitely made of them. In particular, what is God's holiness? It is not a standard of living that God keeps, but it is God Himself; He is the standard of holiness.

About that time a man I had not been conscious of contributing before spoke up and said, "Chaplain, that holiness is not something in our outward flesh, is it? Doesn't it come from within us? When God saved me I was changed from the inside out. Immediately I had no more desire to smoke or to look at those dirty magazines, and it was coming from inside of me. A man came to our cell door and wanted to show me and my cell mate some pictures out of a dirty magazine and we both together at the same time told him we didn't have any interest in looking at them. Then we turned in surprise to each other and asked each other where that came from. And it's not just what I don't do, either, because I'm doing things I never had any interest in before. I've been waking up every morning at 2:00 with a desire to get out beside my bed and pray. I'm afraid it might disturb my cell mate a little, but I want to do it to meet with God." Do you see why I love these precious brothers?

The situation in the political atmosphere is not improving. We are trying to wait on God and hope that with a new administration in the state capital taking place in the new year perhaps things will improve. The officers have not been put back into our chapel areas and so we are really crippled in many areas of effective teaching without our books and materials and equipment. We don't want to move it to another area if there is any chance that there will be a change of direction and the officers be replaced, so we are just doing our best for now.

The academic area of each facility has vacant classrooms that would work just fine for our classes, but the educational supervisor, for whatever reason, does not want us in there. The officer in charge was very open to our coming into one of the classrooms, and after all, it is academic; but the educational supervisor went in and told him not to let us use that area. He then said we could have a room in the vocational area. It is a bare walled room with no floor covering, no ceiling, no equipment, etc., and very unsuitable for classes, but that is all he will agree to.

If that is all we are going to get, we will thank God for a hole in the wall and continue to grow in Him, but it becomes more and more obvious that they want to just crowd religious services out.

Many states no longer have chaplains and many just subcontract to outside agencies for chaplaincy services. Those agencies do not want any chaplain that would be definitively anything; they would only hire ecumenical social workers from recognized liberal organizations. As chaplains in New Jersey retire or quit they are not being replaced, so the whole situation needs a covering of prayer that God will have His way in it all.

It is extremely hard to imagine that He would abandon the many hungry hearts that are reaching for Him from within prison, but the enemy hates to see a soul rescued from his clutches, too, so we are in a battle. As long as there was a man in Trenton who was sympathetic to Christianity, that had an effect even in the administrators of our prison, but he retired and now the administrators seem without any backbone at all to stand up to the inroads of the antichrist. My supervisor did all he could to try to talk with the administrator and the answer was, "It's done, get used to it." Only God sees tomorrow; we don't, but will you help us pray?

We plan to spend a lot of extra time during the month of December in one on one talks with the men in our classes. There are over 100 of them enrolled right now, so that is another request for prayer that God will grant us wisdom, love, grace, anointing and all else that is needed for these visits. I am looking forward to them, but leaning hard on God for help.

From myself and the men you are praying for, we once again with all of our hearts thank you each one for those prayers, and then we want to wish each of you a most Blessed Christmas.

William Cawman

5
"AND SUCH WERE SOME OF YOU...BUT!"

January 1, 2010

It is hard to imagine that the first decade of the new millennium is already history. It has been during this last decade that all but one of these prayer letters have been written, which total in number now to one hundred and twenty-one, not including this one. Many requests for prayer have been included in them, and in answer to those prayer requests many of you have responded by praying, and consequently there have been also many victories to share.

Thank you, each one, for the many prayers that have been sent to our Father's throne up in heaven in behalf of these precious men in prison. I must tell you that God has heard and is hearing them and He has not forgotten one of them.

Very early in the history of these prayer letters from the prison here, a particular man that we designated as C——, was brought to your attention, both as a miracle and also as a need for prayer. C—— was born in Newark, NJ, but was unwanted from birth and was dumped into a household of lesbians to take care of him. When about seven years of age his mother would come and get him and put him on street corners to make drug deals for her. He remembers when he was about eight years of age, his mother was living in a shabby apartment with hardly anything except a mattress on the floor, trying to take care of him and his brother and their cousin.

One day the door broke down and a huge black man entered demanding the jewelry she had stolen from him and sold for drugs. She didn't have them, so he kicked her in the mouth and smashed every one of her teeth right out of her head. C—— recalls gathering up fragments of her teeth in his hands. He would often sit by his mother's bed and give her injections of drugs and then closely monitor her so that she would not go over the edge while trying to come to the state she wanted.

Often he recalls asking himself, "What am I doing this for?" "But," he said, "it was my mother." At the age of seventeen he was driving a stolen car, taking his mother out for a drug deal, when they were arrested and both put in prison. After serving some time he got out and four days later made a deal from which his mother bought drugs and took an overdose and died. From that time on most of his life has been in and out of prison—most of the time in.

He remembers the first time he met me in the detention center, or the "hole," as they call it in prison. He was working there as an inmate paralegal. After watching me for a time he wanted to talk. He told me some of his life's history and then said that even though trusted in the prison, he had been a steady addict to heroine for over twenty years. But a month or two before talking to me he had become so sick of his life that he went into his cell and locked the door and began reading his Bible.

For several days he read and suddenly realized that all desire for heroine was gone. Not only did God instantly deliver him from heroine, but He also completely healed him of AIDS and hepatitis C. He had at one point been so sick with it that he didn't know if he would even live. From that moment he became a student of the Bible and came to a firm belief in the way of holiness. He even preached it to others and led others to come into the light of it, but there was always something missing in his own inner being.

Little by little he became taken up with trying to obtain a change of custody and get out of his uncomfortable surroundings. We tried to warn him that he was not ready to leave and that the devil was trying to detour him from what he knew he needed, but he thought he knew better and obtained a change to another prison and from there parole.

Very shortly afterward he made contact with his ex-wife, who was still hooked on drink and drugs, and she led him right back into it all. In desperation, because he knew there was something better, he turned himself in and went back to prison. For the next several years he was in and out of prison several times, and even tried to slit his wrist at least twice. Life turned sharply downhill and we seldom heard from him.

But many prayers had gone up for him. My own dear mother prayed for him as if he were her own son. God remembered, and a few months ago we began to hear from him again, and the whole tenor of his letters was changed. He told us how he had determined that he was ready to listen and obey God and get his life right.

He was released from prison the day before Thanksgiving and within a few days came to our church and began to place himself before the brethren for prayer and instruction and help. God began answering long bottled-up prayers and he began confessing that for a long time he had been keeping secret closets of wrong hidden within him, but he was done with it. He wanted to really find the relationship with God that he knew he could have and then get fully sanctified. It seems that God is moving mightily in his behalf.

It is almost impossible in today's economy and tracing of everyone's track records for a man coming out of prison to find a job, but he has a good job already, as well as a place to live directly across the road from the church. I say with all my heart, "Thank you for every prayer for him, and Praise the

Lord!" Please keep praying that he will never stop but become the man completely that God wants him to be.

Another man who has been in prison for years also needs much prayer, not that God will do His part—for He is and has for a long time—but that this man will quit giving in to discouragement and really settle it to go all the way with God. The other day he brought me a letter that I asked him if he minded me sharing with others as a prayer request. I will give you the letter here with his permission.

The girl writing the letter is his youngest of two daughters and she is now seventeen. Right after she was born he was sent to prison with drug related charges. His life in early childhood had been in a family that used witchcraft and was very godless. He remembers as a child having dreams that he was in a corner, faced with evil spirits that he now looks back on and wonders at. He spent several years in prison and was then let out on parole.

He said that as soon as he was released, it was just as if a demon entered into him and he hit the streets and his old life-style and never even went home to his wife and two little girls. He went back to prison again in no time with fresh charges and several more years to serve. This is the point in his life when I first met him. He was such a broken man that for a long time it seemed his emotions would never stabilize.

He felt so terrible about what he had done to his family, for his wife said to him, "All I wanted is for you to come home to me." She had faithfully brought the girls to visit him during the first sentence, but after this she only came twice and then dropped off and divorced him.

Ten years have gone by and now he received this letter which I'm sure will pull your heart out for both of them. I include it for two reasons: (1) To help you pray for both him and his family, and (2) To give you a little picture of the suffering selfish sin brings into every life around it.

Dad, I am writing because your letters keep me unsatisfied

and enraged. You constantly say how much you love and miss me and yet you cannot seem to relay that in the way you choose to live. Do I not matter enough? I would have loved to have you in my life at one point but now seeing what you are it would seem to have only been as unfulfilling as the letters you send. You fill these letters with verses, scriptures, and testimonies, but I am not entirely sure why. You consider yourself a man of God, but you can't even stay out of jail long enough to get to know your own daughter. I understand that God forgives and I am sure He forgives you for the many mistakes you have made, but can I? That is a question I cannot even answer. There is a part of me that wants to love you entirely and another that wants nothing to do with you. I just wish you could have been a man and stepped up to the plate as a father. Could you have kept yourself out of jail or would that have been asking too much?

Perhaps there is nothing that would help this man more to get established spiritually than for a family to support him, but here you can see the other side of the picture too. Sin is so cruel! It is so selfish! It is hideous beyond all power of description, yet men hug it to their bosoms, loath to give it up for the beauty of the Christ-filled life. Such is the blindness of sin.

This poor girl's heart is aching for a father; a father's heart is aching for his daughter; but do you think this moves the heart of the devil? He laughs with hellish delight while he savors the delicious thought that after all this pain there yet awaits an eternity of anguish beyond all imagination of man. Oh, the unfathomable gulf that sin brings between an immortal soul and a loving God who created it. Pray on, Dear Friends. If we can snatch a few more from his clutches before Jesus comes it will be worth it all.

I need not tell you that true godliness and holiness always stirs up the wrath of hypocritical religious professors. My supervisor sat down to lunch with me the other day and said,

"One of the religious volunteers has been complaining to the volunteer coordinator that there seems to be something like a holiness group spreading their doctrines around and many of the men are being affected by it." I said, "Chaplain, I'm sure the complaint could go the other way, too?" He smiled and shook his head.

I told him that I would talk to the men and let them know it will not help anything for them to counter in a public setting what one man is teaching by what another one is teaching, but I also told him that perhaps some of the volunteers needed a little instruction also; that others had just as much right to teach the truth the way they believe it as they do. He agreed to that also, so we'll see what that does.

There is strong pressure coming from many sectors of the volunteer groups who come in from other churches to replace the chaplain supervisor with a black charismatic preacher. And indeed such preachers can get a response from the crowd. They no sooner stand up before a group than they have them shouting and swaying and smiling and waving their hands in the air with enthusiastic response, but as soon as it's over the sinning business goes right on. Satan loves it; no wonder it seems at times to be winning the day.

But— "This is my Father's world; Oh let me ne'er forget, that though the wrong seems oft so strong, God is the Ruler yet. This is my Father's world, the battle is not done; Jesus who died shall be satisfied, and earth and heaven be one." Doesn't your heart cry out, "Oh God, hasten the day?" He will.

Just as He sent His Son into the world the first time "in the fullness of time," so again He will. Not a moment too early, not a moment too late, He will send Him back to completely cleanse this old world of every little smudge print of Satan's work, and "the earth [shall be] the Lord's, and the fullness thereof." Until then, let's carry on, and enter into this yet another year of God's infinite mercy to see as many more come to Him as we can. The part you are doing in prayer is ever so vital, and without it, all that we are trying to accomplish would be worthless.

Thank you so much and let's go forward.

Your Brother,
William Cawman

┼┼┼

February 1, 2010

WHAT A MONTH! WHERE should I begin? For all the things which have transpired it seems like a long time since the last letter. In part it is because we have suffered another tragic attack of Satan who never gives up those he thinks are his.

In the last letter we wrote about a man we have known and for whom prayer has been made for years, and how God was helping him, and He was. For a period of a few weeks he was a changed man inasmuch as he had made a choice to listen and take help from the brethren in the church and was so encouraging as he sought the Lord. At the turn of the year we had a New Year's Holiness Convention in the church and during that time God was really dealing heavily with him. He talked to some of us one afternoon after we had been in prayer and told us that he had never been so close to the power of the Blood. He also told us that a couple of things kept coming into his mind, but he didn't know if it was from God. He said if he would open up about them he would definitely go back to prison.

We probably didn't realize just then what a crisis this was, but in a few days it became obvious that he had lost his desire to seek after God and was going backwards. Different ones tried to help him but he began to quickly drift back into the same man he had been many times before. Then one weekend he began to evade us and not show up for church.

He began to have severe stomach upsets and turn a gray color, and we had fears he had gone back to drugs again. When we asked him about it he very emphatically denied it but then admitted he had lied to us out of necessity a couple times. He is still in the area but is evading us and he even stated that he doesn't believe there is such a thing as the witness of the Spirit or holiness of heart because he had sought it fervently and couldn't find it.

Oh, how painful it is to watch someone turn away from the one golden opportunity in their life to find the right way and make it to heaven, and instead turn again as a dog to its vomit. The Sunday night it became obvious that he was definitely on the way back down, a number of us gathered in the church and prayed for him until nearly midnight. He knows that, but is choosing to listen to a lying spirit instead of the only people in the world that truly love him.

Such is the awful disease of sin! Will we give up? No! We did not enter this battlefield under our own ideas or our own orders, and we will not give up. The next day as I was walking through the prison compound the enemy was tormenting my mind, "Just get out of here! Give them up! All you're doing is creating heartache and problems for everyone!"

Then I entered the room to visit with a man for the first time. He began to tell his story. He was a cop in a nearby town and had fallen into a trap and committed crime. He is in his early fifties and has a wife and a high-school-age daughter. Now his world is collapsed and he is locked up. As he related his tale, he stopped and said, "Chaplain, I don't have the problems that some men in here do. My wife and daughter are standing firm behind me and I don't really have anything at home to worry about but..." and here his voice broke and he began to sob almost uncontrollably.

For several moments he couldn't speak, but finally gaining a little control he said, "I have a deep empty vacancy way down inside of me and I don't know what it is." Then he sobbed some more. I said, "Let me tell you exactly what that vacancy is. Your life has finally been brought to a standstill until you can hear Jesus knocking at your door, telling you that you need Him to come in. You were not created to live without

Him and you are feeling His absence in your life."

I went on to beg him to not ignore or get used to that ache, but to really seek God for a living relationship with Him. He told me he had always been a Catholic, but that didn't matter, he was willing to seek God. We had prayer and I begged him to get alone and seek after God and we would get back together in a few days. He said, "Good, I want you to do that."

Right on the heels of the attack of Satan over his own dirty work, God allowed this hungry soul to open up in such a way that my heart settled it all over again to just be right where God wanted me to be. As he left and I remembered what Satan had said I prayed, "God, I would rather be shot dead than to stay away from a hungry soul like that!" And I would, and I mean it!

No matter how many times Satan lays a blow at God's work, the Blood of Jesus is going to win this battle and we are not backing out. And then my heart began to reflect on Jesus' ministry. For three years He lived and talked and walked and slept and worked miracles and taught twelve men. Near the end of that time— as He, with passion and love, broke bread and shared the emblem of His broken body and shed Blood with those men — they were having a discussion among themselves which of them should be the greatest.

What must Jesus' heart have felt, having left the glorious throne of His Father's heaven and all of the worthy angels who are totally dedicated to the Father's will, and now his entire ministry on earth was grinding around in the basement of carnality in all of its ugliness? Yet, without a thought of forsaking and giving them up John tells us that "…having loved his own which were in the world, he loved them unto the end." My heart looked up and I prayed, "Jesus, give me more of Your heart; of Your passion; of Your love. And Jesus, give it to me *unto the end!*"

The man who sang songs in the dumpster because of the realization that nothing ugly was coming out of his heart anymore is conspicuously growing in the love of Jesus and the beauty of holiness. In class one day he had to testify. He told us that he has just settled it that if anything brings the least cloud between him and Jesus, he will have nothing to do with it again. Later he was talking to me alone and told me that he doesn't know just what God is about to do, but that he hadn't been able to sleep for three nights with excitement. He said, "Do you know, when I was a boy I could never go to sleep on Christmas Eve, because I was so excited about what was going to happen the next day. I feel that way now. I just am excited to see what God is going to do next."

They moved a young man into the cell with him that said he didn't believe in God. This made him eager to talk to him and he said they started talking about God at nine o'clock at night and talked about Him until three in the morning. He enjoyed it immensely, and the other man—well, we will see, won't we? He told me this: "I am just not having a problem anymore with sin in my life; I'm just not! But I am so grieved over most of what is being taught in the Sunday night services that I hardly ever go anymore."

I happen to know what kind of a diet it is; the devil himself could do no more to rip Christ down from the Cross and promote living in sin. One would wonder how a holy God in heaven can bear to hear such things and not strike it with His wrath. But Satan's day is coming and coming soon! Next Sunday is my turn. Pray for me!

This man is a lover of truth, and he is experiencing the preciousness of just what Jesus promised, "When He is come, He will guide you into all truth." My heart burns and rejoices as I sit with him and listen to all that God is revealing to his hungry heart. He is being led into the deeper truths that so few never get near, and it is a blessing to be with him.

The last couple of months, as often as I am at home, I have been randomly calling men from my classes in to get acquainted and know them better. When a man walks through the door I never know what I am in for. There are men that I would guess are really gaining ground from the classes, but when I sit with them and they begin to share themselves, I marvel at how little they have absorbed.

Then another man will come in that I have wondered in looking on whether he was getting it, and lo and behold, he has been going way up the road from where I would have guessed. There is one thing about my job—and I actually do get paid by the State of New Jersey for this—I get to hear stories day after day. If I want to hear some more stories all I have to do is put a few new names down on the appointment sheet for the day and there they are!

What a variety of pathways life can hold! A very pleasant and docile looking young black man came in and thanked me for putting his name on the list as he had wanted to talk with me. Almost two years ago, living completely for the devil in Elizabeth, NJ, he had driven his car away from a bar and he became aware that another car was following him. It pulled up alongside of him and he could see guns pointed at him. He jumped into the back seat and out the opposite back door and started to run.

He doesn't know how many there were in the other car, but they shot him in the leg and dropped him to the ground. He was then looking up at a man or men with guns and they shot him five times. One of the bullets went in right along the edge of his right eye and came out on the left side of his neck. Another one went right into his head above his right eye. He said his vision blurred for a minute and then he saw them running back to get into their car.

He noticed he had his cell phone in his hand so he called his girl-friend and she went into hysterics. He called another friend and asked them to send the ambulance. When the ambulance got there he said they put him out and he came to the next morning in a hospital after surgery to remove the bullet in his head. He said doctors were standing all around him and kept coming in to see him all day long, amazed at the miracle that he was alive.

He was sent to prison over the incident and after he came

to prison he turned to Jesus for the first time in his life. He said, "I have not changed my mind and I know that God hears me when I pray, but I am bothered because I don't feel I have the clearness and closeness to God that I had when I first came to Him. I think it is partly because I have been hanging around the wrong people." I urged him to do something desperate about that and immediately cry to God to bring him back to a real knowledge of acceptance with Him. He said he would do exactly that.

Then he told me a little more about his earlier life. He is 32 years old now, and he has only met his father about five times in his life. He has three brothers and not one of them has the same father as the next one. His father gave him his phone number once but he really didn't have any connection that would make him want to know him. His younger brother is also in prison.

During his growing up years his mother was so spaced out on drugs that he would work to pay for her rent so she would have a place to live. He would take care of her and wash her clothes for her and she would just live bombed out on drugs. After a time she went to a rehab but recently he received a letter from her that she had relapsed and the letter was so depressing that he has fears she may do herself in. She is now just living in a homeless shelter.

Brothers and sisters, if you came from a Christian home or even a somewhat structured home, even though it may have been less than perfect, do you realize what you have been saved from? And can we who have had so much more than our share of good things not do all we can to lift up those who have had not even the faintest resemblance to anything called a "chance?"

The dear man I told you about recently who broke down and cried over how good God is treating him has heard nothing as yet from his mother, who was living on the outskirts of Port-au-Prince in Haiti when the earthquake hit. Pray for him if you will.

The month that lies ahead is as unknown to us as this one was one month ago. I have not the slightest thought as to what will be in the next letter. It may depend much on your prayers.
Thank you.
William Cawman

March 1, 2010

MANY YEARS AGO I actually did study theology from many different aspects, but never did I learn the views I am learning now. Come with me to a visit from a man who has been smiling at me for about four years in my classes and Bible studies and listen in for a refresher course. "Chaplain, this is my third time now in prison. I did two other bids that were about two years each and now I am four years into a ten year bid, but God knows it's all part of the ingredients He needed to give me to make me what I'm supposed to be.

"It's like when you bake a cake, ya know. You put in the flour and the milk and the sugar and the nutmeg and then after that you have to bake it. See, before God was giving me the ingredients and now He's giving me another ten years. It's sort of like He has me in the oven and He's turned the volume up; but I know I'm going to be all right. Ya know what I mean?" Sure—well, I guess I know.

You've undoubtedly heard it said that "God always knows what He is about," haven't you? Sometimes that requires trust and faith, for eyesight certainly can't see it. Our dear brother that I have written about several times, and most often have referred to as the dumpster singer, is leaving us. In just the last letter I told you how he is not only growing remarkably in his walk with God, but has also been very excited over something that God was going to do—he didn't know what. Remember, that he is the man who took the place as tier rep for the good Christian inmate who was roughed up by the cops and sent to another prison.

Let me just go back and tell you that the first one I'm referring to struggled for a long time to see the clear light on holiness. He really did seem to love the Lord and had a passion to bring others to Him. He was a blessing in class and a fervent seeker of truth, but just could not seem to grasp that a person could really be cleansed from all sin while living in this mortal body.

One morning after a class when I had felt an unusual degree of the Spirit's help in teaching heart purity here and now, he came to me with his eyes literally bugging out and said, "Chaplain, all the times I have heard you teach about purity of heart it never got through to me like it did this morning. I believe it and I need it."

A couple days later he was suddenly attacked by an officer who did not like him for pointing out to the administration something he was doing wrong (this was his legitimate duty). A code was called and several officers beat him up terribly and then shipped him to another prison where he has been held since, labeled a "cop killer," although many witnesses said he never returned a blow. What transpired in his heart after that class period I do not know, but he has acted the part of a Christian through all that and since. He has written back that he has no ill will in his heart and no unforgiveness, and that God is blessing and using him where he is.

Now back to the man who took his place and has been growing in grace and expecting something great from God. Someone stole an old man's belongings and he went to the man he thought had done it to ask about it. Just like that, four inmates jumped him and beat him up very badly. The officers did not even see it happen but an officer noticed him standing there with blood all over him and his face cut up. They grabbed him and escorted him away and asked him what happened and he just said, "I'll take care of it; I'm not saying anything." They traced a trail of blood and locked a few men up and also put him in solitary confinement.

I went over to visit him a few days later and he came to the food port with his face swollen up but with a smile and thanks to God. He immediately began telling me how very near God's presence had been ever since he landed in confinement. I actually had to ask him why it happened as he didn't even seem concerned about that; he was just overwhelmed with the presence of the Fourth Man with him. He will now be sent away to one of the northern prisons—and I believe he will take the fire of God with him.

Why God allows such rough measures to spread the Word to other men who don't have it is not my business; it's His. I know that in other prisons there is an absolute famine of any truth whatsoever, and if God is scattering His church here through persecution, it wouldn't be the first time He allowed that, would it?

About two weeks later, noticing that he had not yet been sent away to another prison I went again to visit him. His very thick and necessary glasses had been broken when he was jumped and so when he heard me knocking on his cell door, he came over to the window and squinted his eyes through the glass and then saw who it was.

He nearly exploded with excitement as he burst forth with praise and love to God for all He is doing for him. He said, "Chaplain, it has been wonderful! Didn't I tell you I knew God was about to do something wonderful in my life? Now I have had twenty-one days just shut in alone with Him and the Fourth Man has been right by my side. Do you know what? I had about five days to witness to the men who jumped me and I thank God for that opportunity. You know, I have absolutely no anger, or bitterness, or anything like it. My life is completely in God's hands and whatever He sees fit for me to go through, I love Him. Do you know what? They gave me a torn up part of a Bible and it is enough. I have been reading and reading it and as I have read the four gospels I have come to see that if the Holy Spirit does not reveal it to us, we really don't know who Jesus is. I tell you, this whole thing has been a marvelous experience."

I noticed that his face is still swollen from the attack, but that just gives more room for his smile to spread out.

Just about two weeks after this happened, another of our precious Christian men also underwent some persecution and still is. I would suppose the problem came from a gang member, but someone dropped a note that he was planning to kill an officer. Of all the men in this prison he would be the last one probably to be in danger of that. Even the officer on the tier said he is sure he will come out of it all right because everyone knows that is not like him.

Meanwhile, however, he is locked up in detention. When I went over there to visit the first one I mentioned I noticed the officer in charge look at me and later that evening he met me on the compound. He said, "I've never seen you over there before." I said, "Well, I've been there many times in the past twelve years." He said, "I rarely ever see any religious person come over there." I refrained from saying, "Well, you have two very religious inmates right now."

One of the men who has been really seeking to be like Jesus came in the other day and said, "Chaplain, I'd like to ask you something. As well as you know me and for what you see in me, what would you say that I most need to work on or change to be what I ought to be?" Don't you wish everyone was that honest and humble and open? God and the Body of Christ would have no trouble with such lambs as that.

I have been continuing as often as I have time to visit with each of the men in my classes. I have come to a definite conclusion that makes me love my Jesus more than ever before, and that is this: Somewhere, in every single life born into this world, Jesus knocks at their heart's door. And He does it in such a way that they know it is Him.

I am also amazed at how many men will tell of a time, either as a child or later, when they had a definite encounter with Jesus Christ through the faithful Holy Spirit. So many—it is amazing—tell of a time when they were instantaneously changed into a new person, even though few of them went on to walk in that light. No wonder that the last prophetic glimpse we have of Him in relation to the affairs of men on earth is riding in on a white horse with His name clearly blazing: *Faithful and True!*

Rarely, if ever, do I let a man go from a visit without asking him if we can have prayer together. The other day I did. A man who recently asked to join my classes came in and I asked him to tell me anything about his life that would help him or help me to know how to help him. He said, "Well, all right…"

And then for about forty-five minutes he spilled out such a story of how alcohol ruined his life and marriage that it was almost unbelievable. After twenty-six years of marriage and a very successful business enterprise which gained him a half–million-dollar mortgage-free home and a proportionate amount of all the earthly furnishings and trinkets that go with it, drink made a wreck out of both of them.

She is now in a nursing home without half a mind after turning on him and telling the policemen lies about him that put him in prison. He is completely bankrupt and stripped of every penny he had and all of his possessions.

All the while he was telling me about this he was mixing it in with how much he had always loved the Lord and how he now loves Him so much he will never turn away from Him. But as he did so, he also kept cursing and swearing until by the time he was done I absolutely felt checked to even ask to pray with him. I yet don't understand why, but it was strong and I obeyed and let him go back where he came from. Yes, there are some that the Scripture admonishes us to "save with fear, pulling them out of the fire; hating even the garment spotted by the flesh." Are there others (hopefully not many) that the word is: "Depart, I pray you, from the tents of these wicked men…"? I'm glad God is the Judge and it is only ours to obey His promptings.

Sometimes in a ministry like this you come to think that you have met everybody, and then you meet someone else!

Let me quickly introduce you to one of my recent students. He is 78 years old and carries many scars, both physically and emotionally. He was sent to the battle front in the Korean War and on his first day was told to shoot a Korean soldier who was running away. He held up his rifle, but couldn't seem to bring himself to do the job. An officer slapped him on the helmet and said, "I said, shoot!" He shot and then the officer took him over and rolled over the body. He had killed a young woman soldier.

Before long he himself was shot and wounded and crawled into a bunker for safety. Soon he heard another soldier coming into the bunker and so he shot against the wall to scare him away. The soldier threw a hand grenade into the bunker and completely collapsed it on him. He lay there for hours buried alive and badly wounded all over his face until his comrades missed him and came to dig him out.

He came home under a permanent medical discharge, but later enlisted to go to Viet Nam, thinking it would help him recover his nerves. Again he was subjected to severe action and realized he had made a grievous error. He became so traumatized that he wanted to end his life, but God saved him from that. He returned after eight years of service and married and became a criminal defense attorney and a drug counselor for one NJ's counties. He is now in prison after many years of that on drug charges. Why? He says he did what all drug counselors do—supplied a controlled drug to a recovering patient. He loves the classes and says he really loves the Lord. I trust all is well with his soul, but it surely isn't with his emotions. He wakens two or three nights every week screaming with terror as he relives those awful days of battle. His cell mate is very understanding and tries to help him.

News keeps reaching us of men who have gone out to other prisons and are spreading the fire there. Please pray for them that they will not only reach other souls with God's truth, but will keep pure and clean themselves from all the defilement of false religions where they go.

Thank you each one again for praying,
William Cawman

6
"AND YET THERE IS ROOM"

April 1, 2010

LISTEN TO THESE WORDS of Jesus in Luke 14:22,23: "And the servant said, Lord, it is done as thou hast commanded, and yet there is room. And the lord said unto the servant, Go out into the highways and hedges, and compel them to come in, that my house may be filled." Aren't these fascinating words? What man would give out a command such as this in regards to the wedding of his only son? But you see, when men undertake to present a trophy to another, they search with earnest zeal for the most precious materials they can find on earth to make that trophy out of. When God undertakes to make a trophy, He reaches way down below the bottom of any definition of acceptability and lifts a poor lost sinner, undone and completely worthless, and then washes him in the precious Blood of His Son, and then cleanses out of him every single thing the devil put in him, and then fills him with such glorious fullness of His Own abiding Spirit that He is not ashamed to present that trophy to His Son as His bride to sit with Him in His throne for all eternity.

If you don't believe this, just listen a little further to God's words, not mine: "To him that overcometh will I grant to sit with me in my throne, even as I also overcame, and am set down with my Father in his throne." Have you thought that in answer to your prayers Jesus will, for all eternity, have sitting with Him in His throne—which by the way is in His Father's throne—some poor lost prisoner that the devil was quite sure would be damned for all eternity in hell, beyond the reach of the love of God? Shall we pray for more? Shall we believe that more will be saved?

Let me tell you of one of these answers to your prayers. For a short while now, there has been a Mexican man with a very round face and a head of bushy hair who appears to be enjoying every moment of the services. The other day we sat down together and he began to tell me of what Jesus was doing in his heart. His eyes filled with tears and his face beamed with joy as he told me of God's forgiving grace that has changed his life and given him something worth living for. Our time was too short and we will have to continue it again soon, for he had more to tell me that I'm eager to hear.

Let me make this observation: Don't you think that all around the world, hidden away in even some of the most remote corners of it, there are lonely hearts reaching out to Jesus and finding His forgiving touch to their burdened hearts? Why should we believe this? For what other reason would Jesus delay His coming except that He said in the Scripture quoted above that He wants His house filled? Oh, blessed thought—it will be a full house!

I have personally preached in many houses that were not full. In fact, seldom have I preached here on earth to a house that was full. But that great glorious house in heaven where Jesus has gone to prepare a place for us will be filled! And mingled among that great number that no man can count there will be men and women, boys and girls, who have been saved from every sin that Satan made them commit.

Now, one more thought here: Who will be the last name called in order that His house may be filled? It might be that person in front of you in the checkout line that you feel a nudge to say something to about Jesus. It may be that person way off in the middle of an Islamic village somewhere that you prayed for when you didn't even know their name. It may be a man in prison who needs your prayer to help him break through the lies of Satan and touch Jesus. Someone will be the last sheaf gleaned from this harvest field. Let's be faithful to the end. His house will be filled!

Not every man who attends the classes called "Christian Living in Today's World" is getting the message we would like him to, but then perhaps there are also many in our churches on the outside who aren't, either. One such has been coming for several years, but the other day when I inquired of him how his walk with God was going he replied with a very contented attitude: "It's okay, I guess; a little slow, but I'm in no hurry. God waited a long time for me, so I can wait for Him. Sometimes I feel like I deserve to be getting a little more, but I can wait."

I would love to know what you would have told him; perhaps it would help me somewhere along the line. Or would you suddenly feel like you were at a loss for anything to say? I did. I endeavored to regroup, however, and tried to point out that this isn't the way God would have him view his situation.

It is interesting that in any group of people certain expressions develop that are unique from any other group. It is no different in prison culture. Maybe you would be interested if I would share a couple of them with you, but I am not recommending a wider horizon for their usage. "That's when I caught this incident." Or "that's when I caught this charge." It is said with no more gravity than "that's where I caught this cold." It is sad, but there are sectors of our society among whom going to prison even multiple times is considered quite status quo, although inconvenient.

It is not convenient to have a head cold, but then it's not that serious and I'll probably get another one sooner or later. This is just about the level of stigma and shame that accompanies it. One "reverend," leaving from about his third trip through the gates, told us, "I can't wait to get back to my church again; my pulpit's waiting for me." I think my dear mother would have thumped him on the head for a little wake up call, but I guess I'd better not try that.

How desirable it would be if something, or preferably Someone, could revolutionize this mindset and present among these areas of society a "better way." The multitude of programs sponsored by sinners just simply do not change sinners.

Then here's another expression I have heard more than once. "I always turn to God when I feel some sort of way." The problem is that the result of the turning is just as indefinite as is the feeling. Whenever I hear this I begin to think of how many times this is apparently what happens also around many altars of prayer in revival efforts. Somebody begins to feel some sort of way and prays some sort of prayer and then feels some other sort of way and puts the best name on it they can think of.

One time years ago a very small boy was in a service where God was moving hearts in power. He felt some sort of way over it all and went bubbling up to his aunt and shook her hand as he exclaimed, "Insulation!" He put the biggest name he knew to feeling some sort of way he hadn't felt before. We can forgive him and even rejoice with him that his little heart was undoubtedly feeling the genuine presence of God, but it would be well if grown up men could move a little deeper than some sort of a change of emotional atmosphere.

After writing to you about the two Christian inmates who were put in the detention center I went one last time to visit with them on a Sunday afternoon before service time. The second man I wrote about, who had the snitch note dropped on him, was the first one I looked in on. His cell was about six feet by ten feet with a small bed in one corner and a few blankets on it. A pair of flip flops for showering was by his bed. A little box of milk and a little box of orange juice and an apple were sitting on the six-inch-wide window sill. That was all except a large Bible lying right by his pillow.

With a big pleasant smile he walked over to the window in the door and began to rejoice for the bright spot of us visiting him for a few minutes. He began to relate what had happened. "Chaplain, I couldn't understand what was wrong as they cuffed me and led me away to this place, but I just determined to keep a pure heart and let God do whatever He wanted to do with me even though I don't have a clue why I'm here. Jesus has been with me and I just told God that I would take advantage of this time to spend more time with Him. It has been precious, too. I am reading my Bible and do you know what? I don't think we really know who Jesus is until God reveals Him to us through His Word."

With that I had a pretty good idea of Who was talking to him through that precious living Book. If that Book leads us to know Jesus it will certainly take something other than R. C. Sproul's footnotes—no apologies!

I then went down the row to the man who was jumped and had been there longer. Again I listened to a wondrous testimony of how God was keeping him and giving him opportunity to witness for Him. When he heard the voice of the other Christian down the hallway they had prayer together and it brightened the stay for both of them. I stood there in the hallway and prayed and the tier became very quiet.

Many of those men I've never had the chance to pray with before. This man's face was now pretty well healed up, but he still had no glasses to read with. After I had visited with them and prayed with them, I actually felt like I had been the one ministered to. I honestly felt like they were getting so much from God's presence that I almost wanted to change places with them for a while and get some of it, too.

That time may come soon enough according to the prophecies of Jesus. If it does, I tell you that I want to let it bring me into closer union with Jesus, not produce bitterness over my violated rights. My greatest right came not from the Constitution of the USA but from a Blood-purchased inheritance in Jesus—it is the right to keep pure and sweet no matter what else happens! Both men have now been released from there. The first one who was beaten up was sent to one of the northern prisons and I would love to request definite prayer that his lamp will never go out, for it is needed where he has gone. The second one was placed back in the prison system here, but in a different facility.

Usually when we have a revival scheduled in our church we share it with the men in the prison by taking the evangelist into the prison on the last Friday night instead of having a service in the church that night. This past month we did so and my supervisor just happened to be making the rounds for his yearly visit to each service. He sat in the back as the evangelist brought a very fitting and anointed message to the men. Afterward he said, "That was a very clear and good message." He doesn't often get to hear a message like that because he doesn't go where it is preached like that.

He told me some time ago that it is very hard for him to listen to another man preach because all he can do is sit there and think of how much better he could do it himself. I guess what he lacks in humility he makes up for in honesty. Anyway, a few days later he told me, "Chap, I know I tease you a lot about your heresy, but whatever you're doing in here, keep on doing it." Don't forget to pray for him too.

We still remain in limbo as to what the future will hold for our Christian services here. Our chapel officers were removed so that we can no longer use our chapel areas, but have to try to find a place for our classes somewhere else. A new chief of staff was appointed by the governor, and he was supposed to visit our prison a couple of weeks ago. We were hoping he would recognize how much we needed that space and would restore the officers to us, but then he cancelled the trip.

Discrimination against Christianity is definitely felt throughout the prison, but please just pray that whatever God sees fit to do or not do about it, He will use it to deepen the commitment of men who profess to love Him.

Thank you each one again for all your prayers for us.

Your Brother in Jesus,
William Cawman

May 1, 2010

AS WE TRAVEL ABOUT from place to place I am often asked this question: "Are most of the men in the prison where you minister black?" The answer is "Yes." Probably over seventy percent are black. This would be the case all the way from Long Island, NY to the Keys of Florida and for a distance inland. By contrast, I visited a prison in SD and talked to an officer there who told me that their prison population is over sixty-five percent Native American.

You might wonder why the eastern population is so predominately black. I will answer, not just to answer, but to present a situation that desperately needs God's help. If one dares to pull his head out of the sand of "political correctness," (which most generally is synonymous with blind and stupid denial) and face stark reality, a sad but true scene presents itself. And what I am about to say does not in the least dim my ardent love for my many black brethren in the Lord. I love them dearly and they are as close to me as any of my white brethren.

In fact, before I proceed any further with what I was saying, let me tell you that I find the black people most generally have emotional capacities that are far deeper and broader than many white people have. They love with a love I have seldom experienced in even the best of white brethren. They are passionate, both in loyalty and in the enjoyment of their love for Jesus. And it is not shallow emotionalism without substance, either, in many cases. Just to worship with them once in a while or to teach a class to them doesn't always reveal what they really are, but to sit alone with them and hear them pour out their heart in artless and genuine love bonds one to them as true brethren indeed. They do not hide their love when they love you. They tell you so, and they do it in such genuine ways that it is not hard to feel it.

But for all of that, the African-American population along the eastern seaboard of the USA has been deeply wounded for several generations. Scars of the terrible plague of slavery in this country are far from healed, and the longer the wound festers, the more deeply it becomes a part of their mindset and culture. It is, plainly stated, a part of the culture of their neighborhoods and peer pressures to clearly expect to do some time in prison as a normal part of growing into "manhood." There is little if any stigma to going to prison when your brother is already there, your father has been in and out, your uncles and all the male figures in your life that you have been induced to look up to have spent time; and on top of all that, you have heard all your life, "Stop that, or you'll go to prison just like your old man!" Whole neighborhood gangs of boys grow up among each other and among the influences at home as well that perfectly program them to "catch their charge" and "do their bid."

This whole situation makes my heart cry out in pain, "Oh God, who will go and teach them the better way? Who will stop this repetitious and demoralizing mindset that presents a dear little black boy with no greater expectation than the inevitable 'doing his bid' thing?" Is there not a better way? Is there not a way to break this cycle and teach them to expect something better in life than this? Cannot they be challenged to rise out of this devastating program and answer the call to the higher life?

Next time you look with disgust at some upper teenager with his obvious body language calling loudly that he is anti-everything in the whole wide world he knows anything about, and he passes you by without a "good morning" or even a smile, while he wears his pants half off and his hat 90 degrees from straight and his belt twice too long and a comb stuck into his matted coiffure and his body pierced with nails and pins, just think for a moment before becoming too harshly critical—What if I had been raised in his world? Just remember for a moment before developing any attitude toward him that once a short while ago he was a cute little black boy with bright brown eyes and a charming face, but—! This "but" needs to be attacked by grace and compassion like it has never been done yet. O God, help us to do our part!

After two weeks away in revival meetings this month, I returned and as soon as I stepped into the compound a tall officer waved and said, "Chap, I've missed you; haven't seen you lately. Where you been this time?" I told him and he said, "Isn't it wonderful, just out doing God's work? Hey Chap, whenever you see me somewhere don't be in a hurry. Stop and talk to me 'cause I need it. Every time I see you walk by I sense God's presence and I love it. I need to hear what God's doing."

I went a little further and met the Islamic chaplain coming towards me. I stopped to greet him and he couldn't even crack a smile. He just started as usual with a tirade of negativity about everything and everybody. He is anti the people he works with, the men he ministers to, the administration, the government, and everybody else in his life. He is one of the most miserable men I have ever met, and it is always a sound disappointment to try to befriend him or even be civil to him. The saddest part of all is that when his sad, negative, disgruntled life is over he will drop straight into hell for all eternity.

Oh, how I wish that some way I could let him get a taste of how good God is, but he did not get to where he is without many faithful warnings already. His father is the high priest of Islam in Nigeria and had either nineteen or twenty-one sons, I can't remember for sure which. He wanted the boys to receive a better education than normal so sent them to a Baptist school in Nigeria. He has a Bible on his desk along with his Koran. He works with Christian men on a daily basis. But he is a willful sinner of the worst type. He is unfaithful to his wife, he jokes about being the "holy man" with the officers and fits right into the dirtiest of all they want to talk about. Consequently he is very popular with the officers and if I or my supervisor are walking with him across the compound, the officers always greet him "Dr. ——" while completely ignoring either of us.

Such is the leader of the Islamic population in this prison. Such is the example and role model nearly four hundred Muslim inmates have to look up to.

Do you remember from last month's letter that the man who had been accused of wanting to kill a cop and was put in detention for a while was cleared and released back into population? Well, we had a visit afterwards and he told me that he was trying to adjust to the different facility he was placed in, but he said, "If God wants me here to spread His Word, I belong to Him."

They gave him a new cell mate who was a young man just new to the prison. He asked him, "Do you know Jesus?" "Yes." "Have you received Him into your heart?" "Well, yes, but..." Our brother didn't wait for him to explain that but said, "I know what you mean by the 'but.'" "Yea, I've backslid." He started quoting Scripture to him and he told me, "Chaplain, I've never been able to memorize Scripture as much as I've wanted to, and especially the references, but I was amazed at the Scriptures that started coming out of my mouth and I even knew where to point him in the Bible to find them. God is so good!" The young man finally said, "God sent you here on purpose to help me."

After telling me this he suddenly began to break down and sob in his love for Jesus. There is no question but that "the love of God is shed abroad in [his] heart..." He then told me that he carries a heavy heart because ever since the earthquake in Haiti he has heard nothing from his mother who was living in Port-au-Prince. He said with sadness, "I don't know that she was a Christian, and if she wasn't, I'll never see her again."

Tragically, he only met her a few times in his life, as he was raised by his grandmother, but still he feels it keenly.

Let me give you a new prayer request. In the minimum camp there is a man who has put in quite some time there and has steadily been seeking the Lord. He often kneels at his chair for some time in earnest prayer.

A while back he confided in me that he was still struggling with the cigarette habit and really wanted deliverance because he knew it wasn't pleasing to the Lord. I told him to ask a few of the brothers to help him pray and to make himself accountable to them and the Lord and then simply throw them all away and trust God to give him complete deliverance. He did, and God did help him, and in a short time he was completely delivered until he had no desire for them anymore.

He has a little baby girl at home a little over a year old that was born after he came to prison, so he has only seen pictures of her. For a while his wife had cut herself off from him, but just about as he was ready to give up hope, she wrote to him and told him that she wanted their lives to be right and she was going to give him another chance. Please pray that nothing will come between these good desires and intentions and the fulfillment of them.

The first moments, almost, after a man is released can be so critical in which direction he goes. Don't think for a moment that the devil doesn't have a toll booth just on the other side of the prison gate from which he demands just a moment of attention, then another moment, then...

Among all of the men who fail right here, there is a man in our church who didn't, and now stands on ten glorious years of victory over every arrow Satan shot at him. But the moment he passed that toll gate, the devil jumped on both shoulders and began to show him all that he had been missing and what he could now have. For a moment it all sounded so good; and then, the precious Blood "that speaketh better things than that of Abel," rose up and he looked the devil in the face and said, "Old devil, I told you when I was in prison that you could go to hell by yourself, and I mean it now!" Thank God, from there on it has been victory unto victory. Oh, that all of them would do likewise.

We continue to receive encouraging letters from some who were here and now have moved on or been released. Others we so long to hear from but they have gone silent for whatever reason. I know that God has kept a burden, for some of these in particular, on some of your hearts, and I am so thankful. I know it is impossible to express how much we appreciate and depend on the many prayers that go up when you read these letters. I only wish so many times that we could share the reward with you of seeing those prayers answered in so many ways. This I am positive of: every one of you who have prayed will share in the reward someday, for God knows every faithful heart who has even offered one prayer that God has laid on your heart. Until then, thank you! Thank you!

Your fellow laborer in this vineyard,
William Cawman

June 1, 2010

ONE MORNING I WAS SITTING in a room waiting for an inmate to arrive for a visit when I heard the door open and an officer stepped in. I have known this officer for several years and whenever I meet him on the compound he greets me with a smile and a verse of Scripture or else asks me for one for the day. He impresses me as being very sincere and genuine. As he stepped into the room he asked, "Chaplain, how are you today?" I replied, "Officer, there's not the slightest thing between me and Jesus." He grasped my hand and said, "Chap, that's all that matters, and I mean it! More and more that's all that matters to me. I have to be right with God."

I told him I really appreciated those of the officers that would not hide their candle under a bushel and he said, "This is not my job, this is my ministry. Time is short and we must do all we can." He quoted Phil. 1:21, "For to me to live is Christ, and to die is gain." I wish every officer was like him. Perhaps in the Millennium all prison officers will be Christians—oh, no! That's not right, is it? There will be no prisons during the Millennium.

Several months ago I told you about a 47-year-old black minister who is incarcerated and has been doing some serious soul searching. Until we met, I doubt he had ever heard that there is a deliverance from the sinning business, much less a deliverance from the indwelling nature of it. He has listened intently, however, and with deep lines of pondering on his face says repeatedly, "I'm receiving this!"

The last time I visited with him and asked him how he was doing he said with a cover-up smile, "Pretty good. I'm keeping up with my devotions and everything is going pretty well." I said to him, "There are two ways to view contentment: the Scripture tells us that 'godliness with contentment is great gain,' and that is so true. But on the other hand, contentment in a state of relationship to God that is less than perfect is a curse."

He got a very serious look on his face and then immediately let down his guard and started into it more deeply. He looked me in the eye and said, "Chaplain, I feel I can tell you some things that I've never felt free to tell anyone else, and they're bothering me. I keep hanging up on a question. I can't figure out what happened in my life that I'm saddled down with this long charge over me. Everything was going well with my ministry and my wife and my children. I had everything going for me and in my favor. What made me fall into a moment of sin and end up like this?"

I began to explain to him Peter's love for Jesus and how he thought he would be willing to die for Him, but that there was a hidden element of sin in his heart that he was unaware of. Jesus knew it was there and allowed him to enter into a situation that revealed it painfully to Peter. He had to be forgiven for denying His Lord, but then Jesus restored him and sent him to the Upper Room to be cleansed from that seed of sin and failure and be filled with the Holy Spirit.

He listened seriously and then said again, "Chaplain, I'm receiving this." I asked him if he was conscious of the clear witness of the Spirit to his sonship with God and he said he definitely is. I then urged him to seek earnestly to be delivered from sin and to ask God to give him a pure heart, lest that seed of sin rise up again. Please pray for him. It is rare that a preacher of sin-sparing doctrines would humble himself to acknowledge himself in need, but perhaps he, like Paul, "obtained mercy, because [he] did it ignorantly in unbelief." He asked to join my class in Christian Living. Please pray for him.

It had been a few weeks since I had a visit with our good brother who sits by the bedside of dying men and seeks to get them to heaven. Here is a man I can always count on to be living in up-to-date victory. He came into the room with a bright smile and when I asked him how the journey was going he said, "Wonderful. Jesus is so near and if I ever feel that something has obscured Him I'm just like a little child—Mommy! Mommy! — until I find His presence again. I can't live without Him." He carries God's presence wherever he goes and everyone knows it. He has been assigned for a long while to an old Italian man and has come to love him just like he is his father. He literally cares for all his needs and longs to see him know for sure that he is ready for heaven. Great will be his reward in heaven! He is such a blessing to my own heart.

I must tell you a little more about the man I've recently written about who had the note dropped on him and was locked up in detention for a while and then was cleared and sent back. In class we were discussing the subject of "How God forgives," and he raised his hand. He told the class that he had never known the love of a father. His father never held him or hugged him or told him he loved him. He said that he had not even been conscious of it, but deep within there was a hurt that had never gone away that bordered on unforgiveness.

The Sunday night before, a minister had told them how he never knew the love of an earthly father, but how God had healed that lack. He said that as he sat there listening God opened up that secret closet of his heart and revealed to him how that hurt had never been healed and that it was too close to unforgiveness to leave there. He said that as God opened that door he was able to lay it all on Jesus and a healing came to him over it all.

Then he broke down and began to sob quietly. The man next to him touched him and said, "That's all right." Once again I was touched at how God will not leave any hidden areas of our lives to hinder us if we will keep walking in the light. When the Great Physician heals, He keeps on healing until there is nothing remaining that hinders His moving in and through us. Isn't it wonderful?

A young man recently came to the prison from the juvenile one. He is twenty-three years old, but is deeply damaged. He entered the military right out of high school and served three years and nine months. The last seven months of that time he was sent to Iraq and got into some terrible action. He was so traumatized after a few months that they gave him medication and it had no effect, so they gave him a medical discharge and sent him home. There he was admitted to hospitals and they gave him more drugs, but with minimal results. He resorted to street drugs and found heroine the most effective, but realized that it did not take the problem away and it was only worse when he came off of it.

He became violent and was arrested and sent to prison. Any more than that about what he encountered in Iraq he just said, "I don't want to talk about it." He wakes up screaming at night as he relives the awful scenes in his dreams, and many nights he refuses to go to sleep because he cannot bear to face the nightmares again. Any loud noise instantly traumatizes him; anyone approaching him from behind sends him again for a loop. I stood up and put my arms around him and said, "First of all I want to thank you for the sacrifice you have made for my freedom. Some men go and lay down their lives and never come back. Others go and lay down their lives and they do come back, but life will never be the same." I asked him if he ever had any mental disorders or trauma like this before going to Iraq and he said he didn't.

He then began to tell me that while in the juvenile center he had tried to be a Christian, but that it was very hard and he had finally backslidden and now he was just wallowing in sin. He said, "I don't want it to be this way, but yet I would have to say that living in sin is so much easier than it was trying to be a Christian."

I said, "You have just plainly told me that you have never been really born again, for when you are, you will be a new creature in Jesus and it will no longer be hard to be a Christian." I asked him if he had ever tried to make a chicken swim. He smiled and said, "No." I told him that they can do it but they hate every minute of it and it is hard and uncomfortable, but if you could somehow change the chicken into a duck it would cease to be hard and uncomfortable. I told him that is exactly what Jesus does when he really comes into our hearts. He changes our nature until we are no longer trying to be a Christian; we are one.

He said, "I want that." I prayed with him and urged him to seek God until it happened. He said, "How do I do that?" I said, "The Bible tells us two things we must do to be saved: (1) we must confess and forsake our sins, and (2) we must ask and believe God to forgive us and come into our hearts." I told him that if there was any sin he absolutely felt he couldn't forsake and leave to ask God to help him and He would do it.

He left the room promising to do that. I would love to see what God can do through the healing power of the Blood of Jesus in not only his forgiveness and new birth, but in the healing of his mind. He has paid an awful price to serve his country. He even considered taking his life to end the awful nightmares and memories, but he knew that was not the way out. He said he survived Iraq; he doesn't want to go down at his own hand. Please pray for him also.

The other morning in my devotions I read from Psalm 102 these words: "For He hath looked down from the height of His sanctuary; from heaven did the Lord behold the earth; To hear the groaning of the prisoner; to loose those that are appointed to death..." My heart began to feel a pain at how few there are who are cooperating with this Lord; and I'm not talking now about inmates, but about false religious teachers that plague us with "doctrines of devils." The old missionary song says, "Jesus would save, but there's no one to tell them..." Are we short on religious volunteers? Absolutely not. More apply all the time, but so few of them are telling them that Jesus saves!

I thank God for the brethren from our church who fill in the vacancies in my schedule when I am away in meetings, and many of the men in prison thank God for them, too. Sometimes I get a great pleasure out of announcing that next week my pastor will be there, or one of the other men. Then I say, "Is that all right? You love them, don't you?" Quick is the glorious response, "Oh, yes!" What a blessing! But still it is a constant battle with false teachers.

Why on earth a man would desire to preach to others that we cannot live without sin while in the body on earth, when Enoch did it before the Bible was ever written, is more than I can excuse or understand. Please pray for all those who quench smoking flaxes and break bruised reeds. Pray that God will convict them of the serious crime they are committing against the souls of men to stand before a damaged, now awakened, heart and lead them from truth into error like this. May God rebuke them, yet with mercy on their own souls. We will not lose our love for their souls while hating their works.

A man came in the other day and I sensed quickly that he was immersed in human effort rather than empowered by divine life, but it was almost frustrating to try to help him. I tried to open his eyes to the real power of the Christian life and he would say, "Yeah, that's what I'm doing—tryin' to be humble and all and better myself. I've done a couple of bids, but I'm getting it together now." I would go back to first base and try all over again to break into his concepts with what grace can do, but he had for so long been "born of the flesh" that he seemed impenetrable.

Nicodemus was baffled at the thought of being born again. This man doesn't even seem to comprehend it enough to be baffled—he's doing fine— "that which is born of the flesh is flesh," and he seems quite content with flesh. If every man in prison were this way would one feel like Jeremiah trying to preach to them? Thank God that's not the case!

There are more who are hungry—we will go back!

In Christian love,
William Cawman

7
WHEAT AND TARES

July 1, 2010

LET ME QUOTE a few verses from Psalm 119. "Oh how love I Thy law! It is my meditation all the day...I have refrained my feet from every evil way, that I might keep Thy word. I have not departed from Thy judgments; for Thou hast taught me. How sweet are Thy words unto my taste! Yea, sweeter than honey to my mouth! Through Thy precepts I get understanding: therefore *I hate every false way.* Thy word is a lamp unto my feet, and a light unto my path." (emphasis added)

Is it then acceptable that a state prison chaplain also hates every false way? Sometimes I am made to wonder, why do people want to teach others that we are unable to live free from sin, or that once we are saved we are eternally secure of heaven no matter how we live? What is the point of teaching men such nauseating, unbiblical trash? Yet it is a constant battle against these "doctrines of devils."

About a year ago a teacher came in and set up a Bible Institute in one of the facilities. It is a very vibrant and promising program with some sort of a certificate promised at the end. Undiscerning lambs are swallowed up by it. I opened a drawer where the workbooks are kept and the first thing that stared me in the face was the observation that if, when a soul commits sin, it separates him from God, then God must of necessity perform an amputation on His own body, for that soul had become part of the Body of Christ. I couldn't help but wonder what this kind of a god looks like with all these sinning warts all over his body that would require an amputation to get rid of. If sin does not bar us from heaven then Satan himself will be there, for he, too, was once a son of God. This kind of heaven I have no interest in.

Will you help us pray that God will protect His little lambs, that are just beginning to wake up to righteousness, from these wolves? Not all of them come in from the outside, for we have inbred ones, too. One dear soul who is as heathen and untutored as can possibly be imagined came to visit with me and he was all excited because he has a cell mate who is imparting to him "understanding." I really believe the dear man has had a partial awakening and knows he needs a new life, but here he is locked in a cell with a man who never goes to church because he already knows all there is to know. He is apparently a descendant of the prodigy in Scripture of whom it was observed that wisdom dwelt with them.

The poor man was so excited that he wanted to share with me what he was learning and so he grabbed the first piece of paper in sight and began. One verse of the Bible is all you will ever need for it says in Rev. 13:18, "Here is wisdom..." And then of course it goes on to say, "Let him that hath understanding [his cell mate, I learned, has it] count the number of the beast: for it is the number of a man; and his number is Six hundred threescore and six." Now let me share this "understanding" with you and then you will have it, too.

Our illustrious teacher declares that computers are "demoniacal tracking devices," and he proves it by giving to each letter of the alphabet a numerical value; i.e., A=6, B=12, C=18, etc. Now take the word "computer" and give each of the letters their numerical value and they will total 666. Meanwhile the poor victim ensnared by him struggles on in helpless sinning weakness, notwithstanding his new-found *understanding*. Can you detect that *I hate every false way?*

Now for a brighter side—and thank God there is one, Do you remember the young man I told you about who had five bullets pumped into him two years ago; two of them in the head? He is now enjoying a new life in Jesus and growing in it. The other day he told me that in a daily reading he found, on exactly the second anniversary of the bullets, these words from Job: "What? Shall we receive good at the hand of God, and shall we not receive evil?" He said, "What seemed like a tragedy has turned my life around."

I asked him if he would consider praying about writing down his story. He said he had already tried it once and when he got to page fifty he wasn't feeling right about it and threw it away. Then he started again and after page four he felt like he should put that away. I told him that maybe he was writing it without the help of God; to pray and ask God again and if he felt God wanted him to, God would help him write it so that it would magnify God, not him. He agreed to do that, so you might remember him in prayer. He is a living miracle of prevenient grace.

We have a 27-year-old Mexican man who is about as small as adult men come, but he is radiantly enjoying his relationship with the Lord. He wanted to talk to me and he said that he was so happy with his life in Jesus, but wondered what about the thoughts that kept coming to him about his past life. He didn't want to think about those things that once brought him pleasure in sin.

I explained to him that he needed to plead the Blood of Jesus and refuse to accept them, no matter how they seemed to press at his door, and God would keep him free from sin. He just beamed with the instruction and entered into a new liberty.

He came from Mexico at the age of 15 and two years later joined the MS13 gang and has their tattoos all over his arms.

Three years ago this all came to a screeching halt by a prison cell. Another Spanish inmate began to witness to him and he said he didn't want to hear anything about it. He said his heart was as hard as it could be. But little by little the words sank in and his heart began to soften.

One day he said he began to pray and his heart just broke completely and Jesus came in and forgave him. He was happy with the change, but continued to perform the gang activities for a couple of months. Then God began to talk to him and tell him that he could not serve two masters. He wrote letters to the gang leaders and told them that he still wanted to be their friends, but that he had gotten saved and could no longer be a part of the gang or their activity. Amazingly, and all because of the shelter of the Blood, they respected him for it without any repercussions.

Again, I want to request prayer for the 47-year-old minister who is coming into further light. Yesterday in class we were speaking particularly of the necessity of being cleansed from all sin if the Holy Spirit was to flow through us. He came to me after the class and said, "Brother, those were powerful words. Thank you!" Not many who have endorsed a doctrine that excuses and makes provision for continuing in sin ever divorce themselves from it, but I believe here is one who is doing it.

With men like this, I put much more focus on showing them "the better way" than in trying to convince them of their errors. The devil loves any form of godliness that leaves any provision for sin to remain in the heart. False teachers abound who promote such deceiving beliefs.

I often point out to them the Hebrew encampment in the wilderness. Without the camp of Israel was a world of shameful and degrading sin of all kinds. If a person wanted to escape this horrible life, they could become a part of the camp of Israel. Any church atmosphere is better in some respects than a barroom fight or a night lying in gutter vomit with empty pockets. But among the Israelites were a few serious souls who really meant business about keeping right, and they would often visit the tabernacle courtyard where sacrifices were available to atone for their sin. Then, there were those who attended to the duties within the Holy Place and were shut away from much of what was going on in the outer camp. But there was a place that God had Moses erect beyond the veil where, He said, "There I will meet with thee...and I will commune with thee..." This is the privilege of the New Testament Christian, and everything short of that is beneath our Blood-bought inheritance. I ask them what would make them desire to settle down in the outer court or even in the inner circle and not want to enter into the Holy of Holies with God.

About a year ago our pastor was holding one of my classes in my absence, and a young man from Sierra Leone prayed his way into God's presence and was saved. He has been steadily growing in grace ever since, and loves it. He has been telling me that he has a growing desire to go back to his country when he gets out and minister to them. He is fully aware that it may only be his desire and that God may have other plans, but he is hoping that perhaps it would be God's will for him. I know he would be so glad if you would help him pray about this. He was very young when he left there, so it would be very new to him to change cultures, but he really seems to want God's will, whatever that is.

I told our young man who suffered so in Iraq that I would ask you again to pray for him. Just the other day he told me that he only has a few more months to be in prison and he doesn't want to come out until he is really changed. Please pray that his desire will be fully in tune with God's desire for him, not just a desire to escape the trauma of the past. I have tried to point out to him that there is definitely healing in God if he is really willing to be completely God's, but that it would not be love from God to heal him so that he could go back to a life apart from God. He said, "I want that."

We had another occasion for a heavy heart this past month. Several years ago a man came into the prison who also had been a minister of some sort. His ministry was very self-directed and his god very fitted to his sinful passions. I have seen pictures of him standing in his pulpit flanked with helpers while he ministered to others, and all the while he was playing around with several women at a time, none of whom were his wife, although he was married to a second wife.

After he came to prison it seemed that he really began to seek to get right in his heart. I had many a visit with him and finally one day looked at him squarely and said, "There is a hidden closet in your life that you are not coming clean with. You will never be right until you face it and get it clean. I am not eager to hear tales of sins, but I do want to tell you that it will never break our relationship or lower my estimation of you if you will come completely clean with your past life."

He looked at me for a minute and then began to cry. He said, "I have longed for an opportunity like this, but was too afraid of what would happen. I've always been thrown away over everything." He began to belch out the reality of his inner self and God really broke him down and it would have appeared that he came completely clean of it all. It definitely felt like he was growing in grace and becoming a very good man at heart.

When it came time for him to leave the prison I warned him straightforwardly that it would never work for him to try to go out and put new wine into old bottles. I warned him of his former companions in ministry and how they had supported and condoned him while he was living in the most rotten sin imaginable. How disappointing it was that after a visit or two to our church, he returned to the very pit from which he had been rescued. I would doubt if he returned to the low life of before, but neither did he take the highway of holiness. He visited me several times and loved me dearly as far as I could tell, and then I attended his viewing the other evening. Pictures were all over the place magnifying his years of ministry while he was groveling in despicable sin. The Great White Throne will make no mistakes.

Please continue to pray for all of those who are helping in this ministry, that we will do nothing except under the anointing of the Holy Spirit. Thank you for praying.

Your Brother in Jesus,
William Cawman

┼┼┼

August 1, 2010

I HAVE A WONDERFUL BIT of news to start off with. The man who at times has done so wonderfully in his walk with the Lord, but has twice given place to discouragement and dropped out, has caught himself again and come back with deep apology for what he has done. His face is again so radiant with humble desire for God. Have you ever known of people who, while attending an established holiness church for all their life, get a good start, run well for a season, then drop into some trap of Satan, then catch themselves, then do it again, etc.? Well, then, don't be too judgmental over our dear brother, just pray for him. He shows every sign of genuine turning from his fall and has humbled himself and acknowledged that it was wrong.

He wouldn't mind, I am sure, if I told you plainly what his struggle was over. He is serving a life sentence since the age of seventeen, and he is now in his mid-forties. He is surrounded every moment of every day, except for the time in Christian Living class by sin, sin, and more sin. He goes to church and for the most part (say like three or four Sundays out of the month) has to listen to doctrines of devils that condone and promote the liberty to sin.

Fortunately for a while now, our church has one Sunday night a month in his facility, but for a long time we were assigned to the other two and that was all he had. Very few men in his facility are really in tune with the message of full salvation, and I am not aware of any just now in his housing unit that would be living a sanctified life.

Now with all this situation to contend with and no promise

of anything better for the rest of his life, you can see how the devil trains his heavy guns of discouragement directly at him. Discouragement is no small sin to be ignored, for it opens the door to the whole catalog of Satan's wares. In the two times that he has succumbed to the discouragement he has not gone back into outward sin, thank God; but he absolutely shuts himself away and doesn't want to talk about it, which gives the enemy all the more room to work. Please pray that this time he will let God deal with the root problem and come out, never to go under again. He is such a blessing to everyone when he is in victory and such a stumbling-block to his witness when he drops out.

I want to bring another very serious prayer request to you. A few months ago I told you about a man who was propositioned by a female officer after a Sunday night service in the chapel area and how he rejected her and told a sergeant about her. They moved him immediately to another facility in the same prison and did nothing about the female officer. Judge for yourself which one should be on the locked side of the door. From that time on the officers have not ceased to persecute and abuse him with ugly job assignments, long and hard hours, etc.

He has not come to the classes or to church and I was becoming very concerned about him. I put him on the appointment sheet to come and visit me but he didn't come. When I called his unit the officer went to get him but he said that he was all right and didn't want to come down. I waited a month or so and then put him on the appointment sheet again. That time he came just at the end of the time and sat down and told me the following:

"Chaplain, I want to ask you to forgive me for not coming before, and even this time I waited until the very end, but I can't dodge you. I love you, and of all the people I can stay away from, I can't do it to you. I know you care about me, but I have been going through so much that I just feel like completely giving up. I haven't read my Bible or prayed for a long time. I got news that my sister is to have a heart operation and then I found out that I, too, have a heart problem of some sort. I can't seem to escape the persecution that never lets up and I've become so discouraged that I wanted to just give up completely. Just yesterday I opened my Bible for the first in a long time. I felt a little ray of courage to once again look to Jesus. I decided to read Hebrews chapter 12, but I never got there. My eyes fell on the verse, Heb 10:32, "But call to remembrance the former days, in which, after ye were illuminated, ye endured a great fight of afflictions..." I began to think back of those days and how good it was. Had it not been that I prayed yesterday after reading that, I probably would not have come to see you. Chaplain, I want you to know that I never forget you. Your face is always before me. You have shown me the way of a Christian. I love you for what you've meant to me, and I love you for the change I have seen in other men that have known you. I couldn't dodge you forever."

I assured him that we would be praying for him and that it was not the answer to become discouraged and give up. I told him that until that blessed day when he would be enlightened again, I would now and then put his name on the list to see me and that it would not be for the purpose of beating him over the head, but it would be because I love him. He looked at me so tenderly and longingly and said, "I know that."

Would you help us pray that he will not linger in this state but will come back into the joy of the Lord? I well remember the day a couple of years ago when he stood up in class and just honestly confessed his need of something more than an outward form. We got on our knees in that classroom and God came down in a mighty grip of prayer.

I might tell you that as we were praying that day in great earnestness my supervisor and two officers walked through the back of the classroom and that old subtle "angel of light" began to whisper in my ear, "You know if this really breaks loose into a wave of God's reviving power it might not be understood and a damper might be placed on the whole effort here. You might not be able to come in and minister here at all."

It was so real that for a moment or two I almost staggered under the threat, but then the Blood spoke. I almost laughed as I said to that voice, "This is God's business and He can take care of the results or repercussions or whatever else. I am just His servant and He can take care of His own business." Before long that dear man arose a new creature in Christ Jesus. His sins were all pardoned and he had new life within him. He was enlightened and began to endure of course a "great fight of afflictions," but the enlightening was more powerful than the fight and he began to grow in grace. O God, please do it again! Will you pray that it will be so very soon?

Do you remember the young man I told you about who, after leaving a bar in his car, was attacked by guns and was shot five times, twice in the head? He was visiting me on the second anniversary of the shooting and told me that he had picked up a religious periodical that day and read the words from Job's answer to his wife: "What? shall we receive good at the hand of God, and shall we not receive evil?" He said he was so blessed over it because what seemed like a tragedy has turned his life completely around. It was a pretty rough wake-up call, and he knows it, but he is so thankful that God allowed it.

I took the opportunity to press upon him the intensity of the claim that God has on his life. He freely acknowledged it and welcomes it. Pray that he will never take that lightly but will let God completely have His way for the rest of his life.

I must keep our dear preacher brother before you for continued prayer. He is still grasping with hunger the further light of full salvation where he has only known the darkness of sinning religion. So far he has not become offended and backed off, and I hope he will not until he comes clear out into the purity of holiness.

This past month the president of a Bible College has been

here again for a week teaching the few men who have enrolled in correspondence work from the school. What a blessing it has been, and how the men do appreciate that week of being "on the mount" with God. It is such a refreshing blessing to them to stop for a week all that prison life entails and just concentrate on the things of God. Shortly before this week came I felt led to ask this brother if he would be interested in taking the course. He replied, "I would really embrace that opportunity."

I knew that as yet he would not have fully grasped the teaching of Wesleyan Scriptural holiness, but I also felt that I could not be clear and not give him every opportunity to be led into the "better way." I believe it was a week of great light to him and I am sure that if you are acquainted at all with the arrogance that generally attends those who have believed and taught these Calvinistic sinning religions, you know that they defend their positions with whatever carnal traits are left in them (and you also know how many that is!). This man is not doing that. He may at times carry a deep look of pondering on his face, but then when he opens his mouth it is with appreciation for new light. The further he goes the more anxious (is that the word I should use?) I feel "that he which hath begun a good work in you will perform it until the day of Jesus Christ."

Am I wrong to feel a great desire not only for his soul, but also to see God give a rare deliverance from the captivating doctrine that is holding so many outside of the relationship purchased at such awful cost on Calvary? One of the prominent, well-known present proponents of Calvinistic teachings started in the holiness movement and is now one of the most radical teachers of continuing in sin. I'd love to see God raise up a glorious counterpart from among the ranks of Calvin to go forth and proclaim full deliverance from all sin! So be it, dear Lord!

There is a man with a Hispanic name but perhaps of mixed race who has been responding with great interest and delight in the classes. The other day we had a chance to visit and he told me that some time back he had come to a Sunday night service and it was scheduled to serve communion that night. He said that I had told the men before we partook of the communion elements that if they were still struggling with some addiction or sin in their lives and they did not believe that the Blood of Jesus was absolutely sufficient to cleanse them of that, they should not partake of it, as the Bible taught it would be drinking to themselves damnation. But if they truly believed that Jesus' Blood could cleanse away their sin and addictions they could then partake with a clear conscience and it might even strengthen their faith to believe for deliverance.

He said that he had struggled for a long time with a heavy addiction to cigarettes, and nothing could break it. He would try for a while, but to no avail. He just could not get loose from them. That night he looked up to the Blood of Jesus and prayed "Oh Jesus, I can't take communion and then go smoke. Would you please deliver me from this?" He said that instantly he knew he was completely free and has never had the least desire for a smoke since. Now do you understand why all the windows of his heart are open to the extent that it even opens up his face with every new truth? Does it not still work just as it always has, that "If the Son therefore shall make you free, ye shall be free indeed"?

Please pray, in addition to the specific needs mentioned above, that God will give us the Spirit of true revival throughout every class and Bible study and Sunday night service. Without that none of us are sufficient to accomplish the eternal task that looms up before us. I thank God for every brother and sister that is helping us in this little corner of God's great harvest field, but all of us combined are not enough. We need God! Thank you so much for your prayers for us and may the Lord of Harvest reward you openly as only He can.

In Christian love,
William Cawman

☩

September 1, 2010

"FOR THE GRACE OF GOD that bringeth salvation hath appeared to all men, Teaching us..." (Titus 2:11,12) If you wonder why we would start with these words of Paul to Titus and then end them part way through, it is because this is exactly what comes to us as we watch one of our dear brothers in prison. The grace of God is teaching him! And what a teacher! For several years I have watched this man sit quietly in Bible studies and classes without any desire to be seen or heard, and yet grasp Bible truth to the saving and sanctifying of his soul. From that point on there has been no stopping of the great Divine Teacher, the *grace of God*.

The other day we visited again for a while and I just marveled at what grace has taught and is teaching him. He was telling how he attends every Christian service that is held and participates in each Bible study, no matter who the teacher, but just keeps sweet while he sorts out what is Biblical and what is not. This has enabled him to be a father and tutor to many of the men who see the light gleaming in his face and come to him to question things people come in and teach them. He never puts these people in a bad light, but just prays for them perchance they are ignorant of the truth themselves. But then he carefully guides those who come to him into the Biblical pathway. And they come to him all the time. He is a full time missionary within the prison walls. He loves Jesus with all his heart and he loves to lead men to Him.

As he humbly related how God has showed him how to deal with the men without causing them to admit bitterness or arguments into their search for truth, I marveled. I thought to myself, "Lord, I have seen Bible College graduates who do not manifest the wisdom and tact and divine anointing in knowing how to deal with false teachings and damaging doctrines that he does." There is a reason and only one, and that reason is not that he has excluded himself to the classes we teach or the services we hold; the reason is "...the grace of

God that bringeth salvation hath appeared to [him], teaching him." Don't you just love it? Oh, that the whole professed Church of Jesus Christ would receive this promised Teacher!

Let me tell you another miracle of God's doing. About a year ago, more or less, my pastor was taking one of my classes for me while I was gone, and during that class a man who was born in Sierra Leone sought God and was saved. From that time until now he has grown in grace and in his love for Jesus.

As we visited again the other day he told me that all he wants is to be completely like Jesus wants him to be. I asked him if he ever recognizes things still in his inner nature that are not like Jesus and he immediately acknowledged that he does. I urged him to not ignore those signals but to bring it to the same Blood of Jesus that forgave his sins and ask God to remove them.

He then told me that sometimes he feels he would like for God to lead him back to his own country again to tell others, but he is not yet sure what God has in mind for him and he doesn't want to make a mistake. He became eligible for parole, but that would have meant being sent back into the northern New Jersey neighborhood that he came out of and he did not feel that was God's will. He said he prayed but has not yet gotten a clear answer as to what God wants of him so he told the parole board that he wanted to postpone his parole for a while.

I believe with all my heart that God has something in store for this young man that he has no idea of. For him to be willing to forego release from prison in order to have more time to pray and seek God's direction will not be left unnoticed by God. He said that all he wants is God's will, no matter what that may be for him. Will you help him pray until he prays clear through about this? He's a rather bashful, retiring individual, but carries a look of sweet contentment on his countenance and immediately responds with joy to the inquiry as to his peace with God.

Out in the minimum security camp (a 300-bed facility outside the main compound) there is an Italian man with a very bright appearance and a seemingly vibrant personality. He came up to the front after a class and asked if we could sit down and talk. When we came together I was effectively reminded that one cannot judge a book by its cover. Inside of this man and behind this bright face was a seething caldron of deep distress. He began to open up and unload the baggage he was struggling under.

He is a married man with a son not yet in his teens. He has been untrue to his wife and consequently has known for eight months that he is HIV positive besides having hepatitis C. His mind is racing with anxiety over how and when to break the news to his wife and what the results will be. It is plaguing his mind that perhaps he has also made her sick. Then he knows he needs to straighten up so many things from his past life including a broken relationship with his brother.

Now add to all this real trouble the fact that the dirty old devil, once he has accomplished his end-of-the-road program, begins to lay on the lash with a fury that is fatal to any up-look of faith or hope. Blow after blow, night and day alike, hopeless and going down, and that very fast.

For some time I sat and tried my best to point him to the only Source of a sinner's hope, but he was just like a drowning man. He would unload and unload and then when I would try to say something I could tell he was hardly hearing me because of the depths of his anguish. Just as a drowning person fights off their rescuer in their intense desire to be rescued, so he was doing and I could feel it. I felt just as helpless as the rescuer in such a case.

If I suggested that he try to roll his burdens on Jesus and ask Him for forgiveness, hardly would the words be out of my mouth and he would say, "Yea, I do that all the time, but I can't get out of this." If I would suggest that he get alone and really try to pray to God he would say, "I pray to Him all the time, but what can I do with all this?" He would fight me off while at the same time desperately clinging to me.

I went back again for another visit right away because I was going to be away for a few weeks in meetings. He looked at me in desperation and said, "How long will you be gone? What shall I do while you are away? When will you be back, and when can I talk to you again?" My heart bled for him and I wanted so much to help him get to Jesus, the Healer of all our diseases, but he couldn't seem to listen and yet did not want me to leave him at the same time.

Such, friends, is the harvest time that was so artfully sealed from view as Satan advertised his wares. Cruel and unrelenting, the paycheck continues to roll on and on with no pity for the cries of the poor doomed soul. Hope is gone; any ray of light is quickly quenched by the stark reality of the situation; billow after billow of raging waves dash over the soul and break with deafening thunder while Satan and his hellish imps stand back and laugh and mock any faint cry for mercy. Sin is not a toy!

Now let me plead with you, our praying friends. Mark 9:29— "And he said unto them, This kind can come forth by nothing, but by prayer and fasting..." This one is beyond any human help, for as much as he wants some man to help him, he fights them off in his intense desperation to cling to them. But there is a promise that we must plead before the God who gave it: Deuteronomy 4:29— "But if from thence thou shalt seek the LORD thy God, thou shalt find him, if thou seek him with all thy heart and with all thy soul."

But now the fact remains that at this point he is incapable through his deep mental anguish to seek God thus. So we must fall back on another Scriptural example: Mark 2:5— "When Jesus saw *their faith*, he said unto the sick of the palsy, Son, thy sins be forgiven thee." (emphasis added) If this man is rescued out of the hand of the cruel taskmaster he has sold himself to, it may have to be through our prayers. The palsied man could not, absolutely could not, bring himself to Jesus, so his friends brought him. This man seemingly cannot calm the storm of his crippled mind and emotions to make the moral choice to yield himself to God. We may have to pray him into this state.

Oh, how my heart longs, not only to see this precious soul rescued from this downward spiral that will end in hell for all eternity, but also to see God's grace magnified in a fresh application of the precious Blood of Jesus. You, dear friends, have helped to win many a victory over the past years through your prayers. Could we see one more?

Let me make an observation right here; an observation that with every new case becomes more precious. Let it be understood without any question that AIDS is a direct result of a definitive area of rebellion against God's law. Even though it can be transmitted by drug users and dirty needles, etc., it originates in the direct wages of iniquity of the most heinous hue. I can tell you that I have personally known several cases of this devastating disease that were healed when the soul completely turned everything over to the Blood of Jesus. In each of the cases that I have known, the person was not seeking a healing of this disease. They were seeking to be right with God, but as an added kiss of God's forgiving grace, they discovered after they belonged entirely to God that the disease was no longer with them. All glory be to the Blood of Calvary!

Matthew 8:17— "That it might be fulfilled which was spoken by Esaias the prophet, saying, Himself took our infirmities, and bare our sicknesses." It seems God so hates sin that His loving heart is moved to even erase the wages of it many times. Praise His precious name! I might add that if anyone reading this letter has been in that case and has received such love from the forgiving hand of God, they had better fall at His blessed feet and give Him absolutely everything for time and eternity!

It has amazed my heart at how fitting to the lives of these men in prison God can make a book such as *Our Own God* by G.D. Watson. Chapter after chapter has become so pertinent to these men's lives. We recently dwelt on the chapter entitled "Moving in God's Time," and it was very apparent that it touched the quick of many of their lives. Some were eager to identify with it either positively or negatively, and I believe the lesson will be of lasting value to a good many of them.

Again the chapter, "How God Deals with Us" brought out many a comment or question, and I believe was again used of God. Isn't it wonderful that He still takes the loaves and fishes and multiplies them as often and as effectively as He did that lovely day on the hillside near Galilee? His work on earth is finished, but not His work from heaven. He still reaches out those lovely hands to needy men, even behind prison walls.

God is helping the man I have told you about who is so wrecked from a stint in Iraq. Please keep praying for him that he will not take God's help and not receive God. He still needs the complete healing that only a changed nature can bring to him. My heart is more and more convinced that it is either all of God or none of Him. He is not to be mocked by accepting His good gifts and then withholding our all from Him. The greatest percentage of our men in prison are still in need of this complete turnover of their little all to the great God who has touched them in measure.

To this end we will labor and pray, and you are a part of this. Thank You!

Yours in Him,
William Cawman

8
IMPOSSIBILITIES...EXCEPT FOR GOD

October 1, 2010

ARE YOU STILL PRAYING Friends? I am sure you are and I thank you and many men in prison do too. They are also praying for you. I have a very important and urgent request for your prayers just now, and in order to present it effectively I will have to go back and put together a few pieces of a long-standing story, some parts of which I have told you over the past ten years or so.

About that long ago I began ministering to a man here in the prison that still has a few years to go, and after about a year of working with him he came in one day and with a sad countenance told me that his wife had been sent to prison also. He told me the sad details and as I listened to what could well be one of Satan's masterpieces of human and family wreckage, I felt the voice of God clearly whisper to me, "I want to put this one back together to My glory!" It was so clear, that in spite of the many times over these years I have been tempted to question whether I had heard Him right, it has never gone away.

For all these years it has been up and down with him. At

times he would drop out of all classes and Bible studies and would somewhat avoid me, but then would come back again and many times confess that he was getting nowhere. Several years ago he faced his cigarette addiction that he had grappled with almost in vain and by the help of God he was delivered. That was good, but not enough. He reads and reads and thinks and thinks and, to be quite honest, finds it much easier for himself to enjoy his confusion and questions than for him to face himself and get right.

At the time God spoke to me about this situation it was so real to my heart that I expressed it in our church, and one of the ladies came to me and asked if it would be appropriate that she start visiting his wife in the other prison which was two hours away. I certainly thought it would be good and for about five years she faithfully visited her until she was finally sent to a half-way house nearer our church. While there she was able to get to the church and for a short time we wondered just which way she would choose to go. Would she cast in her lot and go all the way with God and bear the reproach of a real Christian or would she try to carve out a god a little more comfortable to her carnal mind and go somewhere else?

Thank God! She cast in her lot! And when she did, God cast in His, too, and a miracle of transformation immediately began. From that time on she has not looked back, but is growing in her love to the Lord as well as in her obedience to Him.

But alas for her poor husband. Now he was not only faced with a chaplain that only saw him every once in a while, but with his own wife. With all the zeal of a new-born creature she began to put him under such conviction that a few times he actually backed off and cut himself away for a while. But before long the Hound of Heaven would bring him back to ask forgiveness and away they would go again. He looked at me in a visit and said with a mischievous grin all over him, "That wife of mine! She sure has gotten a hold of something that changed her!"

Then to her he said, "I don't agree with Chaplain

Cawman's theology, but I wish I had just that much (holding two fingers close together) of what he has." She replied, "Well?" One day he came in and I asked him how he was getting along. He replied, "I'm not getting along at all! There's no use lying about it. I'm not getting anywhere." Often this was the confession, but it seemed he could not move beyond that point. I often faced him with the bare-boned fact that if he didn't have the power to be a child of God, then he needed to be born again, but somehow he kept clinging to a faint hope that somehow, after all—doesn't nearly everyone else teach and preach that this is the normal Christian walk?

Many times after that our visits would be not only about his relationship with God but his relationship with his wife. You see, as I explained to him, this rebuilding of a relationship that had never existed in the first place would of necessity have to be accomplished exactly backwards. The ordinary and desirable method is (even though Solomon himself could not figure it out) that a man and a maid "fall in love," and then begin to express this in a developing relationship that culminates in the marriage vow.

Here was a couple that took the vow with absolutely none of the preceding elements. For some time he would tell me, "In all reality, I don't know that I love her. I never did." "But," I replied, "we have to start with what you have, not what you don't have. You have made a vow and God says she is yours until death parts you. This is the starting point even if it shouldn't have been. No other woman will ever be the right one for you, so here is your starting point. Now ask God for the wisdom and grace to start loving her and God will give you the emotions to do it."

Time after time he would ask, "Aren't you ready to give up on me?" And I would reply, "Never! God never gave up on me! I know all about the barren wilderness you are groping in; I've been there; I've felt its hopelessness, but I can tell you that there is a way out!" He would slap the table and say, "Well, I sure wish I could find it."

The other day we were returning home from a meeting when the cell phone rang and it was his wife. She was excitedly floating on cloud nine as she read to me a letter he had sent her. Together we rejoiced over the radical turn in his language and spirit and agreed to double up in our prayers for him. She agreed that this part of his letter could be shared with you so that you would know better how to pray also. We pray for a person when it seems they are headed the wrong direction; how much more we should gang up on them when we see them make a turn toward the path that leads home. Now listen to what he wrote to his wife.

> To God be the glory! I was sitting here thinking about my life and was tempted to despair, but thanks be to God for His holy Word, the Bible. When I look there, I see how He can restore a willing heart. For instance, God told Israel that if from the place He had them carried away captive after they violated His law, if they repented He would restore their lives but they had to submit to their captors as if to God who was using them as his instruments of punishment. Deuteronomy 30 spells it out real good.
>
> I read that, and I realized that if I turn from my wicked ways in the place where I'm held captive then God will be pleased to restore my life and heart. I am tired of the revolving door of sin, but too often I find myself giving in to my old patterns of sinful behavior. It's been very costly with no benefits. God help me to get it right with Him. I've been too selfish and self-centered for far too long. I really do want what you have in your heart.
>
> I was reading about some of the things we often speak on, and I read I Peter 3:1-12 and thought about us. Maybe your example is starting to win me over. I want it to be real though, not because I'm trying to please you. So I want to be careful that I'm getting down to business with God. I don't want to deceive myself into thinking I'm this or that when I'm really not. I wanted to ask about a comment you made. You said that God had to deal with something in your heart before you could face me

again. When I read that, I thought to myself, "What am I—some kind of monster?" Whatever I did to make you uncomfortable or unloved, please forgive me for that. I was demonstrating my own ignorance and arrogance.

I really want to be a follower of my Lord Jesus who loves Holiness and Righteousness in my heart. God help me! Some of the trouble I have is the way you guys make it seem so easy and instantaneous. What I do know is that I have no success in trying to change myself. How did it happen for you? Do you ever struggle with old inclinations or habits? Since I quit smoking, I realize I'm just a smoke-free sinner. God help me!

Well, Sweetness, I trust that you and the saints are praying for me, and I know I have to do my part too. I ask God daily to make me a real Christian and a Good husband and father for His glory! This is the last chance for me because I know God won't put up with any more jail mess. And I would lose the only child that loves me, S——! I don't know if you would throw in the towel, but I won't take the chance. To God be the glory!

Do you agree that we need to bombard heaven for a miracle that would bring glory to our God and shame to Satan for ever having anything to do with this precious couple? Let's do it. God will do His part, and He is!

Do you remember hearing at times about the man that God saved and sanctified before he ever heard about it? He continues to be such a blessing to everyone as he walks before God and man with not a flicker of anything un-Christ-like. He told me that the man he has been assigned to for a long time now was coming near his end, and that he had really come to love the man and a bond had formed between them as he cared for his every physical and spiritual need.

He had gone back to his own room for a while and when he went back over to the hospital and neared the room he saw a sheet over the window and he knew he was gone. He was immediately overwhelmed with deep feeling and just went back to his room to pray and cry for the dear man.

After a peace had come to him, he went back over and was hoping that they would give him a less intense assignment so that he could again have more liberty to move around among the other patients, but the very next day they assigned him to the room of a young man who had been beaten in the head in another prison until he nearly didn't make it. He was somewhat disappointed at first, but after a few days he felt a clear peaceful witness that he was exactly where God wanted him next.

The young man is slowly gaining some recognition of things and even though he has to tell him his name every day, he remembers him. I know he would ask you to pray that he can lead this young man to Jesus.

Please continue to pray for the young man that was so traumatized in Iraq. The medication he is on is definitely helping him to cope with life, but he told me he only has ten months yet in prison and he doesn't want to go home without God. I told him I would ask you to pray and he wanted me to.

Just in the last few days several new contacts have come to see me with a deep sense of need and lack, and there is no question but what Jesus is knocking at their door. While you pray for them, please pray for me also, for I feel such a need of being so in tune with the Holy Spirit that I am enabled to work with Him, not apart from Him. I often find myself praying silently right in front of a man, "Lord, is this one ready to enter in right now? Is there some key I need to present to him that would close the gap between this seeking soul and a seeking Jesus?"

I know how futile and even damaging it is to crowd a man beyond where the Spirit has been allowed to go in his will, yet if there is somewhere a last step of faith or whatever he needs to take, wouldn't it be God's will to do it now; not tomorrow? I fear intensely any idea that I have what it takes to help a man in this condition; I need the Holy Spirit just as much as he does.

It is He and He alone that is promised to reprove of sin, of righteousness, and of judgment to come. If you can pray for me at all, please pray that I will be in tune with the Holy Spirit. My heart just aches when I sit before a man who from all appearances is, in the words of Jesus, "Thou art not far from the kingdom of God." Please pray that not one of these souls will slip through this time in their life without finding the One who is knocking at their door.

William Cawman

✝✝✝

November 1, 2010

> And Jesus said unto them, Come ye after me, and I will make you to become fishers of men. (Mark 1:17)

THE SUMMER AFTER MY SENIOR year in high school, my brother and I decided to go fishing on the Fourth of July. We rented a small rowboat and packed it with fishing supplies and set out onto the lake to catch fish.

Our success rate was quite similar to the disciples except that we did not fish all night, only part of the morning; but like them we *caught nothing*. Finally a little sunny apparently felt pity for our fruitless toils and jumped up out of the water into our boat with us. With that we gave up the fishing program and jumped overboard to swim with the sunny. Turn about fair play, right?

A number of years later I heard the call of the same Jesus that commissioned the disciples, saying, "Fear not; from henceforth thou shalt catch men." I confess my almost total lack of natural ability to accomplish this. Many times I feel my efforts as fruitless as on that Fourth of July many years ago. But it seems every so often God Himself— who has said to me so lovingly so many times, "Fear not, I am with thee— has compassion on my poverty-stricken efforts and just lets a hungry heart jump over the side of the boat to where I am. He has done this several times of late, and it is my deepest concern and prayer that I will be perfectly in tune with Him as I try to point them, not to me, but to Him.

There are men who possess, from wherever I do not know, some degree of magnetic pull to themselves and can gather a fan club about them, no matter what they themselves are or aren't. I have not one atom of appetite for such a quality, but I do long to have enough of Jesus within that it is He who draws men. Oh, that men could sense enough of His presence that it would produce the same result that it did in Saul of Tarsus, viz. "But what things were gain to me, those I counted loss for Christ."

The Prophet Isaiah, seven hundred years before Christ appeared, uttered this prophecy: "...when we shall see him, there is no beauty that we should desire him." I read those words in family worship several years ago on Christmas morning and I burst into tears. I had to stop and say to my family, "That is, until we know Him." Oh, how my heart longs that men could for a moment see Him with the veil lifted until they *should desire Him.*

One such man comes from the special needs unit, the tier where special drugs are administered to keep the mind and body together, etc. He came to visit with me and was obviously under deep and long-term distress. I asked him what it was in particular that bothered him so much that he had to take medication to control himself. He responded, "My Mother. She was such a good mother, and I can't stop thinking about her and what it would do to her if she knew what I had done and where I am now."

"And where is your mother?" "She died in 2008, and I can't even sleep at night thinking of how it would hurt her if she knew." "Was your mother a Christian?" "Oh, yes, she was a good Christian and taught me right, but I went wrong."

I tried to introduce him to the One who said, "But if from thence thou shalt seek the Lord thy God, thou shalt find him, if thou seek him with all thy heart and with all thy soul." I begged him to bring his whole mess to Jesus and find the peace of forgiveness that only He can give him. I will follow up the visit, and will you pray? You would, I know, if you could have heard his heart cry like I did. But I believe you will anyway.

Again I want to bring the young man who was so traumatized in Iraq to your remembrance, because he wants me to. It is a brand new realm to him to actually pray to God, but he needs this new realm, and he knows it. He doesn't have that much longer in prison and he is afraid to leave without an anchor that he has never had. The medical therapy he is presently taking has calmed his trauma to the point where he can think straighter and sleep at night, but that is a poor substitute indeed for the healing Blood of Jesus.

We have been receiving some good news from an inmate who was here in this prison and then was sent about four years ago to one of the northern prisons. He gave good evidence that God had sanctified his heart before he left here, but then a couple of times since he felt God showed him he had not gone deep enough and again he prayed through.

Just what all this is, only God knows, but he feels he has a clear witness of his sanctification and he is now out on parole and his officer has given him permission to come to our church on Sunday. We are certainly looking forward to having him with us and he is looking forward to it also.

Some of you might remember him as the man who came into my office several years ago after months of vibrant spiritual victory, but now looking rather troubled. When I asked him how he was doing he said, "Well, brother, we need to talk about that. Do you remember a week ago Sunday night when you preached from the words, 'I beseech you therefore, brethren, by the mercies of God, that ye present your bodies a living sacrifice, holy, acceptable unto God, which is your reasonable service'?" I replied that I did. "Well, God put His finger on my life and is asking, 'Will you do it?' Chaplain, I'm in prison over seven ugly charges—they're not good. But that isn't all of them. There are five more that I have never made known, and God is asking me if I will come completely clean with everything. But if I confess those additional things I might lose my go home date."

I looked at him for a moment and then said simply, "And if you don't?"

"No, Chaplain, I'm not willing for that. I want to get sanctified." He got up and walked out of the office. The next day he got up in class and testified to the men about our conversation and then said, "I left the chaplain's office and went straight to my room and I wrote and shed tears and wrote and cried and wrote until I cleared everything up. Then I put it in an envelope and addressed it to the judge and went out and dropped it in the mailbox before I could change my mind. I want to get sanctified."

A week later it really looked like he did, too. He is an extremely sensitive man who wants God's favor more than he wants a profession, and you and I know how the enemy will take advantage of a person like that. So please pray for him that he will learn how to fight his battles and stay right side up and turn out a terror to the devil. Pray also for his wife and daughter, that God will direct their paths until He can be glorified in completely defeating every plan the devil ever had for this family.

Some of you will remember how a few months back a man who we had referred to as C—— in years past had come to church for a while and then fallen back again. He disappeared for a few months but called the pastor again just recently to request prayer. He is out of prison and has a job and an apartment, but he had two bad spells of his hepatitis flaring up again until he was afraid he was dying. In the hospital he begged God not to let him die unprepared and immediately his count went down drastically again.

He begged us to not quit praying for him, so can I pass this request on also? Many prayers have gone up for him over the years, including many from my own dear mother who is now in heaven, and I believe God is still applying the effects of them to his heart. Certainly he would fall directly into the need of Jesus' prayer, "C——, C——, 'behold, Satan hath desired to have you, that he may sift you as wheat...'" but aren't you glad for what follows that? "but I have prayed for thee..." How faithful, how persistent, how patient is that Hound of Heaven! Who cannot but love Him?

Now I must pass another urgent prayer request on to you. Some time back those who have been receiving the letters for a while will probably remember the man who was detained after a Sunday night service at the request of a female officer and then propositioned to sin with her right there in the chapel. He walked out on her just as Joseph did and then reported it to a sergeant.

In a couple of days all the officers seemed to know about it and they moved him to another facility and the female officer remains at her post and whatever she carries on there. From the time he was moved he has endured persecution and insult from the officers. On top of that he lost the fellowship of the other Christian men in the facility where he was and didn't know much of anyone in the new facility. He gave place to discouragement from Satan, although I have never detected that he gave place to bitterness over the mistreatment. He dropped out of church and classes and was overworked by officers giving him lowly assignments that kept him working overtime.

I had put him on the visit list after a time but he didn't come. I did it a second time and he sent word that he was all right and didn't want to visit. I did it a third time and that time he came, broken and discouraged. He told me he could hide from anyone else, but he said, "I can't hide forever from you, because I know you love me." We visited and he more or less expressed the fact that he was on the bottom emotionally, physically, and spiritually. I told him I would be praying for him and others would, too, and that if I put his name on the visit list again I did not want him to avoid me, for I was only there because I really cared about him. He said, "I know that. It is very evident to me."

Several weeks went by and I just yesterday put him on the list again. When he came in he grabbed me and hugged me ferociously and then sat down and began to open up just as bare-boned honest as he could be. "Chaplain, I'm all right physically, but spiritually I'm dead, and I really don't want it that way."

I began to try to rip the cover off of all the lies that Satan was obviously telling him and I saw light beginning to break through again. Finally he said, "I will tell you the honest truth of mainly why I'm not moving forward or praying much; I have been reluctant to face the battles that will come from all the godless people around me if I start going to church and praying again. It just seems easier to let it go for now and not face all that. And then, I can't seem to see anyone around me who I can really fellowship with like I had in the other facility, and I really miss that. There were good brothers there who really helped me, but I can't find anyone here."

I said, "Have you thought of the possibility that there are others here who are also looking for someone they can look up to? Would it be good if you could let God make you that person?" He thought a moment and then began to grin, "Probably so."

"And then," I asked him, "do you enjoy swimming?" "I used to; I haven't for a long time." "Did you ever swim in the ocean?" "Oh yes, a lot." "Did you find it was pretty hard to swim very well in the breakers along the shore? There you just keep getting washed back into shallow water. But out beyond the breakers there is good water to swim in without all the turbulence. Do you know that it is that way spiritually, too? There are several men in this prison who faced into the very opposition you are afraid of. Everyone made fun of them and tormented them for all of the sudden starting down the Christian pathway. But they kept on going and now they are out there swimming in clear water and everyone just knows they are not coming back so they leave them pretty much alone. You will always have battles, but not the battle you are afraid of. I'm going to be in the service Sunday night. Will you come again?"

"Yes, I will. And I see what you are saying is true. I do wish I had what I used to have in my heart." I said I would be looking for him to be in the service Sunday night and that I would expect him to have the joy bells ringing again.

He grabbed me and gave me another violent squeeze and parted with hope in his face. Let me conclude this with something that tears my heart out of me. How many souls are living in emptiness and loneliness on the inside while Jesus, the Friend of sinners, stands on the other side of the door just as lonely to come in? Do you know what stands between the two? One empty lie out of hell! Please pray that in the next letter there will be a shout of victory from this brother. Believe me, I won't be reluctant to share it with you!

Thank you so very much for every time you are true to a burden God lays on your heart for these men who have never had the opportunities that we have. Jesus said, "few there be that find it," but He loves the few who do so much that it makes it worth it all. I confess that I close this letter with a full heart and wet eyes.

Until He comes,
William Cawman

December 1, 2010

ONE HUNDRED THIRTY-THREE of these prayer letters ago this month we wrote the following words: "From time to time we will endeavor to give you accounts of the struggles and victories of inmates within the prison system who could have been you and I had we been raised as they were. In doing so we will for obvious reasons conceal their names and any information which could be vital to their identity or security. These letters will be for one purpose only—to incite to prayer, and to praise

God for His answers... Next month, it may be your prayer that will be answered.

Recently, a prisoner was brightly saved in his first Christian service he had ever attended in his life. Later we found that God had whispered his name to a praying man in another state. He told God he knew of no one by that name, but he prayed for him anyway. We do not intend to pass out names for prayer, but if God whispers a name to you, that's His business—pray!"

Since that letter we have made no attempt to keep a count on the prayers God has answered, but they have been too many for us to back off now! There are still needy souls, and God is still hearing the prayers of those who have been reading these letters and praying for the needs. It melts my heart to travel in and out of the country and hear dear saints of God ask about a certain man and then say, "I have been praying every day for him."

Some of these men have left the prison and I have lost contact with them, but God still has some of them on your hearts. I want to say something to you that I can't say, because "thank you" seems so shallow compared to what I feel toward you. Many of you have certainly become *laborers together with God* in this little harvest corner and I know that you will have a reward I cannot bestow upon you.

The song writer expressed it in these words: "So send I you, to take to souls in bondage, the Word of Truth that sets the captive free; To break the bonds of sin, to loose death's fetters—So send I you, to bring the lost to Me." And another: "Shall I empty handed be, when beside the crystal sea, I shall stand before the everlasting throne? If no soul to me can say, 'I am glad you passed my way; for 'twas you who told me of the sinner's Friend.'" That will be worth it all for you and me, won't it?

I mentioned some time back a little Mexican man who I would rather call a boy. He is so small and has such a young face, notwithstanding his arms being covered with tattoos.

He comes from about halfway down the Gulf coast and is here illegally, but he cannot help that fact for the present. He will probably spend about seven more years in prison here and then be deported back to Mexico. Perhaps because of his small stature he went all the way in joining up with the MS 13 gangs and hence the definitive tattoos all up and down his arms. He would appear to be about 15 years of age and stands out among a crowd of prisoners as not belonging there at all.

Now having endeavored to give you a picture of him let's call to remembrance the Scripture that says, "Wherein in time past ye walked according to the course of this world, according to the prince of the power of the air, the spirit that now worketh in the children of disobedience: Among whom also we all had our conversation in times past in the lusts of our flesh, fulfilling the desires of the flesh and of the mind; and were by nature the children of wrath, even as others. *But God, who is rich in mercy, for his great love wherewith he loved us, Even when we were dead in sins, hath quickened us together with Christ, (by grace ye are saved;)...*" (emphasis added) This, to God be all the glory, is the transformation that has changed him into what he is today.

For some time he has been walking in obvious joy and peace with God, and the light just grows brighter and brighter. I called him down for a visit and into the room came his shining face. "Oh Chaplain, I'm so glad for what God is doing for me—not outside of me, but inside of me;" and he held his hand lovingly over his heart. As he went on to tell me how wonderful it is to have his life completely changed and given over to Jesus I asked him if even with all his heart on fire for God he ever sensed an enemy nature from down inside that bothered him.

"Oh yes," he said, without any hesitation. "I ask God to take that out." I said, "Well, when you do, believe Him to do it, for that is exactly what He came and died on the cross to do—to take out that nature we were born with that is contrary to the love of Jesus within us." He assured me that he was going to do that.

How precious it is to see a bright case of divine love, protesting the very existence of any remains of sin within. Great things are in store for this little brother! Please pray for him.

For several months a missionary from Mexico has been sending us a little eight-page monthly holiness paper and we have been making copies of it and passing it out to the Hispanic men in our classes and Bible studies. It has been a real blessing to them, for I do not know of any other Spanish holiness publications coming into the prison. This little brother told me that he read in that paper about those two sisters who told Mr. Moody that they were praying for him that he would receive the Holy Spirit. It really touched him and he said, "That's what I need, too!"

Another inmate with a shining face told me that he really likes that paper and that after he read it he sent it to his mother. I asked him where his mother was and he said, "In Mexico." I guess that's what one would call a "circular," and a good one, too.

One night recently in Bible study we were talking to the men about what Jesus told us to do when we are enduring persecution. A man I had not noticed particularly before immediately began to respond. He told the men that he had been raised as a Christian, but after going into prison had become a Muslim. He tried that for some time, but one day Jesus spoke again to him and he left it all and "really got saved." (His expression)

He said that his life changed immediately and it was wonderful, but that he began also to encounter persecution from the Muslims. He lost a tooth and had his eye all banged up as they roughed him up, but he said, "So what? It was worth it all because of the joy I had in my heart." He really looked delighted with what God is doing in his life now.

Once in a while things go along rather the same and it could seem almost discouraging, and then someone like this pops up out of seeming nowhere and has already stepped across the great divide and is enjoying the grace of God. This makes it worth every long minute spent with others. One day recently I had the whole day packed with appointments and one after another seemed to be so satisfied with dissatisfaction (how else can I say it?), and then right in the middle of them in came a man all aglow with grace and glory from the presence of Jesus. This same Jesus who gave him this glorious victory also said Himself, "...strait is the gate, and narrow is the way, which leadeth unto life, and few there be that find it."

Oh, how we long that everyone would, but the few are worth more than the whole world, aren't they? I never cease to be amazed over two things: What hinders the light getting through to so many? And then: What a miracle! Where did he come from? Knowing that God is no respecter of persons, there is more than significant weight attached to that first response to divine light.

Before leaving that subject, could I ask a question that completely stumps me? What is it that causes people to be so absolutely and completely satisfied to remain in an absolutely and completely unsatisfactory condition spiritually? In no other area of life would this be the case. Who would put up with a fly swatter that never gets a fly? Who would be satisfied with a car that never starts? Who would continue to climb a ladder that breaks over and over and lets the person fall to the ground? But this is exactly what so many are doing spiritually. Their religious endeavors never give them victory over sin, never bring them into the glorious presence of Jesus, and never bear witness that they are ready to spend eternity in heaven rather than in a burning hell; but they are tenaciously content to continue just as they are.

How absolutely frustrating to try to help a person come into a better way when they insist that they are already doing everything one can suggest would help them. A goose sticking its head through an electric fence demonstrates more learning ability than a human being indwelt by the carnal mind. We fear there are far more of these than the ones we find in prison.

Now on the humorous side (believe it or not, it does come up now and then), since I wrote about our little Mexican brother I saw him again in Bible study last night. His face was still all aglow, but then when he turned around—! It is getting colder outside and so the men were issued coats for the winter. Now whether they did not have a coat small enough for him or whether some officer was deliberately playing with his size, he had a prison-made winter coat that looked large enough for the biggest man in the prison.

From the backside, here was a huge coat, only a few inches from the floor, with a little head sticking out the top and two little feet coming out the bottom. Perhaps little David looked like that after being donned with Saul's armor. I didn't dare look too long for my risibility disorder was beginning to get out of hand. As soon as the coat was put off, there stood our cute little brother again.

Let me share a couple of specific prayer requests. First, during the month of December I am usually home for nearly the whole month and I try to spend some really concentrated effort at getting to personally know the men who are in the classes and Bible studies.

One such man I called in for the first visit and he looked a little mystified or perhaps frightened as he came in, saying, "What did you want to see me for?" I don't know if he had such a history of being a bad boy that he was paranoid or not, but as soon as I told him what he was there for he brightened right up and began to really open his needy heart to me. Now we have had a second visit and he wants more.

Yesterday as we visited he said, "I called my girlfriend and told her that the chaplain wanted to see me again and she said, 'And you didn't even have to ask him?'" As we talked and I sensed his open heart I began to testify to him and the further I went the happier I got, and as I did my best to lay out the invitation into all the perfect will of God

I suddenly felt myself analyzing my own heart— "O God, I really LOVE these men!"

Then I thought of what I used to be and I would rather not describe that here except to say that "self" was filling the whole horizon, and it was simply despicable! But I well remember the first Friday night of a camp meeting many years ago when, after we had sung that precious song "The Holy Life," I was nearly pulled to my feet without an effort by the convulsion of hunger within and I said, "I would give everything I have and am and ever hoped to be if I could have what we just sang about." I did not know at that moment that it was waiting for me just twenty-four hours thence. I can tell you that I have never been back looking for a resurrection of anything that died within me that blessed night, and everything died that was unlike the heart of Jesus.

Since then He has never ceased to mold and chasten me to receive more and more of His great heart of love for His other sheep, no matter what breed they are or what the color of their fleece. Will you please pray that God will anoint and help me this month as I try to lead these men to really see who Jesus is?

Then please help us pray for guidance as to what God would want us to be teaching in the classes and Bible studies this coming year. We don't want to gravitate into a form without power. We really don't!

Thank you, each one, for all your faithful prayers this year!

In Christian love,
William Cawman

9
ONE MORE FOR JESUS

January 1, 2011

HAPPY NEW YEAR TO all of you, and may it be the most blessed year we have ever known. Shouldn't it be so as we draw ever closer to the great Day when our Jesus will return for His Bride? And just think of that Bride! Will there be some with great learning and postgraduate degrees? Oh yes, for He said, "...not many wise men after the flesh, not many mighty, not many noble, are called..." but He didn't say there would be none, thank God.

Will there be any big professors without possession? No, not one. But listen to what He says to them: "Verily I say unto you, That the publicans and the harlots go into the kingdom of God before you." And how? "And such were some of you: but ye are washed, but ye are sanctified, but ye are justified in the name of the Lord Jesus, and by the Spirit of our God." Whether we grew up in a Christian home with an impeccable background or whether we came from just the opposite, in that Great Day we will all be sinners washed in the Blood and made so clean that Jesus will not be ashamed to take us into His throne with Him as He sits down in His Father's throne.

For several years we have made mention now and then of a precious man who was a double murderer, but is now *washed* and *sanctified* and *justified* and lives in continual victory through the Blood of Jesus. I can honestly tell you, without one bit of exaggeration or imagination, that his face shines more and more with the presence and joy and peace of a soul made whole by the Blood. And he knows it is all through the Blood. He has no desire to take the credit or the glory. Other men come to him and he patiently listens to their tales of woe with a heart of deep compassion.

Today as we sat and visited I asked his pardon for using his clear victorious life to point out to other men that they, too, could be living in this prison and have and keep victory. His brow knit for a moment and then he said, "Chaplain, I hear what you just said and it is convicting me a bit. I sit often and listen to men tell all about the trials they are going through and my heart feels for them and I tell them I understand, even though I know that God has lifted me above all those things. I think I have been failing to point them to the Remedy that I have found. I just haven't thought of it that way. I need to do more than just lend a sympathetic ear. I need to tell them where they can find victory over it all."

I am amazed at the level of grace and glory this man is manifesting week after week and year after year without a single lapse into the old pit from whence he came, or any other pit, either. My heart just says a glad "hallelujah" for the keeping grace of Jesus' Blood. Oh, that we had more men just like him in this dark wilderness of sin and despair. There is one other besides him who lives in this Psalm 91 victory. I am not devaluating what others have and are enjoying, but these two stand out like shining lights in a dark night. O God, give us some more of them.

Today I also sat with a man who has come and then not come, back and forth, etc., from classes and Bible studies. He is now 57 years of age and still not serious about his eternal destiny. For several weeks, at least, he has not come to class and so I put him on the appointment sheet for a visit. He came in rather sheepishly and began to say, "Chaplain, I haven't been coming to class—well, I just haven't. I really don't have any excuse so there's no use making one." I said, "I know that, but there's something even more serious and that is, are you getting ready for eternity? God is waiting on you and He is staying on your trail and I will, too. Don't try to hide or I'll be coming after you. You're not young anymore; look at the amount of those gray ones creeping up on you." He smiled and said, "Don't remind me." I said, "I just did. You don't have forever to decide which way you're going to go." He said, "I know that's the truth and I really need to use my will and do what I know I should. I will be in class this afternoon."

He was.

I have tried to give you an update a few times on the Haitian man who has never heard from his mother since the earthquake there. He is such a tender man and loves the Lord, and it is very obvious that the Lord loves him, too. The other day he came in to visit and began to tell me how good God is in his life; then he just broke down and had to choke back tears for a bit before he could continue.

He said that he is actually so glad for this time in his life. God is so near to him every day right in prison and he is certainly growing in grace and Christ-likeness. He told me that he has a young cell mate and that they have begun to study the Word together. Another man would often walk by their cell and see them through the little window in the door and nod his head to them to indicate he liked what he saw. After a while he went and asked the officer if he could visit them in their cell. The officer was very gracious to bend the rules for the purpose he saw it was for and they have been feasting on the joy of leading him to Jesus.

And then another day recently I visited with a Mexican man from Veracruz, and after a half hour with him I felt like I had been with a child of God. Later that afternoon he testified to the Christian Living class. About a year and a half ago he was so sick of his sinful life and the mess he had made of himself and everyone else that he began to truly repent and turn to Jesus. In a moment of contact with the precious Blood of Jesus his addiction to cigarettes was completely broken and a new Life was born within him. He had tried over and over to break the habit, but was helpless until he came to the Blood.

He has been growing in grace ever since and it is not hard to see it. When he came in for the visit I asked him how he was getting along and he stopped with his hand still in mine and looked me right in the eyes. "Chaplain, I want to be completely honest; I am completely blessed. God is doing so much in my life, I just give Him all the praise, and I never want to go back." Then he said, "Please correct me if I'm wrong in this, but I am finding that the Holy Spirit is talking to me about such little things in my life. And yet, as I look at those things I see clearly where they led me in the past. I am so happy with His presence in my heart."

By this time my own heart was burning with joy and I said to him, "Oh Brother, you don't need any correction over that. You just need to completely give place to Him and obey Him. He talks to me about the little things in my life, too, and I love it more and more. Inside and outside, I belong to Him and it is such a delight to have Him tell me anything." I wish you could have seen his face.

I must insert here that for every man like this there are many others who are just as unhappy as he is happy. So many just want to hide behind where they are and make excuses, such as, "You know, Chaplain, it's really tough in here with these people." And then they begin to enumerate all the reasons why (because of where they are and who they live with and are surrounded by) they cannot be expected to be living in victory.

I told some of the men the other day that if they have any thought that they will someday stand before the Great White Throne and tell God that due to where they were they just could not live a victorious Christian life, they would suddenly become aware that they were standing precisely beside someone who had even worse circumstances than they but who triumphed over it all through Him that promised, "Nay, in all these things we are more than conquerors through him that loved us."

My supervisor had planned for the men in his classes to make up a Christmas Eve service for each facility as well as for the minimum camp, and then since two of them would be replacing my regular Friday night Bible studies I would be in charge of those two and he would take the other two. He asked me if I could let the men practice their choir numbers in the two weeks before Christmas Eve.

You would have enjoyed the practice session. Talent was oozing from every pore and they beamed with gratification as they heard themselves. At one point I suggested that if anyone knew how to sing a harmony part it would help make the Christmas carol more beautiful. Immediately, one man verified that he knew how to sing that part. From then on he vociferously sang another part, but it was not one that made it more beautiful. After the next verse the "choir director" (grand titles are bestowed readily when they are self-imposed) stopped the choir and said, "Now I want to hear just my altos and tenors." Obediently the "altos and tenors" sang their part—imaginations willingly translating unison into beautify harmony. The "Director," conspicuously pleased with their progress, as though he had finally been the fortunate artist to discover after all these centuries the famous lost chord, now confirmed that they were ready to join in and sing their respective parts. They set forth again in unison, except that is, for the one who was able to sing "harmony." Please forgive me but it was so rich that at one point I stopped them and looked at the rest of the congregation and said, "Men, don't you think we ought to make a CD?" They had a good laugh at themselves and proceeded forward.

Here are a few lines from the brother who was moved to a northern prison and then got sanctified there:

Greetings in the precious name of our Lord and Savior Jesus Christ. I pray you are well and finding new depths, heights, and ways to love Him more. I can truly say that not a day goes by that he does not instill in me some new way to love Him. Sometimes I have struggled with wondering if He was showing me sin, but I cannot deny the continual cry of my heart against any affront to Him. I am learning much and seeing that it is only in His hands that I find rest and peace. There is no other place I would rather be. I love Him my dear brother, but oh how small my love seems in comparison to the infiniteness of His love. I am committed to doing everything in His power to love Him. (My power can't do it.)...There is a great need for the purity of His love here. Many like the sound of holiness, but few want to live it. The church here is like a little child that wants nothing but icing to eat. The Lord has me learning the importance of prayer. Too often my mind jumped to the outward signs of ministry to solve the lukewarmness here, but the Lord is patiently showing me the power of prayer. I can't thank Him enough.

Today I was visiting with a man for the first time that just came to the prison. He is an Italian man, 45 years of age. This is his first time in prison and this is part of his story. He told me that he had been a very successful business man and had owned a chain of restaurants. He was so busy with making money that he kept putting off getting married and having a family till the next year, then the next, so never has yet.

He then opened up a business in adult entertainment. He says he didn't participate in it himself, but just sat in an office with a couple of secretaries and hooked up lonely men and women. What they did after the hookup was up to them—so he justified himself. Somehow he was put under suspicion because the amount of money he was making made it appear that he was dealing in drugs along with his business.

He ended up losing everything he had and landed in prison, and here he was starting down the road of bitterness toward everyone that had put him there. I interrupted him and told him he might be missing something very important. The adult entertainment business was wrong completely— completely wrong—no way to justify it, and that perhaps God in mercy had brought it all to naught to give him a chance to turn from sin and start preparing for heaven.

I began to testify to him about how perfectly satisfying God's way had been for me when I quit trying to have God with one hand and me with the other. I asked him if he had read the Bible and he said he does some. I went to the story of Saul of Tarsus and how at the height of his self-directed career God brought him to his knees on the Damascus road. He then looked up and said, "Lord, what wilt Thou have me to do?" I then told him that after twenty-six more years rolled by and he had been beaten, stoned, and shipwrecked, and was now a prisoner in a dirty old dungeon, he was called out to stand before a man who in the estimation of the world had made it to the top. Agrippa said, "Paul, thou art permitted to speak for thyself." And the first words out of his mouth were, "I think myself happy!" By this time our Italian man had tears in his eyes and said, "How do I find that?" I will visit with him again soon, and will you pray for him and for me, that I will have God's heart in reaching to him?

With Christian love,
William Cawman

February 1, 2011

I HAVE A CONFESSION to make, first of all. For most of January I left the cold northland to those who stayed by the stuff, and with meetings in Guatemala and Florida, escaped a good bit of the snow and cold. How thankful I am to those volunteers from our church that have a heart to keep up the classes and Bible studies and Sunday night services when I am gone. Even though I experience some seasons of guilt in leaving it to them,

I comfort myself in knowing that it is absolutely a blessing to have others also minister to the men. I have never heard one negative report from the men when I return over any of these my brothers. Thank God for each one of them.

There is a certain and very prevalent battleground that all of us encounter in prison ministry, that in a sense is not much different from any ministry in today's world. It is the battle of self versus Jesus. Why is it that, when there is life in a look to the Blessed Cross of Jesus, men insist to the last ditch on trying to reform themselves? The best that can ever result from self-help is to move across the aisle to another pew in the same church. It all falls so miserably short of the blessed results of one touch of the Blood of Jesus.

I was in a meeting and someone asked me to write to a relative of theirs who was in prison. I did and sent some little booklets to him and shortly received a letter back. While my heart ached for the letter writer, I also felt no little degree of indignation toward the tidal wave of self-help religious programming that has pointed men everywhere else other than the Fountain that was opened in the house of David for all sin and all uncleanness. Would you bear with me if I insert that letter here? This letter is so typical of exactly what we face in so many we try to help that it might help you better understand the battle we are in. Here it is:

> Thank you very much for the booklets that you sent me. They are helpful and are helping me get a better understanding of God and how to build my faith. For a long time I didn't really believe in God. As I got older I started questioning why I didn't and I believe it's just that I didn't understand Him. I am now trying to turn my life around and I think that I needed to start with God. I started to read the Bible and attend Bible study and I realized it wasn't that I didn't believe in God, it was that I didn't want to. Now that I am getting a better understanding of Him and all that He has done for us, I got some hope for myself that I can be a better person. I still struggle daily with not sinning but I do try and I hope that is a good start. I have made a

lot of bad choices to end up here and I know I have to start making better choices to stay out of here. I learned I can't do it by myself, so I decided to ask God for help. Although this is a path I'm not used to it is one I want and need to try. I have done wrong so long it is hard to start doing right but I am trying and I'm trying to build my faith up so it isn't so hard. I still don't understand God but I know it will take time to understand completely and at least now I believe there is a God and He loves me. Now I'm trying to love myself and others the way I'm supposed to and these booklets you sent are helping me to strengthen my foundation. You do a very great thing for people in my position and I wanted to thank you and tell you I greatly appreciate it. I have been getting moved around a little because I got a new case put on me and am getting it taken care of now. I believe this is a little test to see if I want to continue in a new direction or go back to my old ways and I am staying strong in my new beliefs that this will end in making me stronger. My mail will follow me and I hope I could write you if I have questions or to let you know how I'm doing. If there is anything that you think I should know or would help on this new journey I would greatly appreciate it....I know it will take time but I want God in my life. If there is anything you think would help on my journey I would enjoy learning. Thank you for your time and God bless you.

Do you see any similarity here with a man long ago by the name of Nicodemus? Would you agree with the suggestion that every single question he has and every struggle he is having could be answered in a moment if he could only experience what Jesus told Nicodemus: "Verily, verily, I say unto thee,...ye must be born again"?

This, friends, in a nutshell is where we are hung up in the vast majority of men everywhere. They have never been born again. Satan will almost (should I take the "almost" out?) promote and help them out in the exercise of the very manipulations quoted above in the letter. We hear such expressions over and over and they have come directly out of the lips of false teachers who themselves have never been born again: "I'm trying to build my faith." "I'm trying to walk the new walk, but it will take time." "I've done wrong so long you can't expect me to change overnight."

Why not? Try the Blood cure! What on earth do you mean about this building your faith thing when faith is a gift of God? Did it take the lame man at the temple gate "time" to leap and walk and praise God? Forgive me, but I just can't help inserting here that story in Acts chapter three as it would have been written by all this self-help programming. "And Peter and John looked upon the lame man and said, 'Look on us. Try wiggling your right big toe like this. Now practice that until we come back tomorrow for another lesson, but don't worry if you continue to feel lame as this will take some time. We'll be back tomorrow and see if you are ready to move your second toe. You need to build your faith that you can do it if you just practice enough.'"

Hallelujah, no! From a state of absolute infirmity he leaped into a most glorious walk with God. This is our greatest need in prison, and out of it, too. We so seldom witness the power promised to those who receive Him. We are beholding the pathetic spectacle of the weak and insipid religious programs that encourage a man to believe he is something he is not. It works just as effectively as making a rattlesnake believe he can fly two miles high like the eagle. He was not born an eagle and so he cannot fly like one. Until these men are born again they are sinners and will act like one. Please help us pray for some more new births.

Encouragingly, amidst all this stash of religious fluff, every once in a while some hungry soul really does pray through to the Blood of Jesus and is born again. Do you know what? They can't hide that any more than the others can hide the fact that they have never been born again. We have had a few new babies born into the kingdom lately, but we need far more. Why, oh why, will men try so arduously to be Christians when they have not been born one? I'll tell you why: the deceiver of the souls of men will do anything, even that which is strenuously religious, to see hearts detoured around the cure Jesus provided. We have no record of what Nicodemus did after he left Jesus.

What makes my heart hate Satan with all there is of me is that we do have the record over and over and over of what men are doing with the clear and simple words of Jesus: "Ye must be born again." They seem to let it go in one ear and out the other and try the harder to make themselves Christians while still sinners. So the booklets are helping our dear new contact to understand God better, but it will take a long time to understand Him completely. Jesus, please help this dear man to look up to Thee with a poverty-stricken soul and trust the Blood that was shed for him. He will go to bed that night "understanding" God in fuller measure than years of mental and emotional manipulation would ever come close to. While my heart bleeds for the victims of such lying programs, I hate the cunning Satan who as an angel of light spread such self-help theology so far and near.

I wish you could have one of the half hours I enjoy sitting with our dear Haitian brother—the one who has never heard from his mother in Haiti since the earthquake. He grows sweeter and more loving all the time as he walks with God and obeys His Word. The other day he was telling me again how God took away his heart of stone and…tears began to flow again, and without trying to hide them he said, "Now I cry a lot just because I love God so much."

He is the one who first asked for some Bible and theology courses as he felt it would please God if he studied more. He expressed to me that it is not always easy for him but he loves it and just wants to keep going because he knows it pleases God. He says he wants to live for God more and more. There is just no doubt as to what Spirit dwells within him. He goes to work in the industrial building within the prison each day and there receives criticism and persecution, but it only seems to make him all the sweeter. Maybe you don't think that is an appropriate word to use for a man. All I can reply is that you have not met him yet.

As last year drew to a close I sensed the need for a change in our weekly Bible studies. The men would come each week with no need of preparation and just listen for an hour to what we had to say and we felt it would be profitable if they had something to study all week. We ordered Sunday School quarterlies and decided to see how well they would be able to understand the material and how it would work.

I confess again my weak faith. I was amazed at the first study session after they had received the quarterlies. They immediately began to voice their delight with them and I noticed some of them had the lesson all marked up and were ready to discuss it. One man said, "This was really good. I read it five times, it was so good!" My first thought was, "O Lord, forgive us who have had this all of our lives and have gone perhaps weeks without a thought of expressing thanks for our Sunday School lesson!" Needless to say, the class time is too short for all the questions and discussion. Please help us pray that they will continue to be a great blessing.

In His love,
William Cawman

March 1, 2011

NEAR THE BEGINNING of our ministry in the prison a dear man got saved and immediately started walking the pathway to heaven. As soon as he heard of another work of God that would take care of the sinful nature within him, he started seeking it earnestly, just the way any really born-again soul will do. For several months we sat together on a very regular schedule and talked and prayed about this great work of God within the heart of the believer. One Friday afternoon as we talked and prayed the atmosphere was heavy with divine expectancy.

Suddenly he got up and just walked out of the room.

On Monday he came back to see me and apologized for leaving that way but said he was just in such a grip of desire that he hardly knew he did it. He had gone straight to his cell and all weekend had sought God for a clean heart. Now on Monday he looked at me with a puzzled expression and said, "I don't know what to think; three times this weekend God has said, 'Son, the work is done.'" I looked at him for a moment and then said, "Well, do you suppose it is time you acknowledged that?" Never will I forget the sudden change on his countenance as faith leaped up to grasp what God had done: "I think it is!"

From that day until the present moment God has kept him in victory without a single relapse. All glory be to God! Ten years have passed by and he is now the Sunday School Superintendent of our church (you must understand I have never been allowed to use names in these letters by state instructions). He has become a brother indeed to all of us.

For some time now he has been accompanying another couple as they go in on Thursday evenings to a county jail to minister. The officers have come to know them quite well by now, and one Thursday recently as he entered the jail for the service the Lieutenant looked quite startled and then relieved. "Oh, then it wasn't you," he said. "A man came into jail this week that looks just like you and I thought, 'Oh, no; surely not him! What did he do?'" A sergeant came up behind him and said, "I told you it wasn't him. Our man wouldn't do that."

How it melted all of our hearts with gratitude to God that His keeping power has set an example before the world and the church that by His help men don't have to turn back again. The world is watching us and they would down deep inside be so disappointed in us if we fail, even when they try to get us to do it. How it spoke to all of our hearts that we must be true at any cost.

One of the favorite songs of the men in this prison is "Pass me not, oh gentle Savior; hear my humble cry. While on others Thou art calling, do not pass me by." The other Sunday night my own heart was caught up in the grip of that prayer both for them and for myself. And thank God, He is not passing some of them by. Let me tell you of one.

Several weeks ago a man came in to see me, who was the picture of sin's wreckage. He was 39 years of age, but old in the scars of sin. He had gotten into a fight with his girlfriend—who by the way was another man's wife—and had killed her and is serving a long sentence in prison. He sat before me and began to get right to the point, "Chaplain, I don't really know if I'm saved. I try to do what is right but it doesn't last but a day or two and I'm right back where I was. I just cannot stop sinning. I don't want to live like this. I'm tired of it. I'm sure God has something better than this."

I was quite sure of it, too, and so we went to prayer and tried to point him to the Blood of Jesus. He left much lighter and a week later came back with a smile. "Chaplain, God is delivering me! Every addiction is gone! The cigarettes are gone; the pornography is gone; I'm not sinning, and I have peace within my heart!" Guess what? Jesus cannot and did not pass him by. Hallelujah for the Blood! When I can't, IT can! Praise God.

Another man has been having quite a struggle lately because he gets so discouraged over all the religious groups that come in on Sunday nights and preach that you cannot live without sin (the Bible calls these "Doctrines of devils") and just carry on an emotional program with no substance at all and then leave them there. He got down under the load of it until he lost the joy of the Lord and was evidencing defeat. I tried to talk to him and others did as well, but it seemed he felt he must carry this burden for the church within the prison.

One day he came to Bible Study and the Sunday School lesson we had for the week was on Psalms of Thanksgiving. At the beginning of the class he stood up and said, "Men, I need to say something. I need to ask the Chaplain and all of you to forgive me. This Sunday School lesson has deeply convicted me and then God has shown me that I am not bringing any glory to Him because I have been under a burden for something that is none of my business to change anyway, and I have not been shining for Jesus. I want you to forgive me and I'm learning my lesson." Oh, what a change in the atmosphere it brought. Thank God for that SS lesson!

The problem he was facing, however, still remains and really is a battle for the few men who really have a spiritual vision. One of our other brothers— who has already passed through some of that battleground and has learned to walk in victory in spite of it all— came to me also and said, "There's hardly anything in the services except what your group brings us. I don't mean to be critical or complaining, but really the minister who came last Sunday simply gave us the message: 'Keep plugging along, men, it could be worse.' I said, 'Yes, I guess in his Bible John 3:16 would read, "For God so loved the world that he gave His only Begotten Son to lift our chins and tell us it could be worse."'"

How much worse can it be than "having no hope and without God in the world"? Here's a forty-plus man telling me his story after hearing about the plugging-along program. His dad walked out on his mother for over twenty years, living with another woman. He now has dementia and so the other woman doesn't want him anymore and kicked him out, so his mother took him back in, by now a total care case who cannot even control or clean up after his own body functions. She is 77 years old and is also caring for the twin sister of the man in prison who was in a car wreck at 18 and now has the mind of a 12-year-old. The twin brother sitting before me was so wasted in his mind over drugs that he burned his mother's house down when the police surrounded it to try to arrest him.

But the Sunday night message was to "keep plugging along, it could be worse."

Who, I wonder, will have the hottest bed in hell— the poor victim of society's sin, or the false prophets who offer nothing more than nothing? To try to follow up the mess they leave poor deluded souls in is indeed uphill business. So often when we try to point men to a better way, they have been so dulled by false teachers that salve over their consciences with human programs that they cannot conceive they are not all right, notwithstanding they have no joy, no testimony, no peace within, and no power to live above sin.

But again I say, He is not passing all of them by. He is hearing the cry of every broken and contrite heart. A recent addition to my classes seemed to be a very zealous and vivacious short little man who always greeted me with deep reverence, "Good morning, man of God." I sat down to visit with him and asked him how it was with his soul. "Chaplain, in 2009 I thought I got saved, but in 2010 I got saved! He cleansed me! Every addiction was broken in one moment and He came into my heart!" And with that tears squirted from his eyes without an effort and he began to just laugh with joy. "Chaplain, it's wonderful. I love Him, I really do."

Well, I found I just loved Him more than ever about then, too! I am fully convinced that the Holy Spirit is brooding with one last longing effort over this old world. Behind the faces you meet everywhere you go, you may be surprised at how many hearts He is knocking at and how many are letting Him come in. I cannot express how gloriously rewarding it is to go for some time without too many visible results and then all of the sudden realize that someone you never guessed it of has begun a walk with Jesus and made a start for heaven.

Another recent arrival told me his story. He was born into a mixed marriage and then adopted out at the age of two. He grew up in a very hostile racial section of Newark where the Bloods (a very bad gang) were constantly fighting and carrying out racial violence. He was early given a street name that indicated he was a mongrel and at a young age began to hang out with the gangs. After his first prison sentence, of which he has had three so far, he formally joined the Bloods and had his back tattooed with their emblems. I believe it was between his second and third sentences that he fathered a little girl.

After being imprisoned the third time he says he began to hear God knocking at his door. He began to think about his little girl growing up like he did, without a father and without a home. He became more and more serious until he fully sensed his need of getting his life really straightened out. He went to God in prayer and told Him he was going to give his heart to Him and asked Him to protect him from the gangs. He knew he could not ride the fence and try to serve God under cover and so he went to the gangs and told them he was getting right with God and was leaving them.

He also told God that since He had done so much for him he wanted to ask God to let him lead three times as many souls to Jesus as he had led into the gangs, and he said God is helping him to talk to others. It surely felt like he was genuine and had a real love for Jesus. You might remember him in your prayers.

I have another special prayer request that covers the next two months. I try to be conscientious about leaving space between evangelistic meetings to keep time open for the prison ministry, but I began receiving some rather plaintive calls from my baby daughter, whose letters you also find with these. She is getting ready to move up into Malawi in late March and all of the sudden felt she needed her daddy. This made it necessary to crowd up some previously scheduled meetings until I will be gone from the prison for about six weeks from March 6 to April 18, the period in Africa being March 14-April 6. This will make a heavier load for the volunteers from our church who so faithfully fill in all they can for us.

Will you please pray that the Lord will protect on our journey, giving His leadership and guidance every step of the way, and at the same time, reward these our precious brethren who are willing to give their time to back us up? We would deeply appreciate it, as I have never left the prison for that long and will try to not do it again, unless the Lord so leads.

Thank you so very much for all your prayers,

William Cawman

10
PRISON AND BEYOND

April 1, 2011

MY SUPERVISOR IN CHAPLAINCY writes thus to me: "I envy you; here you are spreading the gospel on the mission field while I'm preparing to sit in on a Jumah prayer service. It isn't fair!" Pray for him as he endeavors to keep the door open to the gospel in the prison against increasing pressures from every direction without anyone to turn to except God.

I am not implying that God is a last resort. I'm only saying that our state government has been stripped in the last few years of any support whatsoever for anything related to Christianity. The antichrist is gaining momentum rapidly and it is very obvious that it is not anti-anything other than Jesus Christ, the Son of God.

And with that bit of prison news could I beg a brief absence and double up on African News? The reason for this is that for the best part of a month that is where I have been instead of prison. My daughter felt the need of help in moving to Malawi and I surely see why now. I am so glad that God allowed the rearranging of meetings, etc., provided for a very reasonable fare and even had some people send in some helpful money towards it.

I left Philadelphia on Monday, March 14 at 7:30 in the evening and spent the next day in Paris, visiting the Palace of Versailles, Notre Dame, the town square where once stood the guillotine, a very ancient cathedral built only about 300 years after Christ, etc. That evening very late we left Paris and flew on down to Johannesburg where my daughter and Pretorius's met me and we spent the rest of that week in Middelburg.

On Thursday evening Sarel took me to a high school where it had been announced that I would be speaking to the young people. Several hundred packed into the auditorium and I spoke to them for about forty-five minutes on the results of following their own choices in life or giving themselves entirely to God and His will. They listened with deep respect and attentiveness and then crowded around me to have their pictures taken with me. How different from America where the God who was once in the school system has been asked to leave.

After preaching for the group in Middleburg on Sunday we left early Monday morning for Malawi and as of the writing of this letter we are several days behind in getting there. I think it was between Maputo and Xai Xai that I was pulled over by a police check. The officer could speak English somewhat and when he looked at my driver's license he wanted to know if it was an international one. I told him that it was just from the USA. He said I couldn't drive in Mozambique with it and I told him no one had ever objected to it before, so he said he would ask his supervisor.

He came back and said that it was all right but that he would have to give me a fine of 1000 meticais because I did not have a blue and yellow triangle on the front of the pickup to pull the trailer. He had me get out and go over to his truck and after examining the papers he insisted that I needed to pay the fine.

I remained very calm and prayerful and respectful to him but told him that in our country if a person offended for the first time and didn't know the law they were only issued a warning and then expected to get it right. I promised him that we would stop at the very next place to get one if he could tell me where that was. He said he didn't know the road ahead of us, and that it is not how it works in Mozambique.

I told him we were missionaries and would he please give us forgiveness this one time and we would get one as soon as possible. He thought a moment and then said, "If you were tourists I would not forgive you, but since you are missionaries and on business for the Lord I will forgive you this time, but could you give me a Bible?"

I looked at my daughter and she said the only spare Bible was the first one we had given her but that his need was more important than her sentiments and I agreed. We gave him the Bible and then he asked me if I would pray with him. I said I would be very glad to and so he put out his hand and I took it and prayed for his salvation right in front of his two colleagues. He thanked me very much and wished us a good journey.

I got back in the car and nearly melted on the inside with gratitude to my Father in heaven for arranging that meeting.

It was absolutely in Divine providence that not just "a" man, but "the" man who did, stopped when we were in trouble. Of course we did not know what the problem was and had he not come just at that moment we would have put a few liters of oil in the truck and gone on down the road to the complete destruction of the engine.

But it was not alone that which made it providential, for this man needed God and he knew it. He had moved up into Mozambique two years before and there was no church that he could really find that was preaching the truth. So he was doing his best but, like Apollos, needed someone to show him the way. They had bought a house that they gladly shared with us as well as the best of their food, but they said when they moved into the house they found it completely possessed by black magic and demonical powers.

They had a woman come to help them and she went through the house knowing just what to look for and even began to tell the couple things about themselves that only they knew up to that point. They felt she had done a good job of cleansing out the demons, but Sarel, very knowledgeable about such things, plainly told them that they had only had the black magic subdued by white magic, which the Charismatic churches are based on.

I got up the next morning quite early and read my Bible for a while and then went outside to walk and pray, but soon the man and his wife called to me and for nearly an hour we sat on the front porch talking about the way of truth and God's holiness. I began to understand why we were there and my heart felt so at ease with the way God was leading us.

They then served us a delicious breakfast and then he went to the mechanic he had engaged to find out what all was wrong with the pickup. The mechanic had started working at 4:00 that morning because he knew we were eager to not be delayed any longer than needful. By then he had discovered the damages done and so the man we were staying with and my daughter and I went to a bank and transferred some money to cover the damages. Then they had to order the parts from South Africa.

Our host said he would take us to Zavora and then when the pickup was finished he would bring it up to us along with the mechanic so that they could be sure everything was satisfactory. Sarel, Lintie, and my daughter insisted that I had to ride up in the cab with him so that we could talk about the Lord. And we did.

No sooner were we on the road pulling the trailer behind us than I began to open up to him the ways of God and how completely different they are from the way of the modern churches. It seemed like no time at all before we were seeing the sign for Inharrime, only 14 kilometers from Zavora. As we turned off onto the dirt road to the mission, he said, "I want you to know that any time you are in this area my house is your house, and I mean that." I told him that there was a house in New Jersey that was the same to him.

In a couple of days he called to say that they had found a few other parts that were needed and so he had gone to Maputo to wait for a friend to bring them to him from South Africa because the other parts had already left. Sarel took the call and he told Sarel that he was putting some of his own money into the repairs but he would not tell him how much, and then he told Sarel that he wanted him to come up and hold a series of meetings for him.

When I heard that I again was melted to tears to see how God was arranging every detail of even the discomforts of our plans. I told the people here about an Italian electrician that I knew well. When his son went to high school he came home to his father with news he had newly discovered from his higher education. He said, "Dad, I have some rights of my own around here." His father replied, "That is right, my son, your rights around here are to say 'Yes, Sir!'" I told them I wanted no right whatsoever with my Heavenly Father except the right to say, "Yes, Sir!"

Before I ever left America I felt some discomfort over the short time we would have with the brethren in Zavora. I felt God giving me several areas of truth I so wanted to share with them, but we would only have one day and evening to give them. Now I understand why God gave them to me; He knew all the time that we would be detained several days and even over Sunday with them.

As soon as I met Salatiel he said to me, "I cannot believe it is really you again. God has allowed the truck to break so that you could talk more with us." I told him that God had given me some messages for them and he said, "I am hungry for that." We have had several times to just sit together and I felt the Holy Spirit sitting right with us. I will tell you that I marvel at what God can do when the indwelling Spirit is present.

As I opened up some of the things God had given me for them, I kept expecting to have to explain further or to come at it from different angles, etc., but such was not the case. These precious men had heard the Good News and were welcoming the Comforter, whom Jesus said will guide us into all truth, and they immediately grasped every word I was telling them.

They began to really open up their deep concerns over those who had turned to the Charismatic way which they can plainly see is just another form of witchcraft. They were not bitter; they were not critical; they were burdened but very outspoken that they saw it as wrong. They were concerned about the division in the church.

I listened to them and then warned them of the dangers on both sides of the road, how they could see the wrong and become bitter against it and fight it in their own efforts and end up just as bad as the others were, or they could just compromise to keep peace like the opposition wanted them to do. The others are talking about "Unity, unity." I told them we can never compromise purity for unity for we would lose purity as well as unity. There is no unity among carnal hearts. They readily agreed and the more we talked of the way of truth in all these things, the more I marveled at the Divine wisdom and grace God was giving them.

Your prayers for Zavora have not been in vain! God has established a holiness beachhead in this little spot on earth and these men have settled it to be true to God's holy way. Holiness works! I have felt it; I have seen it! There is no other gospel that is worth living and preaching.

By the way, when we were here two years ago we would go to sleep several nights listening to the beat of the witch doctor's drums. They never hear them anymore! Thank God! That does not mean that all witchcraft is gone, by any means. Mario came up to take me somewhere when he got a call that they needed an ambulance service from the clinic to the hospital in Inharrime. He invited me to go along so we picked up an intern doctor from Holland and the mother and infant and another woman. They were afraid they could not make it in time as the baby was very dehydrated and unresponsive.

The young student was doing his best to get fluid into the baby but did not have a small enough needle. Mario was driving at 140 kilometers an hour (almost 90 miles an hour) and a policeman began to hold up his radar gun. Mario shouted out the window, "Sick baby," and they waved us on. Then the intern said, "Mario, this baby has something around her belly from the witch doctor. Should I take it off?" Mario said, "Yes, by all means. That may be why she isn't getting well." We did make it to the hospital and she pulled through.

The heat has really been a battle for us all; it is so draining. I went with Azarias yesterday to a service out in the bush and enjoyed it immensely, but it was so hot. It will be even hotter in Malawi. Hopefully the pickup will be here by Saturday night. We will proceed the long, hard two day trip on up to Malawi and spend the rest of that week getting my daughter settled in. Through all of this I can testify that I stand in awe of my Heavenly Father as never before and only pray that I will never lift a thought or a choice or anything else to hinder His perfect will.

In His glad service,
William Cawman

May 1, 2011

SINCE OUR STAY IN AFRICA ran over into this month let me just tell you a couple items of follow-up to last month's letter before I become incarcerated again. The time spent with the people in Zavora, Mozambique, was certainly a blessing both to them and to us. It is very clear that grace and holiness are working among the people there, despite the severe opposition to it. God is giving the brethren there such an amazing blessing of Christ-likeness and common sense as to how to keep walking in the light they have received while being opposed by enemies all around them. It was such a blessing to see God's grace working in and among them.

We were there through Sunday and then started north toward Malawi around 4:00 am on Monday. We had gone only a short distance and the rebuilt engine in the pickup began to heat up. This time we knew it because the temperature gauge, that had not been working before, was working now. We pulled over and called back to Zavora. Fortunately a very able mechanic from Durban, SA, was there. He and another man came up and couldn't find anything wrong, so they told us to keep it in lower gears and go on. That only lasted a few more miles and we knew we could never make it like that.

They came back and the mechanic told us he thought he knew what the problem was: the cooling fan was not working properly and was not speeding up as the temperature rose. He took it apart and cut out a piece of metal roofing material and locked it in place so that it would turn as fast as the engine did and now it seemed all was fixed. We went on our way for a day and a half and had just crossed the great Zambezi River and were about a half hour on the other side. Suddenly the temperature gauge shot up again to the danger point and we barely made it to the side of the road before it boiled over completely dry.

The temperature outside was nearly 100 degrees. We were in an area of completely uninhabited wilderness where it was unsafe to even walk away from the roadway, because Mozambique has never had the funds to remove all the land mines placed promiscuously throughout the country during their civil war.

All of the sudden I realized that Satan was leveling every piece of artillery he had at my own heart. I got out and began to walk up and down the roadside while lifting my heart earnestly to God. "O Lord, are we out of Your will? Have we missed Your leadership somewhere? Lord, we are never going to get there like this. Something is wrong. Could You please speak anything to my heart?" I had no question at all that either we were missing it somewhere or else Satan was mightily angry that we were going.

Suddenly—and here I am totally lost for words to describe what took place—the agony of distress gave way instantly to the sweetest assurance from Heaven with the words, "Son, Satan is fighting, but you are perfectly in the center of My will and it will all come out right."

Satan fled while my soul entered into a perfect sense of rest in God's sweet will. I believe I experienced just a little of what the three Hebrews felt in the burning furnace, for I knew God was with us even though there was no help in sight and no water to fill the cooling system and no answer yet as to whether the truck would stand the rest of the trip. I would not take back the price of the ticket over there nor anything else for that blessed few moments and the lingering weight of assurance that followed it for days. I could not even talk about it and keep back the tears.

Just then I heard a noise and realized a tractor trailer was coming down the road. I felt impressed to wave to him as he passed. I did not beckon to him; simply waved. He no sooner got past us than he slammed on his brakes and backed up to where we were. He was an over-the-road truck driver with his wife with him and he was a mechanic. We soon learned that we were almost at the summit of the longest, hardest pull in South Africa and that nearly everyone under load overheats coming up it. The truck driver had nothing on that truck except a 55 gallon drum of water he used for showering, and he helped us refill the cooling system. We thanked him ever so much and went on our way again.

Not only for hours after that most exhilarating encounter with God on the side of that road, but for the rest of the time we were there I knew God had again—as He did with every attack of Satan on that trip—turned the battle into a victory that I personally needed.

A few days later I went into a village nearby to the town of

Mangochi, where My daughter is now living, to a Bible study. As the native pastor finished the study a man said, "Oh Pastor, please keep coming to teach us. You know we were raised Muslims, but I never knew that a Redeemer would come from Isaac and that the Blood of Jesus could wash our sins away."

Again, I could hardly hold back the tears of love for these dear people, who in spite of Muslim culture all around them, are deeply hungry at heart. Then I began to put the two together—Satan's attacks and the evident hunger of hearts, and I promised God I could never miss a day nor a prompting to keep my daughter covered with prayer.

The last night in Mangochi before the long bus ride out through Mozambique and Zimbabwe into South Africa I lay on an air mattress with a mosquito net around me in the little house she had rented for $100 a month and tried to get some sleep in the intense heat of the evening. I listened to the sounds—the eerie loudspeaker giving out the Muslim call to prayer, the wild music coming from the market place nearby, and then the deep bass grunts of a hippopotamus that had wandered up into town from the river not far away.

I had a deep down feeling that I was dropping my daughter off in the middle of a lion's den, but then had the assurance that Daniel never spent a safer night than the one he spent with the lions. And wherever God's will is for any of us, there is no safer place in all the world.

And so now—would I rather be in Africa or in prison? I would rather be in the center of God's will than anywhere else in the entire world, no matter where that may be.

There is a letter I received lately that I want to share with you who are praying. I hope it will encourage you that God is hearing and answering your prayers. This is from a man who was in our prison and is now in one of the northern ones, but who prayed through to holiness after he was sent there.

Dear Beloved Brother,
It is with great pleasure that I write this letter, and send my

10: Prison and Beyond

greetings. I am truly blessed by Him that is best, and Oh, what praise fills my soul! Alleluia!

A few days ago I received a bunch of tracts from the Old Paths Tract Society. Amongst a sample pack were several tracts on the sin of television. A couple days later I read a couple and decided that it was time to repent of watching tv. I unplugged it, boxed it up, and put it in storage as soon as I was able. (I would of smashed it, but I didn't wish to offend the souls around me. I'm in a dorm of 50 men.) Right away joy sprung up in my soul, and it has been growing since. Alleluia!

Brother, what a shameful waste tv watching is. No man would willingly rummage around in a land fill for a meal, but any saved soul is doing worse if they are looking to glorify God and watch tv. I deeply regret my tithe to Satan, but I promise to never give him another moment before one of his altars. (I said tithe because I did the math. If I only watched 3 hrs of tv every day, versus the 6 or so most people do, then I gave Satan 1/8 of my devotion. That's more than 10%; the basic tithe!) What a waste. I thank God He can rebuild the old waste places.

Brother, since that blessed day of tearing down Satan's altar I have been so blessed that I wish I never watched tv, ever. As great as the blessing He has given me is, it is so much greater how He has given me for others. I have witnessed and encouraged more souls in the Lord these past several days than I have in at least the past year's total! Alleluia! I am handing out 10-20 tracts a day, and I know a revival is coming. Oh what a mighty God we serve. I will keep you posted.

Please thank the brethren and all those who have tarried in prayer for the souls here and myself. A fire storm is coming and there is plenty of kindling to be burnt up. Just like a fire is needed to encourage new life in pine forests, so too we need a Holy Ghost Fire storm to run through this place and consume all the dross. He is able and I am willing. Even so come Lord, come! Alleluia! (I hope you don't mind me using a little zealous quoting of Scripture a little prematurely and out of Rev. 22:20's direct context.)

Brother, I thank God for being able to share this victory and testimony with you and I look forward to all He is going to do. Please share my appreciation and love with all those who have left all and chosen the better...best part. God bless you and all the saints.

Your brother and son in the Faith.

Could I tell you that I am well aware of our state prescribed boundary lines that dictate that we are to form no intimate personal relationships with the men. While aware of this, I tell the men every once in a while that if I am really doing my state paid job rightly, they and I become blood brothers—the most intimate relationship known this side of eternity. Recently my heart was so warmed as one of them was praying and said to God, "Lord, thank you for our chaplain. He's not just our chaplain, he's our brother." No paycheck can begin to reward like this. I thank God for these men who (in answer to your prayers) are taking the highway of holiness and it is working!

In Him,
William Cawman

┼┼┼

June 1, 2011

BEYOND ALL DOUBT the next best thing to having a living and real relationship with God in your own heart is to watch another soul come into a relationship like that and then grow in it. Peter felt this when he said, "...to them that have obtained like precious faith with us through the righteousness of God and our Savior Jesus Christ."

Such a blessing has been our dear brother from Haiti who has been "...grow[ing] in grace, and in the knowledge of our Lord and Savior Jesus Christ." In our recent revival in our church we took the evangelist and his wife into the prison for the weekly classes and what a blessing the men received from it.

On Wednesday of that week this man was in the class. After the evangelist had given a message to the men our brother raised his hand and began to express his love of the truth they had just heard, and how it witnessed to him. He told how God had already convicted him of something a few days before and how yielding to God fully in it had brought such a peace to his heart. He had broken the band on his watch and so another inmate made him a band, but it was made in such a way that it violated prison rules. He felt a little uncomfortable with it, but when the sergeant passed him and looked at it he didn't say anything so he just let it go for a few days. Several more times the sergeant looked at it but said nothing.

Suddenly he realized that there was a cloud between him and God and that watch was bringing it. He took it off and threw the whole watch away with that violence that only a redeemed soul knows: "…yea, what revenge!" Instantly he felt the peace of God sweep through his heart and he said, "What do I need a watch for in prison, anyway?" As he told this incident his voice broke with emotion and tears began to flow. God's presence descended in the room until his blessing became a blessing to all of us.

A couple weeks later in a Sunday night service I asked if anyone had a testimony. He came to the front and with the beauty of grace all over his face said, "Brothers, it's a beautiful thing to be a child of God…" and then gratitude began to flow from his heart for everything and everyone around him. It was a beautiful thing to listen to a child of God, too, and I couldn't help but feel for all those who are struggling with their surroundings that are the same as his and are being cheated out of the grace he is finding.

So now let me go across the aisle in the same church and tell you of something quite the opposite. Another man who has been there for several years now, immediately embraced the message of holiness when he first heard it. At times he appears to have wonderful victory and when he does he is a blessing to others also. But he seems to have a pattern of thinking that leads him over and over into spiritual darkness and it shows all over him.

Outside of the few men that preach the way of holiness and deliverance from all sin, the whole smorgasbord of religious teachers not only condone sin in a believer (if such can even be called a believer) but promote it. One man taught them with these exact words: "We all know that after a person is born again, he still continues to sin." 1 John 5:18 however says, "We know that whosoever is born of God sinneth not; but he that is begotten of God keepeth himself, and that wicked one toucheth him not."

So these dear souls must sit and listen to such "doctrines of devils" that flatly and unashamedly contradict the written Word of God. This troubles his spirit (rightly so) but he does not catch the danger point where righteous indignation can open a door of the will to the entrance of fretting that leads to bitterness. David said, "Fret not thyself because of evildoers…" The angel to the church of Ephesus said, "I know thy works, and thy labour, and thy patience, and how thou canst not bear them which are evil: and thou hast tried them which say they are apostles, and are not, and hast found them liars: And hast borne, and hast patience, and for my name's sake hast laboured, and hast not fainted. Nevertheless I have somewhat against thee, *because thou hast left thy first love.*" (emphasis added)

Our dear brother cannot seem to leave in God's hands what only God can handle. The angel to the churches did not condemn Ephesus for discerning false prophets; He did not condemn them for not being able to "bear them which are evil," but He did condemn them because while so doing they had lost their love. This is exactly what has happened to our brother too many times now. It seems that for a while he will catch himself and do better but then falls back into the same trap of Satan.

About a month or so ago we were studying a Sunday School lesson about being thankful to God. He stood up in the class and told with tears how God had convicted his heart over the lesson; that he had allowed things that are taking place in the church, which God was not asking him to handle, to rob him of the joy of the Lord. He asked the men to forgive him and I hoped he had caught the secret of his repetitive spiritual failure and that things would be different.

For a week or so he had a shining face again, but then it seemed he fell harder than ever, even writing a grievance letter to the administration of the prison regarding the head chaplain. He says that he spends more time trying to counteract what those teaching holiness of heart and life are teaching than teaching anything himself. This may be, but that is God's business, not mine or his. Even if it is the truth, my supervisor loves me dearly and makes it known in private and in public.

I called our brother in and tried to show him how every time he takes things out of God's hands into his own he loses the glow of his relationship with God and loses his joy. He needs your prayers. He does seem to want God. He does want to live free from sin and be pure in heart. But he has a very weak spot in his defense against Satan and he needs prayer.

The Scripture tells us, "We then that are strong ought to bear the infirmities of the weak…," and this certainly is his weakness. Others around him, such as the man we told you about just before this one, are living under the same circumstances. They are keeping victory and growing in grace, but our dear weak brother has almost formed an addiction to stumbling over this pitfall of Satan. I hate the devil with all my heart and I hate his work on others just as much as what he tries on me. He doesn't care one bit what causes us to live with less than perfect clearness with God. He will grasp any handle he sees that will give him entrance to our wills.

Perhaps you might wonder if there is such a thing as a typical day in the life of a chaplain in a prison. Perhaps there is, but it doesn't seem to come too often. On a Friday recently I had planned to put in one of my longer days—9:00 am to 9:00 pm, ending with two Bible studies in two different locations.

I had scheduled at 9:00 am the man who I had told you

about months ago that was accosted after a Sunday night service by a female officer wanting him to sin with her in the chapel after all the others were gone. He refused, and like Joseph fled the place, but when he reported it to the sergeant in charge, they moved him to another facility and did nothing about the officer. Word followed him to the other facility and he began to suffer persecution from the officers there. He became discouraged (discouragement is no small tool of Satan for it will open the door to all other sins) and just went into hiding. I have tried several times to get a visit with him, but only once did he come. That time he let me know he loved me and didn't want to lose his soul, but the price of living a Christian life with all the persecution seemed too big at the time.

I scheduled him again for that morning but then found he had another appointment at the same time that didn't show up in the computer when I scheduled him. I went over to my supervisor's office and he asked what I had going, and I told him I had a cancellation and did not have another appointment until 10:00. He asked if I could help him out by taking the chaplain position in the weekly new man orientation up in the visit hall. He said he had asked the Islamic chaplain to do it but he had just called in with a weak croaky voice saying he was so sick he couldn't do it. I agreed to fill in and when I went up front there was the Islamic chaplain visiting very animatedly with a couple of officers—voice and all in very good shape. I suppose it is just perfectly acceptable with Allah to tell black lies due to the fact that Allah never was, is not, and never will be. His prophet is dead and rotten and in hell suffering for all his demoniacal sins, including his thirteen wives, the youngest of which was 9 years old.

Well, I did the new man orientation and went back to my next interview. Can you figure out why this is the fastest growing, most aggressive "religion" in the world, and why our national leaders are bowing their heads and letting it rip away all that has made America the Great, great? As our hearts cry to

God over this situation, let's not fall into the trap of our weak brother and fret because of evil and lose our love!

Some months ago we had mentioned the need of prayer for a place to have our classes because they had removed the officer from our chapels except for Sunday night services. God has answered and we are now being given a very nice classroom in the academic area of the educational building in all three facilities which is well suited to our purpose. Two out of the three officers in charge are extremely good to work with, claiming to be Christians themselves, and the other one who is not so friendly is moving to a different spot in just a week or so. Please pray that we will get a third one as good as the other two.

Different times over the years I have mentioned a small black man who is serving a long sentence for murder but who is such a blessing as he lives a holy life with victory over all sin. He has been a teacher's aide for a long time in the academic department and the officer in charge has utmost respect for him. The first time I went to that area to have class there, the officer showed me to a room and then asked if there was anything else he could do for me, because, he said, "If I don't, I have to answer to you know who!" The dear shining brother was standing right behind him grinning from ear to ear.

We still have our Sunday night services in the chapel and then an assembly room (the room that was our chapel when the prison first opened) in the administration area is available for Friday night Bible studies. "Hitherto hath the Lord helped us!" To Him be all the glory, and to each of you be thanks abundant for your many prayers.

Every time I feel a surge of anxiety over how long the door will stay open I remember that it was opened to begin with only by God and so He can keep it open as long as He has work for us to do there. When I think of the few precious men who are walking so brightly with God in the beauty of holiness I think of a part of the Angel's message to the church at Sardis: "Thou hast a few names even in Sardis [Southwoods

State Prison] which have not defiled their garments; and they shall walk with me in white: for they are worthy." Surely I do not believe God is going to forsake these and leave them with only promoters of sinful living. This, too, is worthy of your prayers, for I know you are aware of the escalating encroachments of the anti-Christ spirit.

Let us continue to work while it is day.

With Christian love,
William Cawman

11
Department of Corrections, They Call This

July 1, 2011

Actually it is July 5 already before I am sitting down to type this letter. I am pretty sure that in twelve years or so it is the first time I have not had it typed out before the end of the month, but this month held some very unexpected details besides the planned schedule. My wife and I were in South Dakota in a revival, then we flew home for two weeks and then flew back out and picked up our vehicle and trailer and went to a camp meeting also in SD. From there we were supposed to drive back to Kentucky to our own camp, and then home on the Fourth of July to be incarcerated for five weeks straight.

On the morning we were to leave for Kentucky we got word that my wife's almost lifelong friend who had lived with them from girlhood had passed away. We immediately changed plans and left our trailer in SD and drove for two days to Yakima, WA for her funeral on Wednesday. Then we left early Thursday morning and drove for three days back to KY to be there for the last Sunday of camp. We returned home yesterday. Breaking all records for our wandering to and fro upon the face of the earth, we covered by land well over 3600 miles in five days of driving.

But now we plan to spend several weeks with our prison family and we are so glad that God is planning to spend time with them, too. Let me begin by sharing a part of a letter from our former Mormon—do you remember him? Here it is:

> My warmest greetings to you in the name of our dear Savior, Jesus Christ. He is truly letting His grace abound all around us. That is truly amazing to a beggar and pauper like me. Bless His mercy and His name forever!
>
> ...I've memorized the words to the hymn, "Thy Will Be Done." Like many beautiful hymns I've encountered, I don't know the melody, but the words are moving and marvelous just by themselves.
>
> ...There's a scripture I read every day on a little card: Deuteronomy 1:21, "Behold, the Lord your God has set the land before you; go up and possess it, as the Lord, the God of your fathers, has said unto you, 'Fear not, neither be dismayed.'" I wondered many times about "the God of your fathers" because the God I know now is certainly not the God of my fathers. They believe in a very different "God." But I've come to think of you and men like you...as my "fathers" because personally, or by their lives, they've given me true direction toward the true God.
>
> Maybe you'll forgive this, but in my own mind I refer to you as the "apostrophetics." That word sounds like apostles and prophets (perhaps intentionally), but what it actually refers to is that you added an apostrophe. My false spiritual fathers said:
>
> "We are Gods."
>
> But you and other true spiritual fathers have said:
>
> "We are God's."
>
> You added an apostrophe to the falsehood. And to me that's just the way God works; He adds one little thing, one little bit of leaven or a jot or tittle and changes everything; changes decades of falsehood into burning truth! Imagine how my goals in life have changed by adding that apostrophe; the change in

who I look to as a role model, how it's changed my relationship with Jesus and taken me into His heart and He into mine. Praise the Lord!

Thank you for this, and for your role as a Father in Israel in guiding me toward the true Gospel and the good news of Jesus Christ. That is with me all the time. Certainly the Lord has blessed us by His grace, with His Son, His teachings, and His hope. I pray for you and for your family and ministry, and for all the men at Southwoods who are being drawn by the Lord.

In His love, ———

And then here are a few lines from a letter by the dumpster singer—and do you remember him? He is in a northern prison, but not the same one as the man whose letter I've already quoted. He writes:

I pray this letter finds you doing well in health and at peace with our Father...Brother Cawman, in this season of my life I'm experiencing so much peace. It's a joy to live in God! There is such a joy in knowing our Savior. I'm learning to trust Him in all that I do. Sometimes I forget that I'm in prison!

...So my Brother, keep preaching the way of Holiness! Continue loving God and His people. Thank you for sharing your adventures in ministry with us. Please give all the Brothers my love.

I'm praying for your daughter in her new mission field. I am always blessed to hear how God is using her! Extend my greetings to her!

In closing may God's love continue to surround you and His peace keep you until His appearing.

Last month I wrote to you of a man who was accosted by a female officer and in rejecting her he found himself moved to another facility in the prison and was subjected to a good deal of persecution. A few days after what I told you in the last letter he saw me on the compound and apologized for missing the visit and so I put him on again. He came down and I asked him how he was getting along. He said, "Chaplain, you know I've always been honest with you; I'm not getting along at all. I've just given up. I'm not reading my Bible or praying—I've just given up."

I said, "My brother, do you want to end your life like you are now living it?" "Oh no, I don't." "Do you know when you will end it?" "No, I don't know that either." I said, "Jesus has been waiting a long time now to hear from you again. Don't you think He ought to?" He said, "Chaplain, I see love coming out all over you. Nobody ever loved me like you do and I miss it. Put me back on the list for all the classes and Bible studies and I promise you I will dust off my Bible and come back."

I said, "Thank you, but I'd like to ask you something else; will you begin reading that Bible again and spending time in prayer to Jesus?" "Yes, Chaplain, I will." True to his word he has been coming and his face is already brighter. Now please pray that he will not stop short of a full cure for all that would ever turn back again.

He also told me during this visit that he does not go to the Sunday night services because they are so foreign to the truth he has heard from us. I just told him to follow his heart and seek after God. I believe statistics would bear out that over 70% of our inmates are in from drug related charges, but the greatest enemy we face in prison is not drugs or gangs, but false "christs."

One day recently my pastor had a very good class in one of the facilities and a young man was really moved on and was seeking God. The men were supporting him and it all seemed like a new open door. A week later I was visiting with him and he was already finding great comfort in a shelf full of books he had collected of Joyce Meyers' writings. We have plenty of her new age, self-help propaganda available, for she has the money to send the books in by the boxes full. Everything I tried to point out to the young man of the need yet in his life that only Jesus could supply he seemed to have already found or was finding in Joyce Meyers. He told me the books were making him feel so good about himself. I asked him if he really had a direct relationship with Jesus. "Oh yes." I talked to him about the need of allowing God to cleanse out all of the nature of sin that we were born with and that has given us all the trouble we ever got into. "Oh, I think He's already done that. I'm feeling so good now." These cursed "doctrines of devils" (1 Timothy 4:1) are leading people directly away from the convicting finger of the promised Holy Spirit. I hesitate not to say that we are engaged in a royal war, and we need prayer as never before.

Please pray for the next few weeks as I will be planning to spend more time than usual in the hospital. I went over there and visited around recently and I knew I needed to be there more often. You never know what will be the response as you open a door and walk into one of the hospital cells.

First there is an older man who has been in prison for years and he is so glad to see me and begs me to come back again. He does feel he has been forgiven and loves for me to talk about the Lord.

Next is a cell where there is not much response, for the dear soul has already used up all but perhaps a flickering chance to choose his forever hereafter. What he has done with his power of choice it is already too late to know, but at least I try to pray with him and hope he is able to hear and still make that response without which eternity will be ever so horrible.

Then in the next cell there is a young man sitting on the edge of his bed looking at his television. I introduce myself and he takes one very quick look at me and then turns his head again to his television. I try to get acquainted; I try to ask if he would like prayer; I try to ask his name; he never looks at me again, but simply fixes his eyes on his television. Will I go back again? Yes, will you pray for him?

Then I enter another cell. On the edge of the bunk sits a young man with a trachea in his throat and I see him pulling it in and out to suction his lungs out. I think he is busy so I don't approach him until he finishes as he does not even look at me. Then when I do begin to speak I discover that he is totally blind. I ask him how long he has been blind and he says for about a year. It is the result of his diabetes. I ask him about his lungs and he tells me that he got double pneumonia in January and can't get over it so he has to keep suctioning fluid off of his lungs through that device. But when I ask him if I can pray with him, he is ever so ready. He responds as I do so and then asks me if he can somehow get a digital Bible that he can listen to as he wants to hear it so badly. I promise him I will do something about it and when I inquire they tell me one is on order for him.

Time is so short and the needs are everywhere. As the old poem so effectively states: "The work that centuries might have done, must crowd the hour of setting sun." I know many of you are praying for us. I thank you. Jesus thanks you. The men in prison thank you. GOD ANSWERS PRAYER! So let's pray on.

With love & gratitude,
William Cawman

August 1, 2011

AT TIMES WE ARE REMINDED in such simple, yet heart-warming, ways that God is constantly doing His very best to make Himself known to every man. This may seem to be a small incident, or else a coincidence to some of you, but it wasn't to the men who witnessed it, and I, too, felt it a direct voice of God to aid the faith of the men present.

We had gathered for class in the minimum camp and the inmate who prepared the room set up ten chairs. Nine men came in and sat down. We then stood for prayer and sang a few choruses and just before we sat down to begin our study I felt impressed to pray for whoever should be in the vacant chair. I had never had that impression before in any setting whatsoever. I said, "Men, before we sit down let's join in a prayer for whoever in this camp should be sitting in this vacant chair." I asked one of them to pray and I really sensed the seriousness of their desires as they prayed to God for whoever that was.

As the "amen" to that prayer was no more than said, the door opened and a tenth man walked in and began to go get another chair. The man next to the vacant one went and took him by the arm and ushered him into the prayed-for chair. There swept through the room an audible expression that said very clearly without the words, "Lord, You answered, didn't You?" I believe God saw those men needed a fresh revelation of the fact that He is real, and He surely gave it in a simple way they could grasp.

The next week the set-up man put out twelve chairs.

Some of you will remember the little Mexican man I have written about who radiates the joy of the Lord even through his many gang related tattoos. He is the one who received the size XXXL coat last fall and caused me no little amusement as he entered Bible study with only a wee head and two little feet projecting from the massive rear view.

Well, Friday night after the Bible study, which was taken from a Sunday school lesson on the Successes and Failures of Israel, he came to me and with a happy yet hungry face said,"Chaplain, would you please ask your church to pray for me, because I want to get sanctified like you are talking about." He is so sweetly enjoying the first work I would love to see what the fullness of the Indwelling Spirit would do to him.

Will you help us pray that he will follow the faithful Holy Spirit into the full cleansing of his heart? I personally will have no problem witnessing a sanctified heart shining out from behind MS Thirteen gang tattoos. After all, Paul said to the Corinthians, "And such were some of you: but ye are washed, but ye are sanctified, but ye are justified in the name of the Lord Jesus, and by the Spirit of our God."

Last month I asked prayer for some extra hospital visitation I had planned for this month and I thank you for praying. Our attendance at the services and Bible studies there is increasing and another service has been added each month. Again, I must tell you that it is one of the most fast-changing atmospheres you can imagine, to walk from one cell to another with no premonition as to what will be encountered.

I did revisit the young man at the end of the hallway and again he ignored me with hardly a word except a wave of hand toward the door showing me the way out. I laid my hand on his shoulder and told him I cared about him and would pray for him and he motioned a second time toward the door. I plan to return in a few days.

Then there is a man who was on death row for many years but is now serving life, because a few years ago the governor abolished the death sentence in New Jersey. He is an extremely talented artist even though he has had no schooling for that at all. He can take a picture of a person and with a ball point pen make a black and white drawing that exactly matches the photograph, even making the eyes more vivid or else changing the direction they are looking. He showed me the artwork he had underway and then we spent over an hour visiting.

He told me that even while he was on death row a number of years ago, things were so different back then that the warden would let him out day after day on furlough to sell his artwork as long as he was back in his cell at night. He would be free on the town and was even invited to dinners, etc., and then would return to his prison cell to sleep. He is very pleasant and enjoys someone to visit with but seems to have no spiritual desires that I can detect, even though he is now seventy-nine years of age.

He is six foot five and has a very deeply distinguished look in his face, but all he will say about his soul is that he doesn't object to religion, he has just never been religious. He reminds me of the eagle that groveled so long with the chickens that he forgot he was an eagle. Oh, that he would "come to himself" before he passes from almost a life in prison to a lost eternity. What a waste of what God had in mind when He said, "Let's make man!"

But then I walked into another cell and there lay a black man wasting away in what might be his last effort to live. I bent over him and began to speak to him and he said, "I don't speak English much." I asked him what he spoke and he said "Spanish." He was from Cuba. I switched and tried to converse a bit in my limited Spanish and before long he was holding my hand between his and tears were flowing down his old black face. I just let him hold my hand for a while and talked with him and prayed for him. It was hard to leave him when he wanted a friend so deeply, but he did tell me that Jesus is in his heart and he prays to Him all the time.

Oh, what a revelation awaits us on the other side when we begin to find out where all Jesus is extracting His bride from. Again let me quote: "Full many a gem the dark, unfathomed caves of ocean bear; full many a flower is born to blush unseen and waste its sweetness on the desert air." Surely tucked away in some of the most unlikely places on this earth there are precious gems awaiting their place in the crown of glory that will adorn the Savior's brow, in place of the crown of thorns we placed upon Him.

Don't you want to be there when the Father crowns His precious Son, not alone "with the glory which I had with Thee before the world was," but with the Bride that He has rescued from every dirty hog pen imaginable on earth, and has washed her in His precious blood until so clean He is not ashamed to take her into His throne with Him as He again sits down with His Father in His throne? Oh friends, we dare not miss that glorious, grand coronation day, do we?

And do you care who it is that stands beside you as we join that great anthem, "Thou art worthy to take the book; and to open the seals thereof: for Thou was slain, and hast redeemed us to God by Thy blood out of every kindred, and tongue, and people, and nation; and hast made us kings and priests: and we shall reign on the earth "? I can tell you that I would be just as thrilled to be standing beside a man from death row as beside the greatest preacher earth has known. And by the way, there will be no big heads in heaven. We will all be sinners saved by grace! Oh, excuse me, I am supposed to be writing a prayer letter, not preaching, am I not?

Before I relate the next story I would want to be very sensitive to any of my brethren who have been in active military service and would find this account unnerving. Please just skip the rest of this paragraph if it would bother you that way. We move on to another cell and find a man who did come to one of the services but doesn't very often. He is a sad, yet perplexing case. He sits in his wheelchair with three colored ports hanging from one arm through which he receives all the nourishment he gets.

He was in Viet Nam and was in some pretty rough action. He is now suffering from diseases known only to the military medical staff, for it is a combination of reactions to the chemical weaponry used and the jungle bugs he encountered. I asked him if he is able to enjoy any food at all through normal appetite and he said, "What appetite?"

He was a helicopter pilot in the army and yet saw a lot of ground action. When he was discharged he applied for a job opportunity in the paper for a medevac pilot and got the first position he applied for. Life was going well for a while and he was making good money, etc.

One day he landed his copter on a road at the scene of an accident and as he did he spotted what looked like a baby doll on the road quite a distance from the rest of the accident. Just then he saw it move an arm and realized it was a real baby. He started for it as no one else even seemed to notice it, but just before he could reach it a tractor trailer ran over it. He said he had seen "hell" in all forms in Viet Nam— had even held his buddy's brains in his hands— but when he saw that happen to that baby he came completely unglued on the inside. The only way he could cope with the trauma was to start using drugs, and that is why he is in prison.

But the saddest part of his life is a part that I honestly don't understand nor know how to break through. When I ask him about his relationship with God he immediately responds, "Oh, yeah, I made my peace with God a number of years ago. He and I have an understanding and everything is all right. I don't need a lot of church or prayer or Bible. God and I understand each other. You see, God doesn't want me in heaven because He knows I would steal the pearly gates, and the devil doesn't want me in hell because I would run off with the keys to the place, so I've got it all arranged for."

To get past this front I know not how. Is it a false facade, or has he really sealed his choice into a willful blindness such as this? I don't know, but I will visit him more, for you and I both know that such a philosophy, or whatever you might call it, will never hold up on that great day not so far hence.

The Sunday School quarterlies and the lessons in them have been having a real impact for good in the Bible study times. This quarter has been focusing on Israel's possessing the Land of Canaan, and it has really been getting through to the men that those inhabitants of the land are not to be left behind without disastrous results. After one study one could hear the comments all over the room as they were leaving as to how deeply they had been convicted. One man said, "That was a pretty heavy plate full, Chaplain."

Of course, by God's help we are endeavoring to waste no means available to crowd the sin issue to the wall. After all, why are they in prison to start with? The place where we are holding these studies is called a "Correctional Facility." Is it not appropriate to put two and two together and get corrected what they are here for? There are such programs available as "Behavior Modification" and "Anger Management" and a few others, but does modification correct? Does management deliver? Oh, for a sweeping revival of deep, pungent, Holy Ghost conviction to "reprove the world of sin, and of righteousness, and of judgment to come."

While it is true that we are without doubt living under the

commission in this age of "Go out quickly into the streets and lanes of the city, and bring in hither the poor, and the maimed, and the halt, and the blind..." yet where we are to bring them to has not changed. There has ever been but one (and that an all-effective one) cure for the sin problem, and that is the precious Blood of Jesus that saves from all sin.

I can tell you that opposition surfaces from everywhere and from the most unexpected places to the reality of a Savior who can cleanse from all sin, but He can still do it, and He will continue to do it until old Satan's last word has been forever silenced. There is nowhere else to go; the Blood is enough! Hallelujah! I'm getting happier by the minute writing about it! I must confess with shame that I tried "anger management" and "behavior modification," but I was never able to keep the weeds from sprouting again until the Blood of Jesus Christ eradicated them! How can I advocate anything else to others?

With Christian love and joy,
William Cawman

†††

September 1, 2011

UNBELIEVERS AND DISOBEDIENT hearts say as they tremble before Satan's power, "Who can stand before the children of Anak!" (Deuteronomy 9:2) But all unknown to them, Satan trembles as he says, "Who can stand before his indignation? and who can abide in the fierceness of his anger? his fury is poured out like fire, and the rocks are thrown down by him." (Nahum 1:6) Please keep this in mind as we relate the following prayer request.

About three weeks ago I received a written request from a man I had not talked to before and as he sat down, rather nervously, in front of me I noticed that he was heavily tattooed with satanic symbols and cultish emblems. He wasted no time getting to the point. "Chaplain, I have been deeply involved in satanic worship and in the occult. I have read the satanic bible and have gotten myself tattooed with symbols and I've gotten caught up in mystical and magical activities and now I'm scared. Is there any hope that God would want me now? I actually sold my soul to Satan. Is there any way out? I'm scared."

I looked at him and instantly my heart went out in longing to him as I said, "The first thing you need to do is get on your knees and thank God that you are scared. If there were no hope for you in God you wouldn't be sitting there asking me if there was. The very fact that you are scared and want to approach God is proof that He is knocking at your door." "Oh, what a relief. I was afraid I had gone too far. But what shall I do about going to church with all these satanic tattoos on my body?" I said, "Do you have a long-sleeved shirt?" "Yes, I do." "Then put it on and keep the sleeves down and go to church." "Oh, all right, I can do that." And all this while his face was becoming more and more relaxed from the anxiety he had come in with. I enrolled him in the classes and services and the next time I visited with him he said he was finding light from God.

Please pray that he will not stop short of a complete spiritual blood transfusion and become a "new creature in Christ Jesus." I told him about a young man in Guatemala who once motioned for me to come where he was kneeling at the altar. He told me that there was a time in his life when he told Satan that he could have all there was of him. He said the months that followed that were horrible beyond description, but that he had there that night told Jesus He could have all there was of him and the spell of Satan was broken off of him.

Thank God there is no point a soul can go to that is beyond Deuteronomy 4:29— "But if from *thence* [find that if you can] thou shalt seek the LORD thy God, thou shalt find him, if thou seek him with all thy heart and with all thy soul."

Another new contact this month also pulls on my heart. A man wanted to see me who had just come into the prison and was still healing up from his latest encounter with the police. His head was split open and his wrist was broken from the scuffle they went through to arrest him. He has a history of drugs and violent living that is all too common in our inner cities today. He is tired of this lifestyle. Who wouldn't be? The devil's promises burn out very quickly and very disappointingly.

As I began to point him to a new pathway that God would love to lead him into, he looked at me and said, "Chaplain, look at my arms. I have goose bumps all over me. No one ever talked to me like this before. I know there is a reason why I am sitting here in front of you today. This is God's call to me. I really do want to be a new man from what I have been and I know only God can do that for me."

When the law enforcement finally catches up with a man like this, anger boils and "the book is thrown" at him. When the loving Jesus finally catches up with a man like this He so tenderly says, "...it is hard for thee to kick against the pricks." And there is something in the tone of Jesus' words that melt that soul into a humbling acknowledgement, "Yes, Lord, it is; '...what wilt Thou have me do?'" Please pray that he will do it!

I must share a victory with you. Several months ago we mentioned as a prayer request the situation over having a place to hold our classes and Bible studies since the commissioner decided to remove the officers from our chapel areas except on Sunday nights. For a while we were bumped around with a fairly clear message that we were not welcome by many, and we sometimes did not know where we would end up.

We asked you to pray about the situation, for it is very obvious that the "antichrist" is making himself known in the atmosphere about anything that bears the name of Jesus. Thank you so much for your prayers. A short while ago the chief of custody gave orders that we were to be given rooms in the academic area in which to have our classes. These rooms are very well adapted, with all the equipment we might need from time to time and even with individual desks for the students.

Besides God answering that prayer, He allowed us to have

posted officers in both facilities one and two who have proved to be not only friendly to us, but extremely helpful as well. I mentioned this in the June letter and asked you to pray that we would get an officer in facility three who would be just as helpful.

A few weeks ago one was finally selected and after about two classes he asked me if he could have a Bible and one of the text books we were using for our class. Even though our supply of them is limited, how could I do other than to give them to him when you had prayed for him? Thank you, every one who prayed. We know better than to settle into much of a comfort zone, even while we enjoy God's provisions, for we have certainly learned the truth here that "...we have no certain dwelling place."

Even with what I have just written, the battle intensifies, and mostly with reference to the Muslim population. I trust it is still safe to write this plainly, but if America does not wake up quickly she will wake up too late. The Muslim influence from the White House down is becoming alarmingly aggressive everywhere it appears.

For perhaps four or five years now, the policy that has been dictated to the administration of this prison is to handle it with care so as not to have any trouble. Satan laughs with hellish laughter when cowards handle him with white gloves, and so does the "religion" he is pushing down sleeping America's throat. As a consequence the prison here has developed an untouchable giant in the person of the Islamic chaplain. No one is allowed to discipline him or dictate to him, not even his supervisor or superiors.

The Muslim population is growing rapidly and we have discovered, almost by accident, that the majority of the tier reps among the inmate population are Muslims. Little by little, yet as aggressively as an angry cancer, they spread their agenda while men sleep. This coming week will see the end of the fast of Ramadan, and the feast of Eid, and it is obvious that the Muslim chaplain is using the occasion to try to make something go wrong so that our supervisor will appear incompetent, for he passionately wants his position.

Perish the thought that he could one day be in charge of all chaplaincy in this prison. One can only think about it for a bit, then we must turn to God and pray, "O Lord, You are the One who opened this door of ministry. You can keep it open just as long as You see fit, regardless of men and Satan." It pains my heart to think of some of my precious brethren who are washed in the Blood and sanctified by the Spirit, left without any help from the outside, but God knows all about this, too. We again request prayer for this most serious condition.

I am happy to tell you that once again our brother who several times has fallen under the enemy's trap of bitterness over the spiritual condition of many of the teachers that come into the prison has caught himself and is humbling his heart before God and others. One thing you will have to say for him is that when God gets through to him he will spare nothing to humble himself and take the right way out.

We had a very good talk today and really, down deep inside, he is so tender and loving and hungry for God. I tried to place myself in his position (a life sentence which started at 17 years of age) and see how he would feel about that viewpoint, but I'm not sure I was successful. I then explained to him that neither could he see things from the perspective of those who were looking at the larger picture he could not get sight of.

He agreed and we resolved to lay aside what we couldn't see and love Jesus and live for Him and love each other. I told him that whenever he gets discouraged over the prevalence of false teaching and goes down under it, one more light for the truth dies and a cloud comes over him. I told him that I appreciate his zeal for God and truth, but that God was not requiring of him what was an impossibility in his position. He recognized that and I hope he remembers it. Do pray for the dear man that he will catch and learn his lesson this time and never fall into that trap again.

As I write this letter (Friday afternoon, August 26) we are

preparing for Hurricane Irene. There is a minimum security prison about fifteen miles from here where about 1200 inmates are housed in trailers. Since they are predicting the possibility of the worst hurricane in decades, all 1200 inmates are being moved from the trailers into other prisons around the state. I have heard conflicting reports of how many are coming here, but just now they are putting mattresses all over the visit halls and at least one of our chapel areas, and tomorrow they will transport men and house them over the weekend in these makeshift huge dormitories.

One can only hope they do not contract an episode of intestinal bacteria or virus during their stay as there will be only two bathrooms for every 100 men. As a consequence of this move, all Sunday night services have been cancelled for this coming Sunday. Somehow I have a feeling that since we have prepared ourselves so well—abandoning the seashore towns, etc.—Irene may decide to take an ocean voyage and leave us to rebalance the state budget for nothing, but I may of course be wrong. I am a chaplain, not a weather forecaster. I'm not sure which of the two needs to be deader to his approval rating.

I interrupted this letter at this point to go to the Bible study in Facility Three. It was a very good lesson and I believe the truth really got home to many of the men. I then went over to Facility One and they were already in lockdown because all available spaces were packed with rubber mattresses for the incoming inmates tomorrow. It seems they are bringing anywhere from 500 to 900 men in and bedding them down like sardines (hopefully without the mustard). We will see by Monday morning what the condition is.

Please pray for our new prison administrator. Our former one retired the first of August and we have a new one just arrived a few days ago. Politics has no inherent properties for self-cleansing or for growth in Christian graces—none! Therefore it is so important that he see things the way he should. Evil and wrong is viciously aggressive and already it is evident that his ears are hearing from sources that could set us back even further in our ability to keep the Gospel door open. Please pray that He who holds the hearts of kings in His hands will rule and overrule until His will can continue to be done.

Thank you for your prayers,
William Cawman

12
MY SAVIOR HAS MY TREASURE

October 1, 2011

SOMETIMES WE ARE REMINDED quite effectively that we are working among "tattered garments" of humanity. We who have been raised in sheltered Christian homes and taught from early youth principles of truth and honesty learn with difficulty that not everyone shares those values and that the old chains do not break as easily as we could wish.

One day recently the men started coming into the classroom for Christian Living class and after only two or three had entered I noticed a tall, thin, young black man sobbing hysterically with his head bowed over his desk. One of the other men had noticed it first and was laying his hand on his back very gently, so I went over and said a short prayer for him and then leaned down and asked him if it was something he wanted to share with us. He shook his head "yes" and then told me in broken sobs that his five-year-old daughter had just been hit by a car and they didn't know if she would make it.

We all felt so moved for him and gathered around. First I prayed, then one man after another prayed for him in a bond of real brotherly love. After we finished and went to our seats, he tried to stand up and started to fall over backwards. A couple of the men caught him and took him into the hall to the drinking fountain, but he still felt quite faint, so they began to escort him out of the building and up the alley to the medical facility. A sergeant saw them and asked them why there had been no code 53 (medical emergency) called and they stopped to explain just how it happened and he told them to go ahead.

When they got to the clinic the nurse asked him what had brought it on and so he told her about his daughter. The nurse then looked up his records and he had no biological children on record. I will have to stop the story there—sorry—for that is all that I know, except to say that he is back in class again. All one can do is wonder.

Please do pray especially for the man we have mentioned several times who was doing so well until propositioned by a female officer. He has really struggled ever since and is still struggling. Recently he did start coming back and doing better, but he is dropping out again and has told me that he is just so powerless to live above sin. He is dodging me again when I call him down for a visit and I think it is because he feels so discouraged, hopeless, and ashamed. He knows I love him and he will not stay away forever but oh, how I long to see him break through to real victory again.

I see more and more that discouragement is one of Satan's most frequently successful weapons to defeat souls. If he can get a person's ear in discouragement he then throws all of his other artful arrows in right behind it. One could wonder how many souls are in hell whose downward spiral began with giving in to discouragement.

On the brighter side, another man who spent some precious time in giving in to the same tactic of Satan has now come up and out again and is doing so much better. The other day I had a visit with him. Then at the close of it the next man I had on the list came into the room and I just asked them both to stay. I wish you could sit in on one of those visits with these men! It was a precious time of God's presence that came to a close way too soon. I thank God for these lights in a dark place.

Over and over I realize how wonderful it is that God has raised up a band from our church to go in and fill all the vacancies and give the true Gospel from various witnesses, but beyond all that I really thank God that He has a few, even in Sardis, who have not defiled their garments (that is, since He washed them)! They are able to minister in ways that we cannot, for no one can point at them and say, "Oh yes, but you go home every night—we have to stay here!" No, they stay there every night and every day and every moment of those long dreary days, and they keep the glow of inward grace shining upon them. God bless the few who really shine like this. And—they need your prayers, too!

Recently a man joined our class and by his looks I thought he was probably from South America somewhere. I was passing out a little Spanish holiness paper that one of our missionaries in Mexico publishes monthly and I asked him if he could read Spanish. "No, not Spanish—Hebrew. I'm a Jew." "Well, praise the Lord," I said, "I need to have a visit with you." He readily agreed to that and so we shortly after sat down to get acquainted.

Now I must confess that I have a huge soft spot in my heart for our Hebrew brethren. Why should I not? They gave us our Bible, our Faith, our Messiah. True it is that many "received Him not," but some did. The first Christian Church was all Jews. The Bible was entirely written by Jews. Our theology was given to us by Jews. Thank God for the ones who "received Him!" Well, I asked him to tell me about himself and how he had come to be a Christian now.

He was born in Brooklyn and grew up studying the Torah and the Mishna (the huge commentary on the Pentateuch as well as a conglomeration of laws and precepts that the rabbis came up with during the millenium before AD 200). He was sent to Yeshiva (school for Jewish boys) but questions kept coming up in his mind as to why the Bible said one thing and the Jewish interpretations (Mishna) said something else.

One day he was passing through a city park near his home and he saw some rough boys mishandling his neighbor girl. He picked up a stick and went after them, telling them that was no way to treat a girl. When she got home she told her mother and she came out and invited him to come into their home. She began to treat him very kindly and then told him that she knew he was of the Jewish faith, but that she would like to give him a New Testament, telling him that he would find that his Messiah had already come. He began to read it and even more questions came into his mind as he continued his studies at the Yeshiva. His instructors began to question him as to where he was coming up with all these questions and when they discovered him reading the New Testament they kicked him out of the Yeshiva.

After this he went into the Israeli army and there his morals were corrupted and he drifted away from his thoughts about God. After getting out of the army he married and had a daughter, but that only lasted about three years, as he was so deeply involved in drugs and alcohol by this time that it was all he cared about. It wasn't until that landed him in prison that he again began to turn his thoughts toward God.

Now he says he really has a good relationship with God and Jesus is his Savior. He says that he knows that God has forgiven his sins. I will be looking forward to some future visits with him.Of course, he would not be as knowledgeable as the rabbi who was an inmate a few years ago, because he dropped out of their studies as just a young man.

I do trust, however, that his being here will be a means of him getting as intimately acquainted with his Messiah as Jesus wants him to be. Please remember him in your prayers, too.

Often when I have been gone and return I get some feedback from what the other brethren tell them in the interim. After returning the other day I asked the first class I was in if they enjoyed and loved my pastor who had filled in for me.

They shook their heads yes, but one man said, "Oh yeah, I really do love him! Ya' know, he talked to us about what he called 'border-line sins,' ya' know, like—well, he talked to us about commercial sports. I didn't know about that at first, but when I went away and thought about it, ya' know, he was right on. I see exactly what he was talking about now that I've thought about it."

What did we do? Jumped into the open furrow and dug the raw trench some more. We went from there to the entertainment industry. As I described to them how far removed from the image of Jesus a modern entertainer is they began to laugh. I pictured him with his extremely odd clothing, his dirty-looking messed-up hair, his face all sweaty, wearing a guitar strap that was long enough to accommodate the arms of an orangutan, making his guitar dangle down around his knees while he strummed absolutely abominable noise from it that desecrated every rule of harmony and music composition ever known to human art. Then I tried screwing up my face into a distortion of agony such as could be produced by the tortures of the Spanish inquisition techniques—and guess what? I think they began to see it as pretty freakish, too. We then went back to what God had created man for and how far removed from it sin had taken us.

A couple days later we got on the same subject in another facility and after pointing out all the factors that render commercial sports sinful to a Christian, one man tried to close the discussion by turning in his seat to all the class and saying, "What we're saying isn't that it's wrong to watch a football game on television, but just don't make it your idol." I replied, "First of all, get alone with Jesus until you are intensely in love with Him and then see how He feels about that opinion." Do you want to come join us? It will be far more interesting than watching a ball game!

Once again today I sat and listened to the same thing I've heard so many times from men in prison. "Chaplain, I need to ask you a question. You see, I'm soon to go home and my wife is now going to the Jehovah Witness church and she says she doesn't want me coming home and trying to push the Bible and teach them. She says maybe it's best if I don't come home, but we just go our own ways. Do you think that's what I should do? Is it time to just let her go? You know the Bible says, '...if the unbelieving depart, let them depart.'"

I said, "Well, let's back up a step. When the two of you got married had you ever been married to anyone else?" "Oh no, it was a first for both of us." I said, "Then in God's sight you are husband and wife until one of you dies." Immediately I could see the rejection emotion kicking in. "But Chaplain, there's this other good brother and he says that if she departs that's the same as death. That breaks the relationship." I said, "You can twist the words of Jesus and Paul as many others have done and go get another woman if you so desire, but let me tell you what will happen to your relationship with Jesus."

As I went on to point out to him the clarity of God's Word regarding it he began to soften and finally said, "Chaplain, I see it. The Bible is clear and I can't deny what it says."

Then I said, "Now listen a minute; you are soon to go home to your wife who will be your wife until one of you dies. Let's get first things first. You must be true to God, you have to make heaven." "Oh, Chaplain, I must make it to heaven!" "Then don't let anything bring a cloud between you and God. But your next obligation is to be the best husband and father that you can possibly be. Don't argue religion. Don't try to cram your viewpoint onto them. Just live a Christ-like joyful life before them and let me show you what God's Word says may well happen."

Then we went to the Scripture where it says that the unbelieving spouse is sanctified by the believer—that is, nothing will bring them to God quicker than seeing a truly happy Christian. He left the room obviously lighter than when he came in, promising to do all he could to obey God and be a good husband. He will need your prayers too, won't he?

Now we have one more problem we need your prayers

about. If you remember a few months back we had asked you to pray that God would provide a place where we could have our Bible studies and classes because the commissioner had taken away our chapel officers. They gave us the original rooms made in the prison for assemblies like that, but now (and the Sunday School quarterlies are having a lot to do with it) we have outnumbered the occupancy limit for that room by about 130%. The officer is saying we have to do something with the numbers. We think the solution is quite simple—put us back where we belong. Will you pray that they will see this as the solution and not try to limit the men who want to come?

Thank you ever so much for praying for us,
William Cawman

November 1, 2011

HAS OUR GOD EVER failed to keep His own Word? I'm sure without exception you all know what the answer is, and yet it seems we must ever be learning in fresh ways that He is altogether trustworthy. This is exactly what the songwriter was referring to when he wrote the words, "Oh for grace to trust Him more."

Early in life the absolute trust we came into the world with is broken, and continues to be broken in a thousand ways, because of the imperfect world that sin has created. Our greatest area of growth in grace is to learn to trust the never-failing God, for all else does fail.

Last month I told you about a man who had come in wondering if he should let his marriage go since his wife was now a Jehovah Witness and didn't want him preaching the Bible to her and their child. I told him that was definitely not God's will and that God's Word makes no provision for remarriage while both companions are still alive. He sat there and weighed the cost and left saying he was going to mind God, for he had to make it to heaven.

Well, a couple of weeks went by and I'm sure some of you prayed for him as we asked. He came with a big smile and said, "Chaplain, do you know what happened? I called my wife and before I could say anything she said, 'I want to tell you that I have decided to honor our marriage.' Isn't God good?" I agreed He was and I'm glad He answers prayer, too. Had he backed up and counted the cost too great to obey God he would have tied God's hands completely to answer as He did. Now let's pray that God will unite the marriage on solid Biblical Christian living.

Our dear brother from Haiti sat down with me the other day and told me the following account. He had been going through some anxieties over the likelihood that he will be deported back to Haiti when he finishes his sentence, and really it is not anything unusual that he should feel anxious. It has been so long since he was there and things have changed so much. Besides that, most men sense some degree of anxiety or uncertainty when leaving prison anyway, because they are stepping out into such a changing world.

He said that as he brought his feelings to the Lord an old hymn began going over in his mind in French. It was the song, "Trust and Obey." He wanted to find the words in English but old memories of it in French kept coming to him. As he was walking past a trash can he saw an old hymnal lying on the edge of it and he picked it up and started for the index to see if he could find that song. As he did, it fell open to number 349— "Trust and Obey." He began reading it and came to the words, "What He says we will do; where He sends we will go; never fear, only trust and obey." It brought such a confirmation to his heart that his anxieties calmed and he was able to rest in trust, knowing that he would obey. Perhaps God is preparing another missionary for Haiti?

Recently one of the men in Christian Living class had a cell mate who was released and so he began praying that God would send him someone who would be comfortable to live with. One afternoon a young man entered his cell with his bag of possessions and immediately began cursing and ranting and claiming to be a worshipper of Satan, etc. He was anything other than what the other man had been asking God for, but he immediately decided to make the best of it. So he began to speak softly to him and let him know he cared about him.

In a couple of days the young man began to calm down and actually stopped to listen as the other man talked with him about how undesirable it would be to go on in the direction he was going. The young man told him he had dipped deeply into the occult and Wicca and had sold his soul to Satan and all of the practices that go along with it. He said he wasn't happy and asked his cell mate if there was any hope for him to change.

His cell mate brought him down to Bible study that night and got up and told everyone just what condition the young man was in as he sat there and listened. Yet at the same time his cell mate did it with obvious love and concern for him, and I could not detect that he was resenting it at all. When his cell mate finished I asked him if he would like to say anything for himself. He stood up and confirmed what his cell mate had said, but told the men he did not want to go any further in his present state. There was a volume of approval and support that I believe really touched his heart.

He then asked if he could talk with me so I put him on the appointment sheet to come down for a visit. He came right on time and really opened up about his condition. When faced with powers of either the underworld of Satanic involvement or even the deep dregs of sensual sins, I do not pry into it any further than men feel the need of confessing. I firmly believe that God's desire for man from the beginning was to never become knowledgeable of sin at all. There is grave danger to any soul when even a natural curiosity about what goes on behind closed doors is yielded to. Scripture plainly warns us, "Let no man beguile you of your reward in a voluntary humility and worshipping of angels, intruding into those things which he hath not seen..." (Colossians 2:18). We will encounter all of the sin that we need to know about in order to avoid it just by living in this world. With great carefulness we must obey God's warning, "And others save with fear, pulling them out of the fire; hating even the garment spotted by the flesh" (Jude 1:23).

He told me he was fighting fierce battles within as he tried to think about coming away from Satan and turning to God. Even as he sat there he looked out the window at those passing by and said, "See those people out there? Everything inside of me wants to get up and smash that window and really hurt somebody. I'm just raging inside to hurt people. The other day an officer told me that someone had dropped a slip on me that they wanted to hurt me and asked me if I wanted to go to protective custody. I told him I didn't want that and then he asked me if I had done anything to anyone to make them want to hurt me. I said to him, 'Officer, if you will wait right here while I go to my cell, I'll bring you a stack of charges I've received this thick (holding his fingers about 3 inches apart) and then after you read them all you can call me back out and tell me yourself if I have done anything to make someone want to hurt me.'"

I urged him to immediately look to God and plead the Blood of Jesus. I told him not to try to fight this battle against Satan in his own mind or strength or he would lose, but that there is nothing Satan can do against the power in the Blood of Jesus.

Later in prayer for him I was reminded that Jesus our Savior actually invaded Satan's hell and wrenched the keys of both death and hell out of Satan's hands. Surely, to wrench this poor soul who has gone so far into Satan's domain and tasted so much of his hellish power out of Satan's hands needs only his cry for mercy to see it happen.

Oh, how I long to see this man, as well as the one I wrote about a month or two ago, come completely clean just as the Gadarene, "clothed, and in his right mind." I'm glad that God set the boundary line as to how far we could go before He was unable to rescue us. Do you remember where He put it? "But if from thence thou shalt seek the LORD thy God, thou shalt find him, if thou seek him with all thy heart and with all thy soul" (Deuteronomy 4:29). "Thence" is beyond wherever beyond is, isn't that right?

Let me give a little insight into perhaps the fiercest and most frequent battle we fight in prison ministry. You might think it is drug addiction, or pornography, or cigarettes, or drunkenness, etc., but it is none of these, as horrible as they are. It is the damning teachings of a religion that allows sin in a Christian's life. There is not one single foundation for such teaching in the Word of God, but even before the Sacred Book was finished Peter warned that there would be those who would "…wrest, as they do also the other scriptures, unto their own destruction." St. Augustine, for all the good things that he did and said, laid the foundation for this "doctrine of devils." John Calvin, one thousand years later, picked up these seeds of error and formulated a system of doctrine that still bears his name.

Neither of these men ever went on to the destruction of the carnal mind which is "enmity against God," and Satan jumped in right behind them and has infested the huge majority of Christianity to this day with this most damning doctrine. It denies, just as John warned in 1 John 4:3, that "Jesus Christ is come in the flesh." In other words, it denies that Jesus can breathe His nature into our eternal souls and then live His life out through us.

They claim that as long as we are in the flesh we will continue to sin. They ignore the plain truth that Enoch was in the flesh and He pleased God. Jesus was in the flesh and He sinned not. They ignore the clear Biblical statements that the person who sins is of the devil and the child of God does not sin. They insist that once a person is saved they can do nothing to lose their eternal reward in heaven. In fact, one TV evangelist boasted that he would have no fear of dying in the arms of a prostitute, he was so secure of heaven.

It is this tidal wave of Satanic teaching that we encounter over and over. By far the largest majority of men who would attend religious services after coming to prison would have had some degree of church background before they came. Their allowance for sin in a Christian allowed them to come to prison, yet they will still contend that one cannot live free from sin, and that once saved he cannot be lost.

To make the situation even worse, those thus taught—especially those who have really studied it—become very arrogant and untouchable and confrontational. In a few cases I have borne with them patiently for a while and then addressed them in private and asked them to desist their arguing in class as they have not been appointed to teach it. One man, extremely arrogant, replied, "I will speak up because I will stand up for the truth." I returned, "No, you will not, for I am removing your name from the appointment sheet."

Satan is bold enough to appear as the sons of God present themselves before the Lord, as we read in the opening statements of Job. Those who become infested with his spirit develop the same obnoxious attitudes and love to present themselves among the righteous. Sin is its very ugliest when it dresses in a religious garb.

And so, after a time many of these quit coming and resort to the courtyard to catch the ear of weak souls and criticize those preaching the truth. Then for a while we might have a group that is more or less of one accord and wanting to hear the true way of holiness. Then it seems we must fight the battle all over again as new applicants come in, having never heard any other teaching than that we must sin because we are human, but that God understands and forgives it all.

One man actually prayed, "Lord, please forgive us for all the sins we have committed, all the sins we are committing right now, and all the sins we are going to commit." That is no better than the medieval sale of indulgences, whereby a person could buy forgiveness ahead of time for any sin he planned to commit. I must say from experience that it is harder to get a man out of this damning doctrine than out of Roman Catholicism. True grace not only loves sin-destroying truth, but hates contention and strife, and therefore we shall by God's help and grace continue to shine for Jesus and teach that "there [is] a fountain opened in the house of David for all sin and for all uncleanness."

Here and there a truly born-again soul hears, rejoices, and plunges in.

In Him,
William Cawman

Interlude

December 1, 2011

ELEVEN YEARS AGO this month the first prison newsletter was mailed out. There has been one every month since, until now. Please forgive me, but I cannot write about the prison work this time, for my loving Savior has taken my precious wife of forty-one years up home to Himself in heaven. Oh, how much I miss her already, but there is nothing but a greater love for Jesus than I have ever known before in my heart. She has only gone before me and I am on my way.

For many years she has suffered with deep physical infirmities, and just before Christmas of 1992 one of Philadelphia's top surgeons told me, "I've done what I could, but I don't know if she will make it. If she does she will never function again." I lay on my bed that night with hot tears streaming down my cheeks onto the pillow as I looked up into the dark ceiling and said over and over, "God, it's all right. You gave her to me, You can have her." Two days later in answer to prayers around the world from God's great loving family, Jesus came by her side and touched her. In His great love He gave her back to me for the best nineteen years of our lives.

From the moment of that healing she lived a fairly normal

life—absolutely a continuing miracle of divine healing. Doctors would examine her and shake their heads that she was able to absorb any nourishment, but she would smile and say, "But I can."

The last several months again she has been battling with a lung condition, perhaps unrelated to the former battle with Crohn's Disease, but also an auto-immune malfunction. We thought the condition was improving and they were tapering her from the devastating steroids she had to take for it. We were in Colorado Springs, CO, for a revival meeting from Nov 21-30, then came home into a revival meeting being held in our own church. The next day we left for a revival in Tennessee from Nov 7-13, then to another one just west of Pittsburg scheduled Nov 15-20. On Wednesday evening Nov 16 she played the piano and we sang together, never dreaming that by Sunday evening she would be in heaven.

Thursday afternoon she was typing a letter to our daughter in Africa when she said, "I feel like I'm getting the flu." We took her temperature and found she had a high fever and got her to bed. I went on to church and when I came home she was on the couch. As we talked she had a spell that was quite frightening and we sensed her heart was racing. We gave her some more medicine and went to bed, but I had no intention of sleeping—I went there to pray and keep watch over her.

She began coughing more and more and I knew it was getting serious. Up until then I really had very little warning of what was going on. I do remember her saying a day or two earlier that she wondered if the lung condition was coming back. I don't remember what I said to her but I remember her saying in a very low voice, "I don't know if I'm going to live much longer." Of course I didn't hear that.

By one o'clock in the morning on Friday I knew I had to do something. I had been lying there praying for guidance. We were five hours from Jefferson Hospital in Philadelphia where the doctors who knew her were. I considered trying to get her there, but I thank God we did not try it for she would have never made it. I called an ambulance and they took her to a hospital north of Pittsburg.

After a few hours on a C-Pap machine she was only getting worse and so they wanted to put her on a respirator in hopes that they could reverse the chemistry of her lungs and blood. I told her what they wanted to do and she did not want it, but I told her there was a chance they could bring her out. She nodded and they put it in. Within a few hours things looked a little bit encouraging and my hopes were lifted. She was completely sedated, so I left and went back to the church and preached that night.

The next morning when I returned to the hospital and was standing by her bed the lung doctor came in and told me that she was getting worse and he did not think she would make it. Oh, what a knife went through my heart. I just had not let myself be prepared for that.

I called our pastor and the children, and immediately our pastor and his wife got in the car and headed out for us. They arrived about 6:00 Saturday evening and what a blessing to have them with us. My sister and husband and our older daughter, who was about three hours away, came and then the pastor and his wife stayed with me all that night.

About 4:00 am on Sunday she began to take another turn for the worse. About 10:30 that Sunday morning, Nov 20, I asked the nurses to lower her sedation so that I could talk with her. They did but were not sure she would be able to. She opened her eyes and began looking at us. Around her were myself, my sister and her husband, our daughter Grace and a friend that had come with her, and our pastor and wife.

As she began to respond by movements only, I leaned over in her ear and said, "Sweetheart, I wish I could keep you, but it looks like Jesus is ready to take you home to heaven, and it's all right—I told Him He could have you. But Sweetheart, when you see Jesus will you tell Him that I'm coming?" She nodded her head Yes. Then I said, "You love Jesus, don't you?" Again she nodded Yes.

I said a few more heart things to her and then we began to sing— "Jesus is the sweetest name I know; and He's just the same as His lovely name. And that's the reason why I love Him so…" and on that phrase she tried to raise both hands at once. We sang it again and she tried the second time at the same words. I leaned over and said, "Sweetheart, I felt you try to raise your hands; I'll help you." By then she was beginning to spasm and we had to let them turn the sedation up again.

My pastor and wife felt I needed to try to get some rest, and indeed I was emotionally exhausted. I went into the waiting room, but every time I would start to drift off I came to in a panic, "Where is she!?" I gave up and went back and my pastor sat down beside me and asked what we should do.

Just then I realized why I could not rest—hope was gone and now we were allowing them to do what she did not want at all. I realized that it would only be selfish to hold her any longer and not let her go home to Jesus where she wanted to be. When I accepted that a rest came to my agitations and I asked them to lower the sedation one more time so that our son could talk to her on the phone in her ear and that then they could remove the respirator. They did and again she was able to recognize us, but when they removed the respirator she was in heaven within ten minutes.

Friends, I have no options—I must make heaven! As I drove home the next day I promised God as never before that every thought, every action, every choice—my all was entirely His. I promised Him that even my grief was His and that I choose to embrace this painful valley.

As I did so I found and am still finding riches of grace I never knew existed. I have never needed the Comforter as I am finding Him to be now. I am so thankful to God for everything, and there is nothing—nothing at all— in my heart except love to Him. Only God can make bitter sweet. And some of this He does through His wonderful family of loving brothers and sisters. I thank every one of you for each thought, each prayer, each call, each card and text message. I cannot express how much it means to be a part of the family of God. I will obey Him with a greater love than ever before.

Before my precious sweetheart went away I asked her to please tell Jesus for me that I thank Him for giving her to me, such a wonderful wife, and that I thank Him now for taking her home to Himself. While I am stricken with grief, she is basking in the smile of His unclouded face. How can I be selfish and wish it otherwise?

God gave me a precious wife. As I stood by her bedside, this time for the last time, I felt such a wave of rest come over me that in all our lives together there were no scars, no regrets. I thank God and God alone, but I also thank her for her devotion to the Savior she loved. She loved her husband and her family, she loved everyone, but she loved Jesus best of all.

For over forty-one years a plaque given to us for our wedding has hung over our bed which says, "God gives His best to those that leave the choice with Him." How many times one or the other of us over the years have pointed to it and said, "That's true." She just did it a short time ago. He is still giving His best to me, for the song writer said, "My Savior has my treasure, and He will walk with me." I will walk with Him, too. I love Him with all my heart.

Your Brother in Jesus,
William Cawman

13
Dramatized Choices

January 1, 2012

Please suffer a few personal lines before telling you about things in the prison. I want to thank everyone who has sent a card or email or text message or made a call during the past few weeks. Next to God Himself, His precious family has been a support and comfort I cannot place a value on.

As I have continued to embrace my Savior's will, even in this valley, He has become richer to my heart than I have ever known Him before. And through this I believe I have learned a lesson by experience that I only knew perhaps in theology before. It is this: no matter what we as God's children may yet have to pass through before we see His face, there is going to be more than sufficient grace to come through it altogether right with God.

I would never have known this particular grace I am finding so precious without the loss of the dearest on earth to me. I can testify without a shadow that this great work of heart holiness works even in the valley of grief, and I love Jesus with all my heart. A friend sent me the following verse which has been of such unspeakable comfort to me that it is now in my Bible where I turn each day:

> "E'en for the dead I will not bind my soul to grief,
>   Death cannot long divide
> For is it not as though the Rose that climbed my
>   garden wall
>   Has blossomed on the other side?
>   Death doth hide,
>   But not divide;
>   Thou art but on Christ's other side!
>   Thou art with Christ, and Christ with me;
>   In Christ united still are we.

Thank you each one for your prayers. I love each one of you through Jesus. Now let me tell you of what this has done among the men in prison.

When I returned among them I found such love and support and tenderness that one would never have imagined these were men that society has shut away. They had made me several homemade cards which were beautiful with intense artwork, and then many of them had signed their names with a short note of condolence. It made me love them all the more.

But the reactions were not all the same. One man came to see me and sat in front of me and said, "Chaplain, I want to be perfectly honest; I have really been struggling with this. I have actually felt some anger at God for taking your precious wife away. Look at all the marriages out there that are doing nothing for God and doing no good for anyone, and here you and your wife were united in God's work and travelling together and God took her. I just don't understand it."

I looked at him and said, "You don't know Jesus like I do. I feel not one trace of anger or argument with God. Just listen to me now. God gave me a precious gift for over forty-one years. She lived to make it to heaven just like I am doing. God saw that her work here was finished and He took her home to heaven ahead of me and how can I feel anything but love for Him for being so good to my dear wife?"

He looked at me with wonder and said, "I have seen something I never saw before. I want it, too." In so many words several said, "We all feel your pain, but we are all seeing that what you have preached to us works." Lord, whatever it takes. It will be worth it all to make it to where she has gone.

Two weeks before Christmas Sunday I was holding a service in the prison hospital. While we were singing Christmas carols, special investigations personnel were just down the hallway photographing the body of the fifth man to die in four days; the seventh in eleven days. They no sooner left his door than a code 53 was called; another medical emergency was making us wonder if another one was going. I tried to keep the song service going extra long until the activities calmed down, and then preached to them from the Scripture, "Let us now go…and see."

One of the men who had been listening very attentively suddenly spoke up and said, "I know we can find Him, because I did once. Oh, it was so wonderful and real. I knew I had found Him and He was so precious to me for a while, but I don't have that now and I wish I did. When I got out of prison I wanted my girlfriend to know all about it, too, but she handed me a stack of one hundred dollar bills this thick (holding his fingers about two inches apart) and I went right back to the drugs with her again. I wish I could find that again." I did my best to encourage him to really seek expecting God to meet him again and to turn from all sin. Please pray for him.

Early this next Spring will complete fourteen years of ministering in this prison. Let me reflect a little on the direction things are going. When I started we had a Catholic priest who would minister to the Catholics, a Muslim chaplain who would conduct the Muslim prayer services each Friday, and then we had a Protestant chaplain and quite a number of Protestant volunteers. There was very little interface or interference either one between the three groups.

Today the chaplain supervisor is busy absolutely full time with setting up forums for pagan gods and their various requirements. This month there will be the annual celebration for the worshippers of Odin, the chief god of the ancient Scandinavians. They will require a forum to sit around the ancient Yule log (of course it cannot burn here) while they sip nectar and eat pork.

Then we have the Jewish Hanukkah being observed. Then we will have a sweat lodge ceremony for the Native American prison population of our entire state prison system on the 29th of December. It will be in the sweat lodge built with special willow withes after a fire has been built down by the duck pond and rocks have been heated upon which water will be poured to cause the participants to sweat out all their evil spirits. The transportation of the inmates from around the state and adequate supervision for the event will be funded by our taxpayers.

Then we will also have a meeting for the Buddhists in which they will sit around on the bean bags provided, facing their little statue of Buddha and whatever that entails.

You wonder what part of the expense for all of this goes toward Bibles and good Christian books? I think you know.

All this has come about in fourteen years, and yet America blindly goes on this Christmas buying their toys and feasting royally and having their fun. Oh, what is that I hear? "But as the days of Noah were, so shall also the coming of the Son of man be. For as in the days that were before the flood they were eating and drinking, marrying and giving in marriage, until the day that Noah entered into the ark, And knew not until the flood came, and took them all away; so shall also the coming of the Son of man be." What will be the condition of our precious country if Jesus tarries another fourteen years? He may not!

Some of you have asked me about the man I wrote of in the November letter, who had given himself to Satan and was so terribly wrecked by him. While I was away he caused more difficulties (he has no less than fifty-eight institutional charges against him to date) and they moved him to another facility in the prison, and all the officers there were warned about him. He tried to go to church and the officers would not let him. They told him to go back to his cell, that his reputation was too bad for him to be with other men.

As soon as I could I put him on the visit list and when he went to come to me the officers said, "What chaplain wants to see you? What could he want with you?" He sat down and for some time all I could do was to let him vent his anger. He is a seething volcano of rage and anger on the inside. He is the exact opposite of the beauty of Jesus. He wants to hurt anyone he can.

After a while I began to talk to him. "I can see that you are absolutely full of anger, but there is more of you than your wrecked emotions. You also have intelligence. Now I want you to step aside from your emotions and listen to me. You have a choice to make. You will either spiral downward the way you're going and snap and go to hell for all eternity, or you can choose to pray to God that He will come into your heart and change you into a new man. I want you to know that I really care about you and I love you. Will you go and think about this, and then would you want me to call you down again?"

He said he would and that he did want me to talk to him. I prayed with him and hugged him and thought to myself, "If those officers only knew how much I wanted him!"

The next week when I visited him he seemed much calmer and told me that he was finding help to be "more humble" which was so different for him. I told him that the moment we turn from running away from God and righteousness, and begin to face any part of the way that is right, we immediately begin to feel better, but that he must be sure to seek on and find his heart really changed. Oh, how I would love to see him come completely into the heart of Jesus and become a testimony to all who have known his life before, that there is power in the real Jesus to change the worst case into a marvel of His grace. Please help us pray for this miracle.

We came up to Christmas Sunday with some degree of apprehensions as there had been an escalation of fights, deaths and other disturbances. Two Fridays before Christmas I was planning to spend the entire day in the prison followed by two evening Bible studies. About 10:30 in the morning a couple inmates, in order to get themselves initiated into the gang, jumped an officer and beat him up pretty severely. An ambulance was called which in turn called for an airlift as they feared his skull was fractured. It was not, but of course they immediately shut down the whole prison as far as any further activities were concerned, and so about noon I left and went home.

The following Monday I had some interviews inside the main prison and then went out to the minimum camp to hold some there. While I was walking between the two, a code 22 was called, which is a prison-wide stand-up count, where no one is allowed to move until they get whatever is out of order under control. I knew that would possibly take most of the rest of the day, so again I left and went home, thankful that I did not get trapped inside for it.

With all this going on, we were really praying that God would overshadow the service times for Christmas Sunday as our church was to have four of the five services to be held. We decided to try to take everyone in possible, besides the regular volunteers that go in. Now listen to this bright piece of upbeat news after all the down trend I have told you about above.

When I first started ministering in the prison the administrator was a military retiree who was a very level-headed man afraid of nothing—particularly not his political future. I would ask him if we could have a program for Christmas with all of the Christian inmates together (350 approx) and he would just respond, "Whatever you want to do, Reverend." But all that changed with his retirement, and for over ten years politics has been far more important than the welfare of the inmates or the Christian services.

Just recently we got a new younger black man as administrator and I immediately began to recognize a much more sensible view of things in him. I had asked before if I could bring back into the prison a man who had been imprisoned and was now doing so well on the outside and the answer was, "No! Never!" Some time had passed and with the new administrator I decided to give it a try again. Not only this man, but a woman in our church who had also been in prison not that long ago, filled out applications and I turned them in. In two days they were approved, and what a blessing it was to the men to hear from some that had been right where they were and were now happily following the path of holiness and truth without a failure. I thank God and answered prayer for the blessing it was. We will plan to follow that up with a few more visits from them.

Thank you and a Blessed New Year,
W. Cawman

╬

February 1, 2012

Perhaps I can best relate to you the past month's happenings in what I will call "A Tale of Two Masters." You will find an all-too-fitting foundation for this story in Deuteronomy chapter 28. The first fourteen verses tell the tale of the first Master and the rest of the chapter, turning abruptly at verse 15 and laboring on and on, until verse 68 tells the dismal tale of the second master. Over and over in the past fourteen years I have witnessed this chapter played out in living human drama, but just now I want to narrow it down to two men.

The first one is a man I have written about now and then for several years. I have known and visited with him for well over ten years and have watched "…all these blessings…come on thee, and overtake thee…" for just as many years. I will relate some of his story for the purpose of this narrative as well as for those of you who wouldn't have read it from years ago.

He is a white, strawberry-blonde, medium stature man with a glowing face that would make you a total unbeliever regarding his background. He had served in the military and then joined the police force in one of our ocean cities. He had an unhappy marriage, and being a police officer thought he could cover his tracks, and so he killed his wife and his wife's mother. It didn't work like he had planned and he was caught and put in prison in Trenton. One day while he was in the mess hall a huge black man stood up and pointed at him and told what he had been and what he had done and then sat down. Immediately a swat team rushed in and whisked him out because they knew he was in danger of his life. He was put in solitary confinement for seven years. During that time he got on his knees and began to repent and ask God if he could be forgiven. Jesus came into his heart, forgiving all his terrible sins, and giving him a brand-new start.

Now this dear man had never heard a message on holiness and had no idea why God was dealing with him this way, but every so often he would feel the need to set aside a day for fasting and prayer because of what was down inside him that made him commit that crime. On the tenth anniversary of his crime he was fasting and praying to God when Jesus stood beside him and said, "Son, you don't ever have to do this again. I've taken care of it." He had no idea what to call that. He only knew that from that day on his walk with God was so much deeper and fuller and he was not troubled over what might be on the inside.

Soon after that he was moved to the prison where I am and at the turn of the year my supervisor wanted me to switch places with the Bible teacher in that facility. Someone told our brother that Chaplain Cawman was coming over to teach the Bible studies and that he teaches a false doctrine. He teaches that it is possible to live entirely free from sin. (Strange indeed that the exact purpose of Christ's coming should be construed as false doctrine). It troubled him as he did not want to be subjected to false doctrine.

I noticed him as he sat and listened with a puzzled look on his face for several Bible studies, and then the puzzled look began to break into a smile. He asked if he could talk with me and I readily assented. He said that he could not quite figure out the theology I was teaching but that it was making his heart burn within him. I told him to just stay with the burning heart and then I gave him some little booklets on heart holiness. He read them and wanted to see me again.

"Chaplain, I have read those books and I really want to be completely honest; that's what God has done for me! But—I still don't understand—I can't say I don't sin." "Well, Brother," I said, "The door is closed, there's no recorder on, I've heard everything already anyway, so why don't you just tell me what you are doing?" "Well, I still lust." I said, "Can you explain that a little further?" "Well, such awful thoughts come into my mind." I said, "What do you do when they come; do you sit down and entertain them?" "Oh, no!" He said, "I immediately tell them to get away from me."

I looked at him and said, "My dear brother, would you stop calling that 'sin,' since the Bible doesn't? The Bible says that is being tempted, and furthermore it says that "…blessed is the man that endureth temptation…" Now it cannot be sin if it brings God's blessing." As he began to see the truth of this he walked out into new light and liberty and has held fast ever since, and now he is one of the best full-salvation missionaries we have inside of the prison walls.

I just visited with him again yesterday. Read again those first fourteen verses. You say, "That can't be true for a man locked up in prison with a long sentence, can it?" I wish you could have a visit with him. He just told me that more and more he stands in absolute awe at the marvelous keeping grace of God. The blessings are "overtaking" him—I guess that means they jump on our back when we aren't even looking for them; am I correct?

This dear man has settled it that no matter who his cellmate is (and he has had some raunchy ones), no matter what his lot in life, he is going through with God. Now if you can think of a set of circumstances that would render the first fourteen verses null and void any more than his, I don't know what they would be. He is not just finding sufficient grace to make it through; he is finding grace to be more than a conqueror. God bless him.

Tale two: we reluctantly proceed to verse 15. If the rest of the chapter were not written, this verse alone would be one crying reason to change to the first Master, but how horrible beyond words and even imagination are the things that follow—on and on until we come with groaning and tears to verse 44. The soul cries out, "Enough! Enough!" but the fiendish payback of the second master heeds not groaning, crying, nor sobbing in the night. Verse 45: "Moreover…" Verse 48: "Therefore…" Verse 59: "Then…" Verse 60: "Moreover…" Verse 61: "Also…" When, oh when, will the rolling crashing billows of sin's wages ever cease? Not until the soul in bitter anguish turns back to the first Master. But alas, many never do.

In our last letter we wrote to you about the man who has sold his soul to Satan; has delved into Wicca and Voodoo and whatever else. The very afternoon after the visit I wrote about, he was found on the wrong tier and sent to detention. He wanted to see me so I went over and tried to visit with him, but the other inmates on the tier were shouting to each other and through the closed steel door it was very hard to hear each other.

I went and asked the sergeant if when I came back he could provide a forum so that I could have a one-on-one with him as I had been doing. He said to send him an email and he would ask the lieutenant.

I received an email from the lieutenant saying that he would have to deny my request as there were so many departments that required visits with the inmates there that he could not provide it, so I would just have to visit on the tier.

I sent the correspondence to my supervisor with the following observations: "As I understand my position, I am employed by the State of New Jersey in the Department of Corrections. The name would presuppose that there is something or someone that requires correction. The bottom line of what needs to be corrected is sin and the answer to sin is God. It seems strange to me that we are being crippled in performing what we are employed to do." He sent it on to his supervisor.

The next time I was able to have his food port opened although they said an officer would have to stand by. I didn't figure what we had to say would hurt the officer any, so we had a good visit and he promised me that he would really try to get in touch with God. He looked at me through the little opening and said, "Chaplain, a lot of people have told me they care about me, but I know you really do." Then I left for a meeting in Guatemala.

Upon return I found that he had been released from detention, sent back to the tier for four days and then an officer found a letter in his locker, charged him with gang activity and sent him back to detention. This time he will not be returned to our prison, but sent to one of the northern ones. What had he done? Well, did you read verses 15 through 68?

He showed me the letter. It was from his father who apparently is known for his involvement in the gang of the pagans. I could not see anything in the letter that was gang related, but without a doubt the officers had had enough of him and set him up for more trouble— "Moreover...and then..." I could easily detect that he feels it is hopeless.

No matter where he turns or what he does, they have his number and he is "predestined" to these rolling wages of sin. During the four days he was out of detention, he wanted to see the chaplain. The officer said, "What do you want with the chaplain? Aren't you a Wiccan? We know what you're about. You just want to go find a place to burn some incense and carry on your activities and we aren't going to allow it. What do you want to see the chaplain for?" He said, "It's none of your business."

I stopped him and asked him to listen to me a bit. I said, "These kind of responses are why you are keeping yourself in hot water all the time. Let me tell you how to start turning this around. In a few days you are going to be sent to a new place. Do not talk to them like you did to these people here. You should have said, 'Yes, you are right. I have been involved in Wicca and I am trying to change. That's why I'm wanting to see the chaplain and also, officer, I am not here to give you trouble. I am here to be corrected; will you help me?'"

He looked at me in such a way that I knew he had never conceived of such language before and then shook his head and said, "I see what you are saying."

Does he? Will he? God only knows, for often in the downward spiral of those awful rolling billows of sin and its wages the soul reaches the point Satan has been striving to perfect—that point where the turnaround seems hopeless. Is it? Never, for God Himself said, "But if from thence thou shalt seek the LORD thy God, thou shalt find him, if thou seek him with all thy heart and with all thy soul."

But there is a place underneath the smothering, unrelenting wages of iniquity that Satan's lies seem louder than the call of mercy. The more often the soul makes an effort to get up and falls again, the more hopeless the situation seems. The more times hope is dashed against these billows of darkness, the feebler it becomes.

This is exactly where the man of tale two is as I write this letter to you. My heart weeps for him. He loves me and I can feel that he does. He knows I love him and perhaps that is the only straw he is still clinging to that is preventing his going under completely, but will he seek the Lord with all his heart? Please pray that he does.

The officers in the prison soon spread the word around about a man like this. In a way they can't be criticized for it as they do need to have a heads up when a man is this dangerously close to really hurting someone or many. But all this only exemplifies the description in that long ugly prognosis from verse 15 to verse 68. Does it end well? Read verse 67. I have had grown men sit before me with huge tears running down their faces while they cried out, "Chaplain, I know I did wrong, but I don't deserve all this! It never stops! My bank account is gone, my family is gone, my home is gone, and now the nurse tells me I have AIDS. Why is God doing this to me?" "Stop, stop! Do not charge God with the wages of sin. You can choose the pleasures of sin, but you will have no control over the paychecks when they start rolling in."

Can it get any worse? Read verse 68: "...ye shall be sold...and no man shall buy you." Once again the chime sounds out from the prison hospital; another soul has slipped into that great long eternity. Family is notified, but no one cares. He is sent to the crematory and then we carry the little urn of ashes to the prison cemetery where inside a little white picket fence along the edge of a swamp we lower the ashes into a little hole and a four-inch marker with nothing on it but a number is placed over the remains. For sale—but no one wants him. Thus, friends, ends the tale of the second master; that is, except for a long eternity.

Thank you for your prayers,
William Cawman

†††

March 1, 2012

If prison is a mission field, then what about the words of the missionary song that say, "Behold how many thousands still are lying, bound in the darksome prison house of sin, with none to tell them of the Savior's dying, or of the life He died for them to win." This without a question being the picture, what should be our response?

Do you and I have faith enough to sing with confidence, "For the darkness shall turn to dawning, and the dawning to noonday bright, and Christ's great kingdom shall come to earth, the kingdom of love and light?" If we cannot quite pitch ourselves to grasp that, then could we pray, "Lord lay some soul upon my heart, and love that soul through me; and may I ever do my part to win that soul for Thee?" Surely if we love Jesus we can do that, can't we?

It certainly doesn't appear that we are going to win the entire 3500 men in this prison to Jesus. At least I would be honest enough to say that I don't see it happening. But there are a few hungry hearts; a few broken hearts; a few reaching hearts. Could Jesus lay one of them on your heart and another on mine, and through that bring a few more to Him before the night becomes so dark and the darkness so intense that no man can work?

The poor struggling man, who would almost remind one of someone gasping for a last breath of air that we have mentioned to you in the last couple of letters, is now not in this prison anymore. I may never see him or hear of him again; I don't know. But if Jesus lays this product of Satan, lost and undone and crying in the night, upon your heart will you pray for him?

Oh, how I would love to meet him someday in heaven. Didn't Jesus say, "I came not to call the righteous, but sinners to repentance," and did He not say, "They that be whole need not a physician, but they that are sick"? Then this poor soul is a perfect candidate for the redeeming Blood of Jesus.

I will here insert an honest confession from my own life. A number of years ago, before I was even thinking of prison ministry, I was reading some from the life of John Wesley. He told about the first time he went into the district of Cornwall and how utterly God-forsaken and depraved the people were. The adults were drinking and cursing and the children were running naked in the streets.

After he had described his feelings of repulsion at what he witnessed he said, "Surely this place is ripe..." And at that statement my mind ran ahead of him and I expected him to finish with "... for judgment." But instead he said, "Surely this place is ripe for Him who came to call not the righteous but sinners to repentance."

I remember distinctly being so smitten in heart that I laid the book aside and went to my knees in repentance. There is another phrase of an old song we have often sung which says, "God specializes in things thought impossible..." Let's pray for some miracles bigger than the most impossible needs before us, shall we? Dare we? After three years with His disciples and all they had seen, Jesus, about to leave them, said, "Hitherto have ye asked nothing in my name: ask, and ye shall receive, that your joy may be full."

Perhaps you remember that the man we spoke of in the above paragraph was first ministered to by his cellmate, who actually stood up in Bible study and told us what he was. It did seem that God used this man to get through the lies of Satan and start the cords vibrating once again in his heart. While the Wicca man was in detention I discovered that his cellmate was also there.

Often if I am going to go to the detention cells to visit a man I first look up in the state computer to see what he did to get himself there from the officers' viewpoint. I feel it best to be forearmed so as to not swallow too quickly a claim of innocence on the part of the guilty inmate.

I went to see this man and he didn't try to make any claim to innocence. He just began to weep and tell me, "Chap, I am wrong; completely wrong. Someone asked me in the visit hall to hold something for them for a minute or two while they went to do something and I felt a check but I didn't listen. The officer saw it and investigated and I was holding onto drugs. Now, Chap, I can see what you have been telling us is so true. I need to get this thing out of my heart that will cause me to stumble like this. I need a clean heart, I really do."

He was crying tears as he went on, "I don't know what they will do with me now, but I think I heard them say that I will be sent to another prison. What can I say? I did wrong and I knew better." Did I feel a little bit—just a little bit—of what Jesus must have felt as he looked into the tears of Peter as he suddenly discovered, like this man, that he had something on the inside that could not be trusted, and had caused him to grieve his Lord? Both of the men are gone now. O God, did I do my best for them?

For some time there has been a man in prison here that seems very enthusiastic about the church services, etc. After I had preached to them one Sunday night, he signed up for my class "Christian Living in Today's World." He came to the first one and seemed very eager about it.

The second week he came in looking very forlorn and weighted down indeed. I asked if any of them needed a text book and he replied that he would be talking to me about that. I dismissed it and went on with the class, but sadly it seems true that holy fire is not the only fire that is capable of burning inside a man's heart until it cannot be still.

After a few minutes he said, "I was going to talk to you about that textbook, but I think it appropriate to do it publicly. I borrowed a copy of it from one of the other men and I have to say that it is pure heresy. That book is nothing but heresy. Where in the Bible can you justify the concept that sin can be divided into two parts that requires two works of grace to deal with it? Now let me first say that until two years ago during this prison bid my life has been one of backsliding and getting back and then backsliding and getting back. But in the last two years I am really doing well. I have sat under Dr——, and I have worked alongside of Rev. ——, and I was a team member with ministry ——, and ... and ... I feel grieved in my spirit that you are teaching these young men who are inexperienced in these things this type of heresy. Where do you find such in the Bible?"

And my thoughts (unexpressed) were as follows: "Strange indeed that after reciting your recurring backslidings you would dub as heresy what would cure them. Besides 'after that way which they call heresy' was the doctrine which delivered Paul and filled the Bible that you can't find it in. And then too, sir, if you truly had the first work of redeeming grace you would be then able to see the need and the promise of the second one, but right now you are so unlike Jesus and so riled up inside that you cannot see either one of them. And then, whosoever these big men are that you have sat under and worked alongside of remind me of those big men in Jerusalem that Paul said mattered little to him who they were."

But as I endeavored to point out the Scriptural teaching of redemption from sin which is two-fold in nature, he would interrupt and spill out some more acid that was boiling akin to Elihu's seething belly full. He left class and wrote a three or four page letter to my supervisor about the encounter and desired to talk with him about it. My supervisor sat with him and said, "Now, Chaplain Cawman and I have different theological viewpoints but I would certainly not call him a heretic, and right now he has a lot more going for him than you do." For whatever reason, he too was moved on to another prison.

Isn't this good heresy? Don't you love the fact that we can be delivered from sin's guilt, sin's power, and someday soon from even its presence? Hallelujah for "...this way which they call heresy!" I love it! I have lived long enough to witness good old saints go shouting into glory with clean hands and pure hearts. Heaven opened up around their open graves so powerfully that who but a dead soul could not have known where they went.

The grandfather of my ancestor who came over on the Mayflower was burned at the stake in England as a heretic. His dying words were, "Lord Jesus, receive my spirit." My dear Daddy went home as a patriarch because he believed this heresy and plunged into the Jordan River leaving the old man of sin on yonder shore. My Mother followed him just four months to the day, after living in the beauty of holiness (by the way, that's the heresy we are referring to) for just a few months short of sixty years. For all of those blessed years, night and day, summer and winter, this glorious heresy saved her from backsliding.

Almost five years after they passed through the gates, my beloved wife of forty-one years slipped away to join them. Had she lived until August of this year she would have lived 50 years in the blessed state of heresy that saves, from not only the guilt and stain of sin, but from the power of it within. I know this, friends! I lived with them. In forty-one years with my dear wife I have not one single memory of the slightest shadow of a question mark but what this heresy (heart holiness) works, and works well, just like God's Word says it will.

My heart is so persuaded of this holy way that sometimes I feel like I have lost my power of moral choice, but then I must remember that we have been told we are not to go by our feelings. I am supposed to be writing a prayer and newsletter to you, not preaching, but the news is: I am fully persuaded and happy about it. I can hardly see to type for the tears of joy running down my face. My hope of heaven is strong. Then why should I allow men or devils to disturb the joy and peace within? Let's go shouting on. Victory complete is just around the corner!

It is always disappointing when a man walks through the door who had been gone for a few years and now is back in again. One such came back a few weeks ago on a fresh charge. He wanted to talk to me so I called him down and asked him how he was doing. He admitted he was just miserable. I began probing around as to whether he was really seeking God and obeying and it didn't take long to hit the snag. He is still not willing to give up his sin. He has been married and is now divorced, but he has a girlfriend who has Lupus and consequently can get access to prescription medicines which she then sells on the side for really big money. She also has some type of income and so she sends him a very healthy sum, for a man being in prison each week or each month, whichever it is.

He feels justified because she is sending it to him out of her income, not out of her sales of drugs? I began to face him seriously with the choice he is going to have to make: either to give up that woman that he has no business having anything to do with, as well as every other sin in his life, and have God and heaven, or continue on and be more miserable yet and end up in hell forever.

His eyes filled with tears and my heart went out to him, but he stands at the decision point and so far wants God and his sin, too. He did promise that he would pray and seek God and he seemed so reluctant to leave the room. He said, "Chaplain, so many of the men say they feel so much of God when they come around you and they want it and I do, too, but I don't know how to get there." I told him he just could not have God and have his own desires, too, but that God could change his desires until he wouldn't want his sin. Please pray for him.

Here's another little insight into a chaplain's daily encounters. An older black man has been in class for several years now and he seems so kind and gentle. I called him in for a visit and began to inquire into his future and he said he gets out in a few months and his wife wants him to come back home, but he is praying about whether he should go back to his wife or not.

I asked him if it was a first marriage for both of them and yes, they had been married for forty-some years. I said, "Sir, you don't have to have God tell you whether you should go back to your wife. The Bible has already clearly told you that. And furthermore it says, 'Husbands, love your wives.'" "Oh, good," He said, "Then now I know what to do about that." But then, perhaps he has not been a deep student of Biblical ethics and principles. The level of marriage counseling here is many times barely even kindergarten level, but what can one expect from such a bankrupt, selfish generation as we have produced.

I believe I told you around Christmas time that with our new administrator I was finally able to take back into the prison some who had come out of there. While they are under clearance I have been using them, and that to good advantage. Last night, as one man who had once sat among them right where they are, was testifying to them and telling them how gloriously God's grace of salvation and holiness works, I was rejoicing that they had the opportunity to hear from someone that God can keep them true after they get out.

As the men filed into the second service one of them looked very dejected and when I asked him how he was doing he said, "Not good. My father just passed away." We had a special time of prayer for him and I'm sure he could feel their support and love.

Another one of them who was just saved recently was quite moved on and asked for special prayer after the message. Our brother prayed with him and then he told me on the way out the door that he was really struggling and asked for prayer again. He didn't say what the struggle was, but God knows and that is enough for now. Oh, how much these men need some more shining examples to look at. Please pray that God will raise up many more who will prove that He is exactly Who He says He is. I'm glad He is!

Thank you, each one, for all you do in prayer,
William Cawman

14
BROKEN PIECES

April 1, 2012

Early in the year our new administrator sent a heads-up to all of us to be on the alert for any unusual activity or disruptions as they were moving many men around in the state and sending some very bad boys to our prison. The warning was not amiss as we have had more incidents and upheavals of order than I can ever remember since the prison was built. Several classes and Bible studies have just been cancelled because of the disorder.

One morning I went to the minimum unit for a class and the door was surrounded by at least eight police cars with dogs. They told me to wait and they would try to run the class but finally they just shut the place down. Along with the internal disorderliness, we have to send to Trenton each day the total attendance at all of our classes.

One can only wonder if they are not analyzing who to eliminate from the payroll next. I do agree that our governments cannot continue to operate with an ever-slipping red column, but oh, for some godly minds to decide what is necessary and what is not. Please cover this with prayer.

I must tell you of a very vibrant new horizon. I believe I already mentioned an Italian man in his late twenties who was recently saved out of Roman Catholicism and is so very hungry to find more. He is almost covered with very negative tattoos (an Odin axe on his neck and a large dragon on his arm plus many others), but his enthusiasm with his Bible and newfound belief are a real joy to minister to. He of course has so little discernment as yet that he expects everything named "Christian" to be a help to him.

On Monday nights there is a "Bible Institute" held on his unit by a volunteer coming in and so he enrolled in it. The last time he came to visit with me he said, "Chaplain, I want to ask you about something that is being taught to us. We were told that once we receive Jesus we are secure of heaven and can never miss heaven. But we are also being told that we cannot live free from sin in this life. Then the teacher taught us that it would have been impossible for Jesus to sin while He was here on earth because He was God. We brothers have been discussing these things on the tier and we are all confused. Can you explain why this is so confusing?"

My spiritual bloodstream began to writhe under such "doctrines of devils," as the Scripture calls them. It did not take long to clear up the error that we can never miss heaven once we are saved when we pointed out to him that this would mean that Satan would then be in heaven and that every soul that falls away from God and turns to hate Him will bring their hatred and sin into heaven.

Then we went on to talk to him about what a feeble victory Jesus must have won on the cross if the sinning business the devil started cannot be stopped. Again he came clear. The final of the three teachings is one of the most subtle damning errors that man has substituted for the real nature of Jesus. Without one doubt He was fully God; "For in Him dwelleth all the fullness of the godhead bodily." Yet when Jesus left His Father's throne in heaven to become our Savior, He willingly and completely laid aside all reliance upon His divinity. He walked this valley fully man, yet without sin and completely filled with the Holy Spirit. Multitudes of benighted souls are copping out with the oft-quoted statement, "Oh, only Jesus was perfect."

Excuse me, what do you really mean? "Oh, (if they would only be honest) don't expect me to not sin. I am just a man. He was God!" What a flagrant desecration of the holy mission He came to fulfill. The sacred Word says, Heb 2:17, "Wherefore in all things it behoved him to be made like unto his brethren, that he might be a merciful and faithful high priest in things pertaining to God, to make reconciliation for the sins of the people." And again in Heb 2:16, "For verily he took not on him the nature of angels; but he took on him the seed of Abraham." And again, Heb 5:8, "Though he were a Son, yet learned he obedience by the things which he suffered…" Had Jesus relied on His divinity even one time while here on earth, that little ugly statement would be valid, but He did not, thank God! He was "fully man" while here on earth, and He was fully filled with the Holy Spirit. And now—all glory be to God— "And being made perfect, he became the author of eternal salvation unto all them that obey him…" He was tempted in *all points like as we are!* Therefore it was the same divine will that He will now place within us that enabled Him to conquer every temptation known to man. Hallelujah!

With this our dear brother's face was glowing, and so I asked him, "Is what I am telling you confusing you?" "Oh no, Chaplain, it's as clear as it can be and I can feel it down inside. Whenever I come talk to you or sit in your classes I thank God that He has brought you into my life." Well, "God is not the author of confusion, but of peace." And what peace truth brings!

I really enjoyed the visit and it reminded me of something that happened when I was very young. My brother and I had found a baby robin that was far too premature to be out of his nest. We immediately took remedial action and went to the garden and came back with several juicy worms of the larger size. We touched one to the baby robin's beak and open it came as wide as possible. Down went the worm, open came the beak. Two, three, four, five—after either worm five or six we discovered we had missed one vital detail that mother robin knew better than we did: we forgot to chew up the worms. Here was baby robin with mouth wide as ever while several worms were climbing back out. Notwithstanding this minor difficulty baby robin was as ready as ever for the next worm! I confess I love to feed new babes in Christ like this. Is that all right to confess?

Several weeks ago another man in the same area seemed to really find forgiveness of sins, and was also very open and teachable and hungry. He joined the classes and was very bright, but one night after a Bible study he was in tears and asked for prayer. When I followed it up he confessed that he had encountered unexpected stress over the fact that he has sixteen years yet to serve and his mother's health is so poor. He said he yielded to the urge and smoked again and now is struggling to quit. He admitted that the peace he had found and the new life and joy within had grown dim and he knows it and feels it. He promised he is not giving up but is seeking God to restore Him again. He also would be glad of your prayers. I personally thank God that He is a God of second chances.

And then just recently a new middle-aged man joined the class. He has just arrived, either from another prison or from the county. I detected almost immediately an openness and yet a bit of wonderment as we entered the subject material on "The First Work of Grace." I briefly explained why that title, since there are two of them, and he listened with interest and then wanted to visit.

He asked about two works of grace as he had never heard that before, but as I went over the need not only to erase the symptoms of a physical disease but also to get to the very last bit of the virus causing it, he listened intently and smiled so sweetly with acceptance. I believe if he stays around we have another candidate with the need of Apollos. He gives good evidence in his testimony that he has really received the first work, and if so, that is the explicit reason why he is smiling with eagerness over the second.

One day recently as I was having interviews one of the officers on the tier called and asked if I could see a man who had just received hard news and wanted to talk with the chaplain. I assured him I would work him in and so here he came in a wheelchair.

He was really struggling to hold in the tears as he told me that the bad news was about his daughter. His first wife had died some years ago and his second wife had a medical condition that she passed on to their two daughters. One of them died at only four and a half years of age, and now the other one in her late teens was hospitalized for the second time in a week in very serious condition. It seems that they develop an aggressive skin condition that can only be stopped with heavy steroids which in turn causes their lungs to give up.

He was really broken up over it and was not free from some degree of anger at God for allowing it. I began at the bottom of things, asking him how it was with his own soul. He reached into his tee shirt and pulled out a medallion of St. Christopher and said, "See, I wear this to protect me."

I tried to point him gently away from such nonsense to Jesus and he did seem willing to listen. I prayed with him and tried to encourage him to pray to Jesus and get his own heart right and to commit his daughter to a God who will do all things right. He admitted that I was telling him the truth and that maybe all of this was a wake-up call to him and his daughter as well.

I then scheduled him for another visit which we had today. He said that the things I had told him were really going over in his mind and that he really did want to turn his life over to God and receive Jesus into his heart.

He began to tell me of his background—a very successful business owner but connected deeply with the Mafia. He was born in Sicily and carried the ethics from there that have now gotten him where he is. He owned a restaurant, two shops in the casinos and a "gentleman's club." I began to probe around at how serious he was about things in his life that were not pleasing to God. He indicated that he had been seriously thinking about our previous conversation and had decided to do whatever necessary to save his soul.

Then he said, "I have a plan. My wife is coming to see me tomorrow and I will talk to her, because I would like for both of us to receive Jesus the same day. When do you have meetings in your church?" I told him about our Wednesday night service and he said, "All right, could you meet with me again on Wednesday and I will receive Jesus and then I will ask my wife to come to your church that night and ask to receive Him, too?"

I tried to explain that we must come to God on His own terms but at the same time I tried not to break the bruised reed of his reach. I will meet with him on Wednesday and we will see if his wife comes to church on Wednesday. Please pray for this needy family.

I am so glad to tell you that our dear brother (remember I am not to use names in these letters) who has now been out of prison for eleven or twelve years and is now our Sunday School superintendent, has a son and his wife who are now cleared to visit in the prison, and the son wants to become one of our volunteers. I think this is so wonderful that the son of a man who was in prison but really got right with God and brought his family to God can go in and testify to the men of how important it is that they come out right. Pray that God will really use his testimony to speak to the hearts of fathers who perhaps have never felt their responsibility to the lives they have brought into the world.

And then I will close this letter with a bridge to the African news. Late in July a meeting I was scheduled for was cancelled and my little girl in Africa learned of it. She seemed to feel quite strongly that I should pay a visit to Africa again and her reasons were, I will confess, very convincing. The group of preachers and people that she had ministered to in Mozambique have now separated themselves from the work that they were in which is going backwards, desiring to keep the message of holiness clean. They are building a new church on a new property and my daughter feels it is an important time to hold some more holiness meetings and talk with them to be sure they are keeping the vision clear.

I checked airline tickets and they were in line, so now I needed to hear from God as I belong to Him with all my heart and life. I was in Michigan in a meeting and one morning went to the church and sat down in a sunny pew to seek God's direction.

As I got quiet before God after asking Him if He wanted me to go to Africa this summer, He so lovingly and yet with a bit of reproof said, "Now son, you have a gap in your schedule; airline tickets are affordable; your daughter's request is in order; just how difficult do you have to be for Me to tell you to go to Africa?" "Yes, Lord."

I got up and went to town and bought a ticket—July 23-Aug 10. Will our loving Heavenly Father ever exhaust new ways to let us know His sweet will? I mean, even for all eternity? Don't you love Him? I do! I mean, I really do! Thank you for all your faithful prayers. God is hearing them and the answers that have not come yet are on the way. I do believe it, for the battle is not ours, but His.

Your brother in Jesus,
William Cawman

May 1, 2012

Please continue to pray for the Blood of Jesus to continually cover His work here in the prison. We have mentioned before, and it grows rapidly worse, that the Islamic chaplain seems to be on an all-out vendetta to promote himself at anyone's expense. Sadly enough, it seems he has developed a support group which is wide-spread and gaining momentum.

My supervisor followed him into the facility yesterday morning and the officers in Master Center called out, "Hey, Dr. ──, come on in here and have some coffee." They totally and conspicuously ignored his supervisor. How does his and my supervisor handle it? "Chaplain Cawman, I'm growing weary of this battle, but I've given it to the Lord. The only reason I continue fighting is what it does to me when I see your group in here having Bible studies, etc., and I've told God I'll continue as long as He wills." Do pray for him.

And by the way, let me reflect back a few years as to the all-knowing, all-wise God that has made us His children. After a year and a half in the prison as a volunteer with no supervisor and myself the only protestant Christian organizing the services, etc., the position of Chaplain Supervisor came up for applications. Thinking this God's open door I applied. A chaplain from one of the county prisons got the position.

I didn't understand, but trusted that God would take care of me. Just before his probationary period was up he made a very strong racial statement and was escorted out of the prison. The position was posted again and I applied a second time. Another county chaplain got the position, the one who is now my supervisor. I still didn't understand why God had called me there and was not providing any income from it.

A short while after my supervisor was established he and the executive from the department of Chaplaincy in Trenton walked into my office and announced that I was going on the payroll. It has continued to be a provision that simply pays for the hours worked without any other benefits. I gladly accepted God's provision and have lived to bless Him for it.

By today my supervisor's time is largely consumed in making provision for pagan religions to be able to do whatever they do. I am not only completely free from all of that to preach and teach, but am also free to set my own schedule of when I will be there, etc. Thus God arranged, completely without my help, a double ministry of chaplain/evangelist. And since I had nothing to do with it except to say "Yes, Lord," I can also remind Him whenever the stormy winds blow, "Lord, this was Your idea!"

And He so lovingly understands.

But to more positive things. I need to follow up with the man who was so torn between his own desires for the unlawful and the conviction of where he would spend eternity. First of all, can you even faintly imagine what false colors the devil painted for him in this brief scenario?

He is 58 years old and is divorced. He is infatuated with a 70-year-old woman who has Lupus and very likely will die before he puts in the five years ahead of him. She sends him $100 a month out of her drug income. I could not help just bluntly asking him this question: "What will a man give in exchange for his soul?"

I faced him with the distinct possibility that while he lingers in this valley of indecision and unwillingness to break with this unlawful relationship and the money as well, he might lose the desire for God and then lose her, too. And so I said to him, "Let's tally up the exact price tag of your soul. For a woman who is forbidden by God and who may die before you ever are with her again, and for $100 a month, you are willing to spend eternity in hell. Is that what your soul is worth to you?"

He looked at me for a moment with intense alarm and then broke into tears, saying, "Can we pray?" He did pray and as he did God really reached down and touched his blinded eyes. Just whether he got fully saved in that moment time will tell, but He left the room with a smile and tears. Later that day in class I asked him, "Is it settled that you will take God's way?" He replied, "Yes, it is." He also needs prayer.

And then—Oh, thank God for my new Italian brother. What a joy to watch him hunger and thirst to know more of God. He is devouring the Word and finding it so exciting. I have actually watched some people eat in such a disgusting manner that it would take your appetite away. Then I have seen some eat in such an aura of enjoyment that it made you hungry to watch them. He is definitely of the latter category and it is such a blessing to be with him. He is so teachable and hungry at the same time that I don't know how to adequately describe it.

Do pray that, as I warned him, he will keep his desire and hunger directed entirely towards knowing God better, not just understanding mentally the beauties of God's Word and ways. There is an inherent beauty to God's Word even apart from the Spirit's inspiration of it. That is why so many study it so feverishly and then come up with all kinds of twisted theology out of it. Everything God does is beautiful.

David over and over expressed his admiration even of God's judgments, and one need not be alive spiritually at all to enjoy these. Millions of people every year visit scenes of God's severest judgment ever to visit the earth. Why? The Grand Canyon, the strata of rock formations, the great pillars of Zion National Park, are so awesome to behold, and yet they are the marks of God's great hand of judgment. Please help pray that this brother will not get misled by any infatuation with God's Word that will not make him completely what God calls "good."

Do you remember how that on the Day of Pentecost God made the sermon understandable to every language that was present to hear it? Do you know that He continues to do that very thing? I am amazed again and again at how the Sunday School lessons we are using in the Bible studies just fit the need of the hour so exactly and at just the right time.

Many times it is maybe only one or two primary thoughts brought out in the portion of Scripture that open the door to such timely application to their lives. Probably those preparing the lessons never thought once of their relevance to men in prison, but the God who can thrash a mountain with a worm has no problem making the material fit just as if it had been written specifically for them. Isn't He a God worthy of our love and obedience? I hope you screamed, "Yes!"

And here is another heart-warming feature of our Great God, who by the way is the only God of Truth! As we have been looking with great detail at the Scriptural and practical way of salvation and holiness of heart; at the nature of the disease and the consequent nature of the cure; at the only sensible provision of a God that anyone would admit is boundlessly more powerful than the author of sin—I can literally see the clearness of divine truth lighting up countenances all around the room.

False interpretations of God's Word that wrest it into a cover for remaining sin do just the opposite. That, too, I have seen over and over, for we certainly have many opportunities to witness what other teachings produce in these, the subjects of it. When haughty, wicked King Nebuchadnezzar saw the Fourth Man in the fire that he had made seven times hotter he cried out, "…there is no other God that can deliver after this sort."

And the opposite is true, also. There is no other god that rings the bell down in the human heart that He placed there for the express purpose of our knowing Him. And so, perhaps it is not necessary to pray that God will silence all the false teachings so much as to pray that He will give these men *a love of the truth* that will bring them to Him.

W. Cawman

June 1, 2012

LET ME START this letter with a great, huge, PRAISE THE LORD! FOR HE IS GOOD! A few months back I began receiving letters from the car dealer where I had purchased the last automobile, wanting to buy it back. I was puzzled with why, and so I took the letter to another dealer and asked what it was about. He told me it was real because the tsunami a while back in Japan was causing a shortage of that vehicle so they were trying to bring back used inventory. "But," he said, "You don't have to go to that dealer. I'll make you a deal." After he quoted all his terms for a trade I looked at him and said, "Sir, you haven't left me with any options."

Well, a couple of Mondays ago I was leaving from a revival meeting to travel home and I began feeling very keenly the vacant seat across from me where for so many miles the dearest on earth traveled with me. Suddenly Jesus came and sat in that seat and rode all the way home with me. It was such a glorious day that in the middle of it I looked up and said, "Jesus, You are not leaving me with any options. I am Yours completely and forever! Amen!" Now, I didn't mean to take up that much space with personal testimony, but it's because I love Him, and that more than ever before.

But now let me share a couple other testimonies with you. I received some very encouraging letters from men who have been sent to other prisons in the state, so let me give you their testimonies in their own words.

> Dear Brother Cawman,
>
> Greetings in the precious name of our Lord and Savior...Jesus the Christ! I pray this finds you filled with Him. I am well and it is well with my soul. He enables me to walk in the Light and I praise Him because His Blood cleanses me from all sin. I pray that He increases the vessel because there's nothing in-between.
>
> I was unable to see you before I left. You're not far from my thoughts or heart and I thank God for His work through you because it has been paramount in allowing my feet to be placed on a solid foundation! There's a lot of sinking sand here, but He has avenues in place where we don't have to be a captive audience unless we choose the delusion. And I choose Jesus who delivers from sin and not in sin. The lessons I've learned there are being used here to go fishing, and the fish are biting! Praise Jesus, the truth does set men free.
>
> I do miss the class and all the brothers, but all those years weren't spent in vain; many good seeds have taken root and Praise God I'm walking in Victory by His Blood and through His Grace.

You're more of a father to me than I've ever known. I thank God for you and all the love you've shared and lessons I've learned. It seems as if the Lord showed me the need of a pure heart in Trenton State Prison, then He allowed me to learn the doctrine of Jesus and His Blood in Southwoods, and now the rubber meets the road and He is sending me out into the fields. I don't take it lightly; please pray for me! Thank you again for all you have done and all you have allowed the Lord to do through you. I love and miss you.

—Love in Christ, Bro ——

My Dear Brother William Cawman,

Happy greetings to you. Praise Jesus for His absolute victory, and His finished work! Thank you for your letter of Mar 3rd and your encouragement in my walk with Him. It means a great deal to hear from you….Your daughter is in my prayers for safety and success in Mozambique and Malawi. That would certainly be challenging and unusual if you were to spend the summer there. I know if you are led to do it, then the Lord will bless you with safety and victory. It's hard for me to imagine what that would be like for your daughter to do such an important work with her own father there to give advice and counsel, serving the Lord together. I'm sure it would be the highlight of her life.

Thanks for helping me understand how Jesus guides and is involved in the great losses we face. I've wondered about how there is so much of pain and deep grief in life. Deep down I've known that somehow His presence must, at least eventually, circumscribe it; somehow take it into full consideration with us. So it helps to understand the prayer, the reality, and the journey of it that you are going through. It gives me faith in Him and more understanding of how to relate to Him in this area of my life. Loneliness and loss were certainly not unknown territory to Him in His earthly life, and He kept His thoughts right, His focus firm—mostly through intense prayer as far as I can tell. I see how you are doing exactly these same things;

following our Master's example closely. I have no wisdom to bring to this for myself or anyone, only the offer of companionship in looking to Him. I will walk with you, dear brother.

You encourage me to keep my eyes on Him, and that's my heart's desire. There is nowhere else real, nowhere substantial, to look. And He's taking us somewhere glorious. He's taking us deep within ourselves, and deeper into knowing Him, and into a Kingdom He's prepared; and He's walking with us all the way. I really don't believe it's in His nature not to be right there, if I can only see through to Him.

In studying the books on the doctrine of holiness, I think I'm re-learning the meaning of every word that was twisted by the cult I was in. [this man was a third-generation Mormon] I'm making my own little "translation table" (with diagrams and all; it's a mess) because it's a matter of dumping old concepts of everything from salvation to perfect love, and then understanding how the correct, biblical meanings of all these things relate to each other and to the experiences of my personal walk with the Lord. I know you used to be amused sometimes at my attempts to describe things without any vocabulary. The Greeks used to say that "the beginning of all knowledge is the definition of terms;" but fortunately the beginning of life in the Lord can come pouring on whether you know how to describe it or not. Now I'm being blessed because I'm catching up my personal walk with what the Bible says about these things, and I'll be able to communicate more accurately with other Christians. (At least that's the plan…)

You know, I will also do my best to enjoy the journey, as you are doing. I hope to see our Master make His triumphal return soon, but maybe there's a little more to the story yet. I'll do as you say and keep my ear to the still, small Voice. You described Him as the "indwelling Guest of the soul." Now that sounds like something I would say, a description I would come up with (at least before all this study). Interestingly, the message for today, April 11, in My Utmost For His Highest (Oswald Chambers) says: "The Holy Spirit cannot be accepted as a guest in

> merely one room of the house—He invades all of it. And once I decide that my 'old man' (that is, my heredity of sin) should be identified with the death of Jesus, the Holy Spirit invades me. He takes charge of everything. My part is to walk in the light and to obey all that He reveals to me."
>
> …I know we walk together, you and me. My prayers are with you, and with your daughter, for a summer of beautiful and intense work for Him, and relationship with Him.
>
> With gratitude and brotherly love, ———

And then, within the prison here God continues to help all who will open up to Him. Pray that many more will join them.

A recent visit with a precious man I have referred to often told the following: a hospice patient in the hospital was assigned to him. The reason for this one was not that he was dying, but that no one could tolerate him. He was mean and ugly and angry and would demonstrate it without a letup.

Our brother sat with him until he felt he could stand no more and then would go out and walk the hallway in prayer. He said it was one of the keenest trials of his life up to now, but that God was only helping him to grow in grace through it all.

Then he told me, not with criticism, but with deep disappointment, of the Sunday night service before when a man came in from a megachurch in the area and preached such errant doctrine that one could literally commit, and continue to commit, any sin whatever and still be secure of heaven in the end.

It was so rank that inmates began to audibly contest him right in the service until it ended in a shouting match right in church. I think our brother had a right to be grieved sick over it, don't you? It baffles me to no end to try to understand what motivates a person to preach such things as that, and what inspires them to come into a prison and tell men who are shut away for their sins that they can continue to commit them and end up in heaven. Satan is a liar with not one iota of shame over his lies. I hate him! (By the way he lets me know betimes that it is mutual, too.)

Here is a short story that is not finished yet, but needs prayer before it ends up wrong. I received a request from an inmate who wanted to talk to the chaplain. He got right to the point by telling me that he is not really a religious person, but that someone had told him that he could not be forgiven for his sin, it was so bad.

He went on to explain that he is now in the middle of a sixteen-year sentence for the crime of rolling on top of his few-months-old son while sleeping in a drunken stupor and smothering him to death. He has now been in prison for eight years and he wanted to know what to do. Could he be forgiven? Should he continue on with his wife or let her go her way and get it in the past? Then he told me that the week before, his wife had come to visit with him and told him she would forgive him because it was not all his fault. The dead baby had also shown signs of the shaken baby syndrome, and she admitted it was her that did that.

(Let me insert here my inner feelings, although I could be wrong. Did she find out that her baby was going to carry the damage of her actions through life and set up the stage to have her husband carry the blame? Why, after eight years would she bring this up and want to forgive him? Was the guilt more than she could bear? I don't know, I'm just wondering).

At any rate, when she told him that it made him so angry that he just got up and told the officer he had to leave and walked off, leaving her crying. I began to talk with him seriously about God's way out of this deep tragedy. I told him he needed to get on his knees and ask his wife to forgive him, and then they needed together to ask God to heal the past and give them a whole new beginning. He wasn't sure she wanted to go on with him, but I told him that didn't excuse him from doing his best to make the past right. I urged him to begin really seeking God lest his life continue to spiral down such a trail of tragedy.

He did listen well and wants to continue the visits. Please pray—surely this is one of the many cases that only prayer and fasting will afford any light at the end of the tunnel to.

By the way, have you stopped lately and looked up and thanked God for all He has saved you from? Oh, for that soon-coming day, when God by the Word of His mouth will stop Satan's insane wreckage forever and ever!

Yours for Jesus,
William Cawman

15
GRACE GREATER THAN MY SIN

July 1, 2012

I NEED TO GIVE YOU an update on our Blessed Jesus. When He dwelt here below and moved among men He astounded them with His workings, as the following passage says: "And he charged them that they should tell no man: but the more he charged them, so much the more a great deal they published it; And were beyond measure astonished, saying, He hath done all things well: he maketh both the deaf to hear, and the dumb to speak." (Mark 7:36, 37)

I do not understand why He charged them not to tell of His wonders, do you? But obviously He did not condemn them for doing what they could not help but do, and do it "a great deal," for they were "beyond measure astonished." Did you know that He is still completely and always in charming control of His own works, and that many times we do not see what He is doing until way down the road?

Well, let me tell you something from this very day (June 26). I had just returned to the prison class room from a wonderful camp meeting where God moved in mighty power, and so of course I gave the men a report on what

God had done—as if that were possible!

After the class the men said, "Chaplain, may God continue to go with you on these missions, because you have no idea what it does to us when you come and tell us what God is doing out there."

All of the sudden I realized why God in His infinite wisdom opened up a dual ministry back a number of years ago. I have never questioned whether I was in the will of God in a divided ministry, but now I see it is not really divided. It is God's work all the way through and He uses one meeting and His workings in it to minister to another one. No wonder Jesus looked up from His earthly ministry and said, "Even so, Father: for so it seemed good in thy sight."

Friends, what will it be when the last bit of looking "through a glass darkly" is suddenly removed, and we see the whole pathway God has led us through all of our life that was given to Him. The song writer said, "This my song through endless ages; 'Jesus led me all the way.'" Oh, how it makes my heart cry out, "Lord Jesus, draw me ever closer to Thy heart, and help me to never miss a single step or detail of Thy precious will!"

One of the men— who is now out of prison and coming to church and loving Jesus and walking the pathway of light with all his heart and soul— received a letter from a man still in prison, although now in one of the northern ones, who is walking the same pathway. He shared it with me and I cannot help passing it on to you, it is so rich.

How are you my dear brother? I hope you are finding deeper depths and higher heights in Him. There really is no limit to His goodness. Amen. I am doing well, thanks to Jesus. Brother ——, ——, and —— (He will here be speaking of some from the church who went in to visit him) came up here this past Saturday and it was like the balm of Gilead to my soul. I forgot how much I missed the brethren. There are some good brothers here, but you and I both know there is just something so precious about the holiness people. It is a shame that more don't realize the blessed privilege of being holy as He is holy. Sigh; anyway, we had a blessed time. I was so excited that I couldn't stop talking. A couple of times I wondered if I was blabbering on and on, smile. Bless their hearts, they just smiled and let me blabber. When we prayed in the beginning I went to hold ——'s (the wife's) hand, and bless her heart she snuggled up to —— (her husband) instead. It was a precious lesson to realize that there really is no need to hold hands in prayer, especially with someone else's wife. Isn't it wonderful that even a chastisement is precious? Smile.

Brother —— and I had a wonderful time in the Lord. He is a precious saint of God. He has been through so much recently, but bless his heart, he is trusting God through it all. As he told me the sore trials and temptations he has been facing I couldn't stop smiling because of his victorious testimony. It was just so good to hear people making sense again. You know how it is here, it is like everyone is speaking a foreign language. Well, I guess that just means there is work to be done. No sense in lollygagging around, Jesus is waiting.

Lord willing, I will be teaching a class in August here. It is going to be on Biblical deliverance. I know there is no other kind of deliverance, but you have to be specific around these parts or else the devil will get an opportunity. It took some time, but the Lord has put it on my heart not to go head to head with those who resist the truth of sanctification. The truth is the truth and it is up to them to receive it; all I am called to do is be a witness of it. I am going to teach full salvation, but you and I both know that most of the men here aren't even saved so the focus is going to be on salvation.

I'm sure you will pray for him and for God's anointing and wisdom as he tries to teach others of this precious way. It is the most natural thing in the world for a real Christian to tell someone just how precious He is, and then to discover the impossibility of doing it, and then to try it all over again. "The half has never yet been told, of love so full and free. The half has never yet been told; the Blood— it cleanseth me!"

I have a special prayer request. I have told you often lately of the encroaching hindrances that are directly empowered by the advance of the antichrist. The administration has made so many changes lately in where we meet and when, that I am afraid many of the men are just becoming discouraged. Our class attendances have dropped about in half with all of the upsets in schedules and places.

Meanwhile, the Muslim population continues their meetings without disturbance and the numbers continue to grow. A mandatory chaplain training session was scheduled for a date that I was scheduled away in a camp. I sent in my excuse and so missed it. My supervisor tried to describe it to me today in detail. One thing I must say about my supervisor is that he can sit and tell me of attacks to him personally and attacks on our efforts without the slightest ill will or fighting spirit. He has a rare sense of humor that gets him through many a thing that would undo others.

Well, the meeting he said was completely dominated by the Muslim chaplains and the aura of the agenda was definitely oriented to them gaining even more strength. He told me in detail just what they said, but then he said he cannot remember what the "Christian" chaplain said because he didn't have anything to say. "But while men slept, his enemy came and sowed tares among the wheat, and went his way."

If you examine history ever so scantily you will see that in a very weak period of Christianity (AD 500-600) Islam had its birth. Whenever Christianity has been pure and aggressive, Islam has withdrawn into the background, but now? When has the world witnessed a more pathetic and invalid witness of Christ-likeness than we see today?

I said all that to try to picture to you how much we need the covering of prayer as a defense against the tide that is coming in, and that alarmingly fast. God started this work, but surely He is counting on us to hold it up in prayer that the door will stay open until Jesus comes. As much as God comes during our class times and Bible studies and gives His help in very definite ways, it is not time to give up the battle, and we won't! God being our helper!

But now, let me ask prayer from a different angle entirely. Our Muslim chaplain is a Nigerian, and either his father or his grandfather is the high priest of Islam in Nigeria. He has political connections that we do not know about, but is untouchable completely. He is on an all-out mission to get our supervisor removed so that he can be in complete control of the chaplain department here. Unfortunately he has garnered a lot of support for his goal.

Today, however, my supervisor told me he has been becoming more and more aware that this world is coming to an end, and he is concerned about it. He asked the supervisor for a study on Daniel's prophecies as he is trying to correlate them with the teachings of Islam.

My supervisor asked me if I knew of any other studies that might be useful to try to awaken him to the real truth and I suggested a study on Jesus' Olivet Discourse. He said he would never use that as he would not have any use for the New Testament. He teaches that the Old Testament was borrowed from the teachings of Mohammed (figure that one out if you can) and so he is trying to put them together to satisfy himself and those he teaches. He openly professes to be a very sought-after teacher of the Koran.

At the same time, as I followed him through security the other day he was joking so disgustingly with the officers that they should be careful about touching the "Holy Man." He was making a joke of the whole thing, and even at that seems to have everyone bowing to him and giving him whatever he wants.

He is one of the most miserably unhappy, negative men I have ever met. I try whenever I am around him to be friendly and courteous, but he cannot last more than a minute or two on any positive subject. I often wonder just how it feels to be so grouchy and miserable all the time, but would you pray that as he studies the Word of God he will be convicted of his own lost estate before God? I don't know what would ever happen if he would really get under conviction and get right with God, but I would certainly— most certainly indeed— be very willing and happy to find out!

Thank you, every one who is praying and supporting the ministry to men in prison. I am delighted that there are also others who are ministering to men in prison in other states as well. God be with all of them. There is yet a harvest there until Jesus comes.

Your Brother in His great work,
William Cawman

╫

August 1, 2012

OFTEN I WRITE parts of this letter as things happen so that I will not forget, as well as to not leave the whole for the last minute. I want to write this evening, July 12, and introduce you to a (shall I say "typical"— what is that?) morning spent with needy but precious men. Starting at 9:00 am until 10:30, which is lock-up time, and giving a half hour to each man, here is how it went:

(1) This man is 42 years old, Hispanic at least in part, and very good looking. He has never married, but has two girls whom he has hardly ever seen. Drugs and drinking have been his escape from a broken home situation and all of the pain that sin brings into a life, until he was committed to prison.

After getting locked up he began to consider his life and from all evidences he let Jesus come into his heart. It was the best time of his life and he remembers how precious it all became to belong to Jesus. But when he got out of prison he fell and went back into the old habits and all the demons returned. Now he is in prison again, and for a while he tried to live the Christian life without being born again and finally admits he has just become numb with discouragement and hopelessness.

As I began to appeal to him to turn again and really seek for Jesus to come back into his life, he began to choke with tears. "Chaplain, I know exactly what you are talking about for I once had it. I want it again, I really do." He promised to rise up and try again. My heart bled for him. At times like these I have to remind myself that this is God's work, not mine, for everything in me wants to reach out and hang on to him until he finds his way back to Father's house. Please pray for him.

(2) This is an older man with family members in church positions around the area. He grew up knowing. He is not in heathen darkness but now he is labeled for life as a criminal. His eyes also filled with tears as he admitted that this was a wake-up call to him. I asked him if he felt the assurance of sins forgiven and he said very clearly that he does. He recently joined our classes and Bible studies and seems to be so receptive, but pray that he will see the depths of his need and come to God for full cleansing.

(3) Next comes a black man with a lifetime exposure to churchgoing, but without God and comfort. At first he hid behind the typical religious front that the devil pastes over his rotten production, but my heart loves these souls too much to let them hide there. As I began to lovingly probe around his inner heart, he began to show a deep longing in his eyes as we talked about God's grace and forgiveness and the power He gives to live above sin. He didn't have to be told that either he is all God's or not God's at all; he knew that. He became very serious about his condition and behind the long-standing façade tears began to moisten his eyes.

After these three left my heart began to feel so keenly the words of the old song: "Lonely without He's standing; lonely within am I..." So many are in this state. Somewhere along the pathway of life they have come face to face with Jesus Christ and have tasted that He is good; they have felt His touch upon their heart; but now they are so powerless to live the life they know is good. "...the way of transgressors is hard." Yet day after day they go on, hoping someday it will be better. But for many that day never comes and they drop into hell one right after the other. God is still reaching for them, so must we!

But then, some have made the turn and are walking upward in the path to heaven. Our big Italian fellow came into class today and looked so bright and happy that I asked him to pray. "O God, I want to thank You for letting me come to this prison. It stopped all my foolishness and sin and let You come into my heart and life, and I'm so glad for it!"

And then on July 23 I flew again to Africa, so the story will change a bit—just a little bit, for it's all God's work no matter where. Flying Ethiopian Air we landed in Addis Ababa and when we took off for Maputo, Mozambique, a young Ethiopian Muslim man was sitting beside me. He did not appear to be out of his twenties, and as we embarked he pulled out his little prayer book or Koran, one or the other, I could not tell, and began audibly saying his prayers.

As they are at present in the fast of Ramadan, he did not partake of either food or water during the whole flight, but periodically took out his little book and so earnestly prayed. Once he pointed to my watch to know the hour and then continued praying. For a long time he prayed and then when he finished he began sobbing and wiping his eyes and nose with a dirty looking wash cloth. This he kept up for some time and then pulled out the little book again and just bent over it, repeating the words. He wept so intensely that my heart was aching for him, but when I tried to converse there was not a single word we could understand of each other's.

I was thinking, "Dear Lord, beside me in this chariot is sitting an Ethiopian who is also hungry for truth, but someone gave him a Koran instead of Isaiah." I prayed for him and sat there hurting down deep inside to be able to tell him of One who could turn that aching heart into a fountain of joy and praise, but I couldn't. I wonder how many there are during this season of Ramadan who are down deep inside longing for someone to fill the painful void that only Jesus can fill.

Landing in Maputo I was met by Sarel and Lintie, and then we had to wait for a couple of hours for my daughter's plane to arrive from Malawi. Immediately we took off on the five or six-hour drive to Zavora, arriving there around 10:30 that night. Sarel and I were to sleep in a bedroom in Azarias's house (the pastor). There were no mosquito nets but I figured with the preventative meds that my doctor had given me and a smear of repellent I would have nothing to fear. I badly underestimated the power of a mosquito.

I'll jump ahead of my story to tell you that by Saturday night my daughter had come down with Malaria and about 2:00 am Monday morning the little bug got me, too. We were scheduled to travel to Maputo that day to catch a plane for Malawi the next morning. We pulled ourselves together and Jamie agreed to drive us down as opposed to taking a bus, for which we were so thankful.

By the time we got to Maputo we wondered if we should go straight to a clinic, but decided to tough it out until about 7:30 that night. We were both feeling so horribly rotten, for lack of a better term to describe it, that we headed for the clinic. They drew blood to test for Malaria and then we tried alternately to sit, then lie on hard wood slat benches in the waiting room while it seemed the doctor was seeing everyone else but us.

When we finally got in he declared us both attacked with Malaria so we started the medicine for it immediately but began to feel very shaky about flying the next day and then landing where we would have no help or rest.

We called Sarel and Lintie who had returned on Friday to South Africa and they immediately started for the border to pick us up. Such dear people they are indeed! Jamie took us to the border to meet them and they had a bed all prepared in the back of their vehicle where we laid down for the trip to Middelburg.

The next morning both of us felt better and have been improving ever since. We stayed with them until Thursday morning and then took bus for Malawi—a bus trip of two days and one night. After we left Sarel and Lintie, Lintie also came down with malaria and had a worse time than either of us. It is still one of the costly parts of missionary work in these mosquito-infested areas.

The time spent in Zavora was absolutely ordered of God and very precious. We spent much time with the pastors as they poured out their hearts to us in telling of the battles they are facing and begging us to give them all the advice we could. I do not know that I have ever felt more of the anointing of God in preaching anywhere than simply in talking with these dear hungry men. They have not one atom of kickback at all of God's truth, and they desire a pure clean church there in Mozambique.

So that you will know how to pray for this group I will try to tell you the whole story as fully as I can. About thirteen years ago an Afrikaans couple went there and started a work under the auspices of the Assemblies of God. They had come out of the Dutch Reformed Church into the charismatic group. Azarias, the older pastor there, was brought there by them and then they enlisted some other men from the area as pastors. The tragedy is that in most cases of what they called conversion, the people simply stopped (perhaps) their ancestor worship and witchcraft, only to take on the false worship of the charismatic styles. One of the pastors is openly still participating in ancestor worship and is living in multiple adulteries, but he seems to be a favorite of theirs and continues on unrebuked.

When my daughter arrived there five years ago and began teaching the clean pure doctrine of holiness, the Afrikaans man objected and told her not to preach that and then he contracted colon cancer and was dead in months. She went forward teaching it and they loved it and by the time the widow came back it was too late. They had tasted something better and wanted it.

However, since that time the main pastor has proved very untrustworthy and the under-pastors are very concerned because they feel the church is not growing spiritually. These are the matters they wanted to discuss with us and one could feel their deep heart cry for help. As we counseled with them we told them to wait upon God in prayer and then Sarel and Lintie would be coming up to teach them and give them guidance. They might have to just begin to reach into the bush and start a work all over.

The original work was so freighted with birth defects that it will be almost impossible to cleanse it unless all the leaders are agreed. The few men who are pulling for the truth and holiness have a property where a new church can be built, if God so leads that way. It is a beautiful piece of ground which overlooks the Indian Ocean. Please do pray for Sarel and Lintie as they have felt God definitely laying it on their hearts to spend a good portion of their time for a while at least, guiding these dear souls who have received the Light into God's plan for them.

At first we were somewhat disappointed to not get directly to Malawi, but once again we began to recognize the leadership of God in having us in South Africa for a few days with Sarel and Lintie. It was a much-needed time of sharing our hearts regarding the work there in Mozambique and our mutual vision of true holiness. Lintie said people are asking them why they want to move up to the bush and get malaria. She said it is because God is calling them there and that is just part of the price to pay for those souls.

If you could also visit these who have "heard the gospel sound" you would agree that God is definitely not finished with that little spot in Mozambique. While we were there we pulled my daughter's little house trailer, twenty-one feet long, up to a little village where services are being held under a huge spreading tree. They will put in a pit toilet and live in the little trailer and begin teaching the people the way of God. Please do pray for them.

Heading then for Malawi, and after several hours of extremely charismatic "worship" blaring over the bus and shown on the TV screen, we crossed the border into Zimbabwe. I asked my daughter if she had any good CDs along and she had one and so I offered it to the team of bus drivers. They put it in and played it non-stop for almost six hours. A man on the bus wanted it, so we gave it to him. What a licking Satan's atmosphere got for a long while on that bus trip. When they started the trip they asked for someone to volunteer to pray for the trip over the sound system, so I took the microphone and prayed for the trip and for the souls in the bus.

Our time in Malawi was also very profitable, but so short. We got some needed improvements made and were able to get a feel of the work and discuss the future. Thank you each one for your prayers, and please do not forget this little spot on God's great earth.

With love,
William Cawman

┼┼┼

September 1, 2012

IF IT IS INAPPROPRIATE to be excited and happy over holiness of heart and life, then I will just quit writing these letters. We have been studying through a book in our Christian Living Classes called "Bible Lessons." It is simply a skeleton theology from which we have branched out to cover the work of God in all of its aspects. We began some time ago with the typical theological approach as to who God is and what sin is; and then the first work of grace in forgiveness of sins and being born again. Then we dwelt on the subject of backsliding which many teach is impossible and in so doing accomplish what they teach cannot be done.

Then we studied the subject of remaining sin in believers, and are now entering the glorious subject of a second work of grace whereby we are cleansed from every remaining root of sin and filled with the Spirit of God. What other teaching can possibly fit the title of "Redemption," since that word means, "buying back," or "restoring to the original state"?

As we have just begun entering this "Holy of Holies," in the will of God for man, I have found myself approaching a shouting state again and again. Why? Because it is a living reality in my heart and I am as happy as I can be while walking this holy pathway. Thus I am really enjoying this subject more and more. I did not find myself wanting to shout while studying the subject of sin, or of backsliding, but wading through that to the border of Canaan the Promised Land, the atmosphere is becoming charged with the joyous reality that Christ can indeed do all that He came to do.

And all this progress was coming to pass while the Muslims were getting grumpier and more miserable over their observance of Ramadan. Just a day or so before the fast of Ramadan was to end with the Ramadan feast and the Eid Feast, one on Friday and the other on Monday, I received a request slip that was not very clearly written. I thought it was asking for "Jim" the Catholic chaplain and that my supervisor had not noticed and gave it to me and so I put him on the appointment sheet for a visit.

When he came in he told me that the request was for Jumah services; that he had been dropped from the list a few weeks back and wanted to be reinstated. I told him it was a poor time to try to get reinstated as they were in the last hours of Ramadan, but that it would be best for him to wait a week or so and then turn in a slip more clearly specifying what he wanted. Then before he left I asked him if he was finding an answer to his desires in the Muslim religion. He looked at me and said, "Well, I do have a few problems with it. When my grandmother died the brothers told me that it was wrong for me to mourn over her since she was not a Muslim. I didn't like that and didn't think it was right. Now my grandfather has pancreatic cancer and I'm concerned about him and they tell me I must not be concerned because he is not a Muslim. I just don't think that's right at all."

I said to him, "Let me tell you something: you have an individual right to know God as He really is. Would you do something? Would you just hold off from getting reinstated in the Jumah services and really seek after God and ask Him to show you who He really is? Then let me put you back on the appointment sheet again and we will visit and see what you are finding." He said, "Yes, I will do that." Will you pray that he will sincerely seek after God and hear from Him?

In the July letter I put part of a letter written from an inmate who used to be in this prison, but has now been transferred to one further north. Let me give you another part of a more recent letter which certainly evidences a definite growth in grace and holiness.

> Greetings in the holy name of Christ. I am sitting Indian style on my bed right now, thunder is sounding in the heavens, and my heart is hungering and thirsting after righteousness. I wonder how the Israelites felt when God displayed His majesty through mighty works, signs, and wonders? I have always been fascinated by the works of God in nature.
>
> I still remember, vividly, getting on my bike as a child and chasing rainbows after a summer storm. As I got older I became more contemplative, but I still enjoyed watching summer storms come in over the ocean and go out over the bay. There was always such a wondrous beauty in seeing the sky and ocean illuminated by lightning strikes and feeling the thunder roll. The strange calm in the air as the wind picked up, the smell of ozone, the exhilaration as all of creation seemed to pause…I still enjoy thunder storms.
>
> This morning as the sky darkened I thought about the storms we face in life and how I get a similar excitement when they come. I never realized it before, but I am more used to facing storms than the clear blue skies of God's abundant blessings. My mind goes to the scriptures and Paul's testimony in Philippians 4:11-12: "…I have learned, in whatsoever state I am, therewith to be content. I know both how to be abased, and I know how to abound: everywhere and in all things I am in-

structed both to be full and to be hungry, both to abound and suffer need."

It was interesting to see that Paul "learned" how to abound in blessings. He was "instructed." When I realized that I asked God to teach me.

Looking back at my life I can see a pattern of failures that come on the heels of blessings. It makes me think of the proverb: "...give me neither poverty nor riches: feed me with food convenient for me: Lest I be full, and deny Thee, and say, Who is the Lord? Or lest I be poor, and steal, and take the name of my God in vain." (Pr. 30:8,9)

I simply want to honor Him no matter what state I am in.

It has been good to fellowship with the saints that visit. [He is speaking still of the ones we mentioned in the July letter that visited with him] I didn't realize how much I missed the love of the brethren. I wish there were more saints to fellowship with here. Sister —— blessed my heart when she said, "Maybe Jesus wants you all to Himself..." That truly is a wonderful thought.

I am taking a course on Greek and I am enjoying it very much. I love how the aorist tense expresses the doctrine of a second blessing so perfectly. Even the lingua franca of NT times was thought out by God. He is so awesome. It amazes me how people can know Greek and still profess a holiness that is positional only. But that is another topic. Can you please send me a copy of John Wesley's "Plain Account of Christian Perfection?"

I hope all is well with you and the brethren, Grateful, ——

Now let me tell you a wonderfully blessed story of twelve years. Parts of this you would have received back twelve years ago, but it is definitely time for a follow up. Again, I am not to use names in these letters, so you will understand.

Twelve years ago a man who had just received a bright case of sins forgiven heard the good news that he could be fully delivered from all inward sin. He began without delay, just as a born-again soul will do, to seek after it. For several months he stayed right with the leadership of the

Holy Spirit as He showed him his heart and guided him into the truth of holiness.

One glorious day he entered into the blessing and from that moment to the present has never looked back, never cooled off, never lost the glow and wonder of it all. We have watched him grow in grace with a steady pace. Before coming to prison he had fathered two children by a woman he never married and never intended to, and as soon as he was released he went after them. They were in the custody of his mother and so he went there for a while and lived the good life before them, and both of the children entered in and got saved.

He had not seen his father since the day when, at 14 years of age, he had met him in a park and beat him up. Now he wanted to straighten his whole life out and live for Jesus, so he arranged a visit with his father and took him a Bible. His father felt the package and sensed what was in it and said he would open it later. He then went back to Puerto Rico, his native country.

After a time his father became very ill and his son went to Puerto Rico to bring him back to this country. He was deeply into a very debilitating and terminal disease, but nearly every Saturday his son would drive to New York to visit him in the nursing home.

One Saturday he and his two now-saved children were visiting with their father and grandfather and the son said to him, "Dad, if you want Jesus to do for you what He has done for me and your grandchildren He will, but you will have to pray and ask Him." He had never heard his father pray before. In fact, his father was a very deeply-rooted sinner and had been all his life. When he heard what his son said he put his head back in his wheelchair, oxygen tube and all, and began praying out loud. Jesus heard that sinner's prayer as He always does, and he was saved from his sinful life right then and there.

A couple of days later his two sisters came in to see him, bringing him a television. He took one look at it and said,

"Get that out of here, I don't need that!" Twenty-two days later he went to heaven.

The son and his children kept praying for his mother and their grandmother. She too returned to Puerto Rico and after a time became sick. The son went over to get her and brought her back to this country. She went through some medical treatments and recovered quite well, and then knew she needed to stay in this country but needed some type of housing assistance in order to survive.

As God would have it, the only place she could find that was in the very same town where her son was living, which was by now very near the church we attend. She came to stay with her son and his wife (by now he had found him a wonderful wife) and at times would come to church with them. One Sunday night God broke through on her heart and saved her through and through in answer to prayer. She went right on and got fully sanctified just a few months later and has been and still is a blessing to all of us.

Now the story would be wonderful if it ended there, but the part I want to tell you is this: When the man was released from prison his two children were just entering their teen years. They have both taken the way their father went before them and now his son, a young married man with two small children, is going back into the prison his father came out of and giving Bible studies and preaching to the men and they love him!

In case you think that story is too good to be true, you need to think differently, for true it most certainly is. Now aren't you glad you have prayed over the years for the men in prison? Thank you each one.

Your Brother in Jesus,
William Cawman

16
IS IT JUST JAIL-HOUSE RELIGION?

October 1, 2012

PERHAPS IT IS TIME to address a question often asked or referred to, which is, "Do many of the men in prison only receive 'jail house religion'?" The answer to that is "Yes." But it would not be fair to leave it at that simple yet truthful answer, so let me draw a few comparisons. After years of working back and forth between two ministries—that in prison and that of evangelist to churches and mission fields—I would desire to be absolutely honest in making this appraisal. No matter where man is found, the words of Jesus still apply: "few there be that find it."

Now if those words of Jesus were predestinating or in any other way limiting, God would not be good. Jesus was simply stating a fact, not establishing a limiting factor, and so let me continue with a few more observations for those who would wonder about this "jail house religion" thing.

I wonder just what Jesus would say was the proportion in many of our churches of those who truly are born again and know it. How many are there that have a living, vibrant, sin-excluding relationship with an indwelling Comforter? Are there few that find this? Then perhaps it is not strange that many in prison also never go beyond a status quo Christian program.

We hear reports of many turning to Christianity in present-day Iran and other Muslim countries and also in China and other parts of the world. Are all of these genuine new births and a terminus to sin in all of its forms? There have been some huge crusade efforts in which numbers upon numbers have been recorded as "making a decision for Christ," or "accepting the Lord Jesus Christ," or "making a difference." Among these huge numbers we are sure there have been a few that really became followers of Jesus and because they love Him are keeping His commandments, but by and large the great masses are receiving just another brand of "jail house religion."

So what then is "jail house religion."

It is, in a nutshell, religion that works in prison but cannot keep one when he or she gets out. If this kind of religion stands any chance of getting one to heaven, it would be a risk beyond measure to ever let them out of prison, for then they would lose their chance of ever getting there because you see, this only works in prison. Is there any difference in a religion that only works during the days of a revival effort in the church, but when that is over all priorities return to the self-life and the secular interests? If this type of religion stands any chance of getting one to heaven it would be a tragic risk to ever close a revival effort would it not?

Do we see many of the men in prison really getting gloriously saved and sanctified in such a way that the fruit remains? Oh, that we could, but we must honestly say, "No, not really that many." Are you seeing many people saved and sanctified in your church and in your outreach efforts, and do they all stick and make it for God? Perhaps the honest answer here would not be that different from the one we just gave. Shall we then just accept this limitation and settle for it? Never! If we do, we become the greatest and most effective factor in the problem.

An old preacher once said, "God will send to our churches just as much green wood as we have fire to burn." Likely he was not amiss in his appraisal, but oh, how it ought to urge my heart and yours to stir up the fire within. Fire kindles fire, and fire attracts fire. Jesus said with a heart of passion, "I am come to send fire on the earth; and what will I, if it be already kindled?" I believe He said this with longing that it would be so; that when and as He steps up to an empty soul, the glowing face of one of His children would be there right along with it. If we lose the glow of the glorious hope that the very next soul we meet might hear and obey His voice, we effectively destroy the very means He might have used to accomplish that.

And so, after trying to be very honest in what is being accomplished, we are so happy to report to you that amidst all of the "jail house religion" there are some glowing, radiant, genuine Christians among the men in prison who are just as genuine as the best people in your church. We praise the Lord for them and pray that the number will increase.

Just today I asked a man to open our class in prayer. He has attended for some time and I have witnessed him absorbing more and more of the spirit of it all. He is far from the normal run in prison life. He would appear to be an intelligent middle class American whose type for several centuries has formed the backbone of all that America is and what we love it to be. He eagerly assented to open in prayer: "Father, I am so grateful for this wonderful opportunity of gathering here again today with these brothers. But I won't be here but a few more months; my time is drawing to a close..." and then, with a quivering voice, "But Father, I don't want to lose this precious fellowship that I have found. This prison has taught me what I never knew before. I want to keep that."

Such, as nearly as I can recapture them, were his heartfelt words. If our prisons, with all that they so pitifully lack of effective redemption, can cause men to pray like this, what would it be like if God had control of every program and every effort to bring wayward men back to the narrow way?

Can you imagine a life on earth so bankrupt of all that is so meaningful to you that prison life would be a blessing from which you would not want to be released? Do you realize that our today's world is just that empty and disappointing? Not infrequently men are so blessed by being in prison among other men who love them and care about their souls that they cry at the thought of leaving it all. Certainly the Bible does not say in vain, "…the way of transgressors is hard."

I want to tell you a story that should encourage any of you who are passing out gospel tracts or spreading God's Word in any manner. Over a period of thirteen years, God opened a door on the Wildwood, NJ boardwalk for groups of young people to sing and pass out gospel tracts for a week of their summer. At times anywhere from 10,000 to 25,000 people passed by the pavilion where they were singing each night of the week. Besides that, many of these gospel portions have been passed out on street corners and in the Philadelphia street meetings.

One day recently a letter came to the PO box with the news that one of these gospel portions had somehow, somewhere reached a Florida prisoner's mother and she had sent it to him. He wanted to write and thank us and give us a testimony of how he had found God in prison. Doesn't God's Word promise, "Cast thy bread upon the waters: for thou shalt find it after many days"? Furthermore doesn't it say, "So shall my word be that goeth forth out of my mouth: it shall not return unto me void, but it shall accomplish that which I please, and it shall prosper in the thing whereto I sent it." God means what He says and He will fulfill all His promises. Only perhaps when we get to heaven will we find out all the fruit that has come from faithfulness to the Great Commission, but let's continue to be faithful to the end.

Now here is a second letter from the Florida prisoner.

16: Is it Just Jail-House Religion? 285

Dear Brother William,

Thank you for the return letter. It is comforting to know there are others out there that care. You mentioned about your travels to Africa where your daughter is a missionary. My heart rejoices for the work that you do. We as Christians are a living body and a family. We all have our part and place, and I feel we need to stay obedient when we are asked to spread the love of Christ.

I do not feel that because I'm behind bars does that exempt me from spreading the Gospel; if anything, here is where the Word needs to start. As you know some of the most broken people are incarcerated. Not that the other side of the fence everything is "peachy." The lost are lost no matter where in society they live. As I said in my last letter, if it wasn't for prison I would have never given myself to Christ. I was the walking dead! Now with a new heart my eyes are opened to the world and able to receive and give love freely. Praise God for His Grace and Mercy!

I appreciate the offer of books and cd's. I must say your kindness is more than welcome. I cannot receive tapes or cd's, but books are always welcome. I really don't want to be a burden when it comes to stuff like that, so if it is too much aggravation please don't feel obligated. I know there are many con-men out there and they are always looking to get over on people. I see it in here all the time. There are men in here that write to churches just to receive money in their accounts. They also do it to naïve women and older people. Their game is good, they use false testimonies and could lay down Scripture better than most preachers. I want to let you know I have no intention nor will I ever ask for financial assistance in any way to you or anyone for that matter. I wasn't raised that way. I get 3 meals a day, have clothes on my back and a roof over my head. God's great provisions are in abundance in my life. I know there are free men who don't have that. I pray for the ones living on the street. Also the persecuted Church in countries where <u>just owning</u> a Bible is illegal....I just wanted to clear that up before we continue with our correspondence. One of the many struggles I face is accepting gifts of kindness. Your gesture of the books and cd's is, as I'm learning, an offering of love. Normally I would say "no thank you," I'm fine, but I've learned through Christ's love that it is okay to accept gifts. It's definitely a pride issue. God is great! I'm glad He is working on me because I need it. He is my strength…

I appreciate the work you and your church does passing out the booklets and tracts. I'm interested in hearing more of the missionary work you all do. Where have your travels taken you? Do you go as missionary teams or go independently? Is it safe? Do you and your church do any local work? I'm happy to hear of the men that have kept true to the faith even after getting released. They give me hope and it shows there is life after prison.

Please feel free anytime to write and if there are any others that would like to write from the church I would love to hear from them!

Thank you again! Your Brother in Christ Jesus

I know you will pray for him, won't you?
   Thank you each one for all you are doing with us,
              William Cawman

November 1, 2012

"I'M NOT REALLY THAT BAD a person, Chaplain." This I hear so often and it is the very reason that this "not so bad person" cannot become any better. Nicodemus was not so bad a person either, was he? The rich young ruler also had a lot going for him. Yet neither of them was in prison. It seems there is always someone who is worse than myself, which leaves me "not so bad" after all. And so, this is our starting point so many times, shabby platform though it be.

So before me sits an inmate, by request from himself. He is back on a parole violation after his release in 2010. He is now

43 years of age, and still has some lingering hope that things will get better soon. After all, the stint for the violation will be but for a few months, and then he can try once again. The only problem is, by his own admission, he thinks he loves this woman that got him into this mess this time around, and perhaps there is yet hope that he can have her and yet live the good life, too—you know—go to church and "praise" (today's concept of Christianity) and get a decent job and stay away from the drugs on which she is hooked. Just give him one more chance and maybe this time it will all come out all right. He is in debt because he cared so much about this woman that he spent all of his money to get her the drugs she needed to feel the way she wanted to, etc.

And so I listen on and on to his analysis of his state and churn on the inside with absolute abhorrence and hatred for Satan and his garbage can full of slop from the cesspool that he has so garnished as to capture this victim with the vain hope that it will yet come out all right.

Having presented his case I look him squarely in the eyes and respond, "You need to throw this whole mess at Jesus' feet as a guilty sinner and ask Him to completely change you into a new man. You need to forget all about this woman and every other woman for now and get your heart right with God. Life will never get any better trying to patch it up with new efforts and old remedies that haven't worked. You need Jesus! You need to be born again a new creature."

He nodded his head and I began to pray for him. When I finished he was wiping tears from his eyes and promised me that he would really seek God for a change of heart. Please pray for him as God lays him on your heart.

In Christian Living class this past week our dear brother from Haiti asked to give a testimony. With great emotion and tears he testified that he had for some time been struggling with poor health conditions such as diabetes and heart problems. He had taken it to the Lord and asked Him if it was His will to give him a touch. He had run out of medicine for both problems and was unable to see the nurse for some time. When he finally got in to see the nurse she checked his blood sugar and his heart symptoms and they were normal, even though he had not been taking the medicine for them.

I believe God has something special in mind for this dear man. He is such a sweet specimen of redeeming grace and just beams out love and compassion to all around him. Oh, how I wish we had more like him.

Then in that same class we entered into a discussion that led to commercial sports and TV watching. I cleared the deck on that whole business, letting them know that a real love for Jesus would make all of that so obnoxious that they would have no desire for it. It was obvious that some had nowhere approached that level of love for Jesus and so we began to hear some objections. I began to counter them with the fact that a lot of the ball games are on the Lord's Day; that the crowd that gathers in a ball game stadium is not the crowd I would want to be found with when Jesus comes; that sports players become idols and are paid extravagant salaries while many are starving to death in the world, etc., etc.

"Yes, but such and such a team are saying that they are going to give a lot of money to charity—isn't that good?" "Well, it's as good as Paul made it: "...though I bestow all my goods to feed the poor, and though I give my body to be burned, and have not charity, it profiteth me nothing." And right here lays the stumbling block in the whole issue— the love of Christ is not yet shed abroad in their hearts.

The song writer said, "Are temptations so alluring; do earth's pleasures so enthrall; that I cannot love my Savior well enough to leave them all?" I tried to tell them that I was not suffering a single atom of deprivation by not being in love with commercial sports, nor had I any stomach at all to watch television. I am finding in Jesus such utter satisfaction that sometimes it almost hurts. It's a good hurt, though!

Now I must tell you about last week's classes. I was sitting at the desk in the classroom, waiting for the men to come in, and praying for the class about to begin when I glanced down and saw the title of the next chapter in our text book: "The Second Work of Grace." Instantly my heart began to cry out, "O God, I don't want these men to just learn about this; I want them to get it!"

God spoke to me and said, "Then give them your own testimony." After prayer I told them I was going to tell them just how it was in my own life with and without this second work of grace. I told them I would be honest completely even though a part of my life is not pleasant to tell. I went back over the years (shame on me) that I had played around with God's call, wandering in the wilderness and living even my spiritual life to please myself. I confessed how many times I could not tell that I started and then went back; was up and then down; was in love with Jesus and then grew cold in that love; went around and around the same circle of defeat, doubt, laziness and broken vows.

Then I told them of the glorious change that came with the second work of grace. Conviction was deepening all through it and when I finished I said, "Men, how many of you believe you have understood what I have tried to tell you?" Nearly every hand went up. I said, "If anyone, or any atmosphere, or any written page tells you that you cannot experience the same wonderful change, it is a lie out of hell. Now let's quit playing around with God and go after it!"

Let me tell you, I felt as clear as a bell as I left the classroom, but the next afternoon as I was waiting for the next group of men a voice said, "Don't do that again. God won't bless it this time. It is not the class to tell that to. You will not have any help today doing that." The farther it went the more I detected where it was coming from and so I just launched into it again and was helped and blessed and anointed even more than the day before.

Now, why did I tell you that? I told you that for this specific reason: would you help us pray that God will give us some more genuinely sanctified men in the prison? We have a few; thank God for them. One of them was listening as I told them all this and was he ever beaming with delight, but we need some more. I thank God for all whose sins are forgiven, but they will not keep going in that state any more than I was able to if they do not go on into holiness of heart.

The anointing to witness to others was not promised the disciples short of Pentecost. "But ye shall receive power, after that the Holy Ghost is come upon you: and ye shall be witnesses unto me both in Jerusalem, and in all Judaea, and in Samaria, and unto the uttermost part of the earth." And so this of necessity includes Southwoods State Prison, does it not? It has been too long since we have had someone get genuinely sanctified and yet that is the greatest need of this whole ministry. I do not mean to minimize the miracle of any soul getting forgiven and born again, but we must see them go on into the predestinated purpose of God— "to be conformed to the image of His Son."

On Tuesday of last week my supervisor made a trip to Trenton to present some thoughts and desires to the administration. The next day he called me into his office and with a tone of almost hopelessness began to tell me how disappointing the meeting was. He said in plain words, "No one cares about anything!" Politics and salaries are the entire focus and any concern for the welfare of souls is nonexistent. I fear that is just a window into the larger picture of our bankrupt spiritual condition in America. The night is coming. Let's do all we can while the day lasts!

Please pray also for several men who are being released from prison. Several have indicated that they want to come to our church, but wherever they go, pray that they will go on with God and not fail Him again.

Now, I must relate a story of how something in my daughter's newsletter affected the prison. She told you how, within hours of making a decision to purchase an ATV for reaching new areas beyond the river, one of God's children called in and wanted to send the entire amount of the vehicle. How we were rejoicing in God's timing, God's family, God's miracles, etc. It of course would take several days to transfer the money to Africa and in the meantime someone came and offered the man $1000 more for the vehicle and so he sold it.

As soon as I received the news my heart sank. My feelings were: "Dear Lord, I thought we were in the middle of a miracle." After a brief time of this state I began to realize, "Wait a minute. God started this; He always has ways that are higher than our ways and thoughts that are above ours." Two days later our friends in SA located another vehicle of the same make and year, but with the next size engine in it. They went to see it and while there called me on the phone and let the owner talk with me.

He is a dealer and it was his personally and when I asked him if it was in good condition he said it was very good, but had more hours on it than the first one we looked at. He assured me he would make sure it was sound and when I asked him about the tires he said, "They are good, but I will put new ones on it for you." I asked if he knew of any place to get them filled with foam so that she would not have to worry about punctures. He said he did and would take care of that, too. Then I said it would be good if there was a winch on it in case of mudholes and he said he would put that on.

I then told our friends to go ahead and write him a check for it. When he found it was for a missionary, he said that he wanted to become a Christian and would our friend come and help him. Of course he would. Then he said he wanted to help out this missionary all he could and that he would put the vehicle in his shop and replace everything that could be replaced so as to be sure of its fitness and that he would do that at his own expense. Then he said he wanted to have the vehicle sent back to him every six months for service and that he wanted to pay the cost of it.

All right, God, we learn once more that Thy ways are so much higher than ours!

Now, let me get back to prison. As you can imagine I was so

filled with gratitude and wonder at God's marvelous way of answering prayer that I told just about anyone I thought would listen. When I told the men in facility two, I had just gotten to the point where we were actually getting one when our good Haitian brother yelled out, "No! No! No!" and then stood up by the wall and started to cry, looking like he was in shock.

I went over and laid my hand on his shoulder and said, "Oh, ye of little faith...When you have recovered I will finish the story." He sat down still crying and said, "I couldn't see how on earth God could help her to get a vehicle like that and I had given it up." One after another expressed what it did for them to hear of how God worked every particle of it all out and had His hand on a soul that needs to be saved besides. I told it to my supervisor and he looked as though he wanted to cry. I told it to a few of the Christian officers and they just marveled. I told a secretary and she wanted to cry.

So friends, because one of God's children and his wife obeyed the Still Small Voice, they sent shock waves around the world to the glory of God. The end is not yet, for I am not finished telling whoever wants to hear. Who knows how many souls will be touched by that one act of obedience. Do you understand how we are all in this together? As Nehemiah building the wall, each man in his place, and God does all the rest. Oh, let's press on and trust and obey until Jesus returns and the time for work is no more. They are not all in yet. Please pray for the man who sold us this ATV.

William Cawman

December 1, 2012

ON THE EVENING OF November 20, I visited once more the little plot on a hilltop that my great-grandfather purchased in the same year that my wife was born and where lie my precious father and mother and two generations of my father's parents, and where lies the earthly part of the one dearest to me on earth except for Jesus.

As I stood there with fresh tears and such precious memories, the last rays of sunlight were glowing faintly crimson in the western sky. A half-moon was looking down through the hazy darkness. After a while I heard church tower chimes drifting up from the valley below, tolling the hour of five o'clock in the evening. My precious wife had been in heaven for exactly one whole year! What a year of God's unmerited nearness it has been to my heart. His love has poured through my heart in ways that I never knew it could before. His precious family has drawn so close again and again with expressions of love, calls, cards, text messages and promises of prayer. I feel so unworthy of such manifold love, but I thank every one of you, my precious praying family, for it all. With many a card or note fresh tears have come to my eyes and fresh balm to my soul. I cannot express how big my heart has grown in love to all of you too. Thank you, family of God!

I left the spot so dear and made my way to the prison for Bible studies that evening. In each one I just took the time to, first of all, go over simply and plainly what we had endeavored for the past fourteen and a half years to teach the men; that God can indeed so change us by His grace that we are translated from servants of sin into love slaves of Jesus, and that we can then be cleansed from every moral trace of inward sin until clean and pure and pleasing to God here on earth.

Then I told them that I wanted to share a story with them. I told them the life story of my dear wife and how holiness had so worked in her heart and life that I would struggle in vain to come up with a single memory of any flicker of anything that would mar her testimony of holiness. I told them I knew holiness of heart is real and that it works, not only because I have personally found it so, but that I had lived with a shining example of it for over forty-one years. I related again the precious hours of her homegoing and what a cloudless sky she left behind. I told them of how her testimony as the years went by brought more and more inability for me to hold back tears because I knew it was true gold. I told them of how lovingly God has sustained and kept my own heart without the slightest murmur of argument with His sweet will in taking her home.

As the class time drew to a close, tears were streaming down faces and hunger was deeply evident. No sooner had I finished than one dear man broke into sobs as he said, "Chaplain, I was saved a number of years ago, but I have never had such a relationship with God as that. How can I find it?" Then he asked the men to pardon his tears and just sobbed aloud.

I said, "My dear brother, you are on your way to finding it right now. God sees those tears of hunger and He has heard your acknowledgement of need. Just keep right on asking Him to satisfy your heart and He will do it so fully that you will actually hurt with satisfaction." Then I reminded them that they could not hold on to any known sin if they really wanted God to enter into their life and bring them into fellowship with Him.

With that more eyes filled with tears and one of them got up and retrieved a roll of toilet tissue and passed it around. As the men passed from the room they shook hands and hugged me and said, "Thank you for sharing that with us. And may God continue to bless you, Chaplain." One of them said, "Chaplain, I stand amazed at how God has helped you and is helping you through all of this." I frankly admit, I do too, and I love Him for it.

I cannot help quoting a song that expresses at least in measure how my heart responds: "When morning gilds the skies, my heart awakening cries: May Jesus Christ be praised! Alike at work and prayer to Jesus I repair: May Jesus Christ be praised! Does sadness fill my mind? A solace here I find: May Jesus Christ be praised! Or fades my earthly bliss? My comfort still is this: May Jesus Christ be praised! In heaven's eternal bliss the loveliest strain is this:

May Jesus Christ be praised! The powers of darkness fear when this sweet chant they hear: May Jesus Christ be praised! Be this, while life is mine, my canticle divine: May Jesus Christ be praised! Be this the eternal song through all the ages long: May Jesus Christ be praised!" Amen!

One year in heaven! Five minutes will more than repay any sacrifice or suffering or deprivation here below, will it not? If you can think of any consideration, however great or small, that you would place in the other side of the balance against being fully in the clear with God and ready for heaven, I cannot!

One year ago and on the borderland of heaven I asked her if she would tell Jesus when she saw Him that I was coming. She nodded "Yes." From that moment, earth has grown strangely dim. I can think of no other reason to stay here than to win a few more souls for Jesus and to lovingly do His sweet will, however long or short.

Clouds of uncertainty surely hang low over this old world. Let's send all our treasure up above, shall we? There is only one reason Jesus has not returned: they are not all in yet, and some of them are in my prison classes. Thank you for your continued prayers.

And now I must tell you about Thanksgiving Day 2012. Since my Christian family who were eating together chose to have dinner at five o'clock, I asked the sergeant in facility one if he could provide coverage if I would come in and have my Christian Living class. He agreed to cover it, so at 12:30 they called it out and twenty-four men came down. After we had prayed and sung a couple of songs (of course: "Thank You Lord, For Saving My Soul") I told the men that since it was Thanksgiving Day we were going to have a testimony class. Often there were two or three getting up simultaneously to give thanks.

As it went on God came closer and closer. After all, is it not His own Word that says, "Whoso offereth praise glorifieth Me..."? There was no question but that God was pleased with their giving of thanks, because His presence was very near. I began to take some brief notes so that I could share a bit with you of what they were thanking God for. Here is a little brief of it:

A man who had recently arrived from a Texas prison came to the front and told us that he had spent twenty-five years in prison in TX and then had been extradited to NJ to put in another five. He said temptation came to become bitter that they had not counted the twenty-five in TX sufficient for the NJ part too, but that he had deliberately chosen to reject bitterness and yield himself fully to God's will and that he was happy and perfectly content to be a child of God. He couldn't return to his seat for a few moments because of all the intercepting hugs as he went back.

A man who has recently joined our class is quite a sight to look at. He is very dark skinned and then made darker yet by almost complete coverage of his body and face with tattoos. Notwithstanding the outward appearance I have noticed his eager and humble desire as a new-born babe in Christ. He came up and put both hands in the air and said with deep feeling, "Jesus loves me, and I am learning to love Him. When He came into my life it was not hard to pull down the porn and dirty magazines and give myself to Him. Satan has attacked me but I am God's. When I was out on the street I was a loner that didn't want anything to do with anybody, but one day I read Philippians 1:29 and I realized that nobody wants to let a good soldier go, and I was a good one for Satan." He certainly is not a loner now, for his love of the brethren is evident and was reciprocated with many a hug and handshake.

A man on crutches and with a badly damaged eye arose and said, "Men, I want to thank God for His mercy. I was a gang-banger for Satan and served him well. I have been shot five times and stabbed twice and when I landed in the hospital after the last one I began to think of how desperately sick I was of living for the devil. God had mercy and I am looking to Him now and I want more of Him."

With that another man responded from the back of the room, "Thank God, Brother, I know what you are talking about. I was the same mess and I was also shot several times. I have had my friends die and have held their dead bodies in my arms, but I have given it all to God and He has taken it all away. He not only gave me the power to stop all the lust and addictions, but broke the power of them until they are gone completely from my heart."

Then the man right next to him stood up. For a moment he just looked at the floor in thought and then said, "Today is Thanksgiving. I want to thank God for His love, His mercy and His grace. For a long time I was lost, but a year ago I was locked in a cell with this man next to me. I saw Jesus and he began to lead me to Him. I thank God for this brother. God has now forgiven me. I was a member of the Bloods gang for twelve years and there is probably nothing you can talk about of what they do that I am not familiar with, but I am not here to talk about that. God has filled my heart with His Spirit and those things are not part of my life anymore. I'm so glad I have found this better life. We need to be patient with those around us who are still living in all that we once did. Let's pray for them, because I can tell you that I am standing here telling you these things only in answer to prayer."

Then another man stood and said, "Chaplain, I want to thank you for coming in here to teach us this way of holiness. I thank God that I am able to pass on to my family on the outside what you are teaching us in here."

One after another gave thanks to God, to their chaplain, and to each other, and God was honored in it all. The time went by and the men agreed that it was so good to be together like that. It was, too, and I felt personally it was a wonderful Thanksgiving Day, and then that was followed by a meal together with part of my Christian family around our table.

I feel like asking with David, "What shall I render unto the LORD for all his benefits toward me?" Do you remember what answer he gave to that? "I will take the cup of salvation, and call upon the name of the LORD. I will pay my vows unto the LORD now in the presence of all his people." And then the song writer said, "If fellowship here with my Lord can be so inexpressibly sweet, oh what will it be when His face we see when round the white throne we meet?" What a Thanksgiving Day that will be!

Please pray for the upcoming Christmas Eve services. It is up to our church group to provide four services that night plus hospital visitation and we have put out invitations to a few sister churches for any who want to join us. Do you want to come? Can you think of anything more romantically traditional than to go to prison on Christmas Eve?

But then did not He come "...to bind up the brokenhearted, to proclaim liberty to the captives, and the opening of the prison to them that are bound?" (Don't fear, we will not try the physical aspect of the last part of that!) If you cannot join us in person, will you join us in prayer? Wouldn't it be a wonderful Christmas Day for some dear lost soul if they could wake up with Jesus newly born within them? God grant it, for Jesus' sake!

As another year of extended mercy and longsuffering draws to a close, we want to thank again each of you who have been a part of this, either in going or praying. They're not all in yet, so let's keep faithful.

William Cawman

Members of Schmul's Wesleyan Book Club buy these outstanding books at 40% off the retail price.

800-$S_7P_7B_2O_6O_6K_5S_7$

Visit us on the Internet at www.wesleyanbooks.com

Schmul Publishing Company | PO Box 776 | Nicholasville, KY 40340

www.ingramcontent.com/pod-product-compliance
Lightning Source LLC
Chambersburg PA
CBHW071736150426
43191CB00010B/1597